Women, Human Settlements, and Housing

Women, Human Settlements, and Housing

EDITED BY
CAROLINE O.N. MOSER AND
LINDA PEAKE

TAVISTOCK PUBLICATIONS
London and New York

First published in 1987 by
Tavistock Publications
11 New Fetter Lane, London EC4P 4EE

Published in the USA by
Tavistock Publications
in association with Methuen, Inc.
29 West 35th Street, New York, NY 10001

Printed in Great Britain by Biddles Ltd, Guildford and King's Lynn

British Library Cataloguing in Publication Data

Women, human settlements, and housing.
 1. Women — Housing — Developing
 countries
 I. Moser, Caroline   II. Peake, Linda
 363.5'9'091724   HD7391

 ISBN 0–422–61860–8
 ISBN 0–422–61980–9 Pbk

Library of Congress Cataloging in Publication Data

Women, human settlements, and housing.
 Bibliography: p.
 Includes index.
 1. Women in community development — Developing
 countries. 2. Women — Housing — Developing countries.
 I. Moser, Caroline O.N.   II. Peake, Linda, 1956–
 HQ1240.5.D44W66 1987   305.4'2'091724 87–17973

 ISBN 0–422–61860–8
 ISBN 0–422–61980–9 (soft)

Contents

List of contributors

SYLVIA CHANT is a British geographer who is lecturer in the Department of Geography and the Institute of Latin American Studies, University of Liverpool.

MARINA FERNANDO is a Sri Lankan who was director of the US Save the Children Federation in Sri Lanka and is now a consultant in the UK.

LEDA M.V. MACHADO is a Brazilian architect, at present finishing a Ph.D. thesis on women and health mobilization in São Paulo, at the Development Planning Unit, University College London.

CAROLINE O.N. MOSER is a British social anthropologist and currently lecturer in social planning in developing countries in the Department of Social Administration, London School of Economics.

PAULA NIMPUNO-PARENTE is a Mozambiquan social planner doing research at the Housing Research and Development Unit, University of Nairobi, and the Institute of Social Studies, The Hague.

LINDA PEAKE is a British geographer who at present is lecturer in the School of Geography, Kingston Polytechnic.

IRENE VANCE is an Irish social anthropologist who works as a training officer both for housing co-operative groups in London and for the UNCHS (HABITAT).

Acknowledgements

This book represents the culmination of a number of initiatives in the field of women, human settlements, and housing. So many people have played an important part in this long process, that it is not possible to acknowledge them all by name. I should like, however, to express my special gratitude to some of those who have assisted me.

My interest in this field first began when, together with my family, I lived in a bamboo house in *barrio* Indio Guayas, and learnt from my women neighbours the strategies of survival in such conditions. This was further developed during the eight years I worked at the Development Planning Unit, University College London. While there, with the support of Michael Safier and the collaboration of Caren Levy, I developed a short course on 'Planning with women for development', in which many of these themes were first examined. The writings of Marianne Schmink and Maxine Molyneux were important in developing further the conceptual framework of this work.

At the UNCHS (HABITAT) Reinhard Skinner and Yap Kioe Sheng were largely responsible for commissioning a training manual on the participation of women in housing projects, which was written jointly with Sylvia Chant. John Cox, and then Ingrid Munro, as Directors of the International Year of Shelter for the Homeless, requested a policy paper on women and housing. The lack of adequate case studies on women and human settlements led me to persuade a number of colleagues with experience in this field to write up their material. With the support and encouragement of Kate McKee, the Ford Foundation,

New York provided a grant which made possible the publication of thirteen Development Planning Unit Gender and Planning Working Papers. To all these people I owe an enormous debt of gratitude.

Finally, I would like to thank Peter Sollis, and my sons, Titus and Nathaniel, for sharing so much of this with me, while themselves experiencing the vicissitudes of living in an English woman-headed household.

Caroline O.N. Moser

My involvement in the field of women, human settlements, and housing derived from a number of sources. As an urban geographer housing and human settlements have always been a central concern of mine and a series of historical accidents led to this interest being developed in relation to the Caribbean, particularly Guyana. A temporary lectureship in the School of Development Studies, University of East Anglia allowed me to further develop this area of study along a feminist perspective, for which I owe a debt of gratitude to Ruth Pearson. The overlap with Caroline's work culminated in my teaching on the Development Planning Unit short course and my editing the thirteen working papers, nine of which have been rewritten and re-edited for this book. Without Sylvia Fletcher, Eileen Palmer, and Edna Watts, who typed much of the book, we would not have met our deadlines. Their enthusiasm for the project and willingness to keep to tight schedules proved invaluable, as did the assistance of Heather Gibson, our Tavistock editor. Finally, I would like to thank my mother, Marjorie, for never doubting that we would achieve our aim.

Linda Peake
London, April 1987

Introduction

CAROLINE O.N. MOSER

This book examines the role of women in human settlements and housing in the Third World. The importance of focusing specifically on women relates both to the central role that housing and infrastructural services, such as water, electricity, and sewerage, play in their lives, and to the fact that this tends to be ignored by those involved in the planning of human settlements. The increasing concern during the past decade of both governments and international agencies with the provision of shelter for low-income populations of the Third World has firmly placed the issue on the political agenda. This has resulted in large-scale investment in a diversity of housing projects, particularly site and service and squatter upgrading. These developments make it critical to examine how far the needs of women are being addressed in the planning of human settlements and housing.

Background to the issues

WOMEN, EMPLOYMENT, AND HOUSING
It is important to start by clarifying the distinction between housing and human settlements. While the term 'housing' is often used to refer to the physical fabric of the house, and the land on which it is built, the term 'human settlements' includes not only housing but also the wider area in which it is located. Consequently it also refers to infrastructure and other neighbourhood and community-level facilities. The focus throughout

is principally on the urban sector, although many of the issues raised are as important in rural areas. This bias is because most housing and human settlement policy to date has been concerned almost exclusively with urban areas.

The important but often invisible role of women in the economic and social development of their countries and communities, and the plight of low-income women in Third World economies, has been highlighted and publicized by the United Nations Decade for Women (1976–85). During this period both academic research and policy-making have been concerned with women's economic contribution to development. Moving away from a preoccupation with the role of women within the family, academic researchers have documented in both rural and urban areas the complexities of women's employment, as waged workers and in informal sector activities, and identified the importance of their paid 'productive' work to Third World economies.[1]

Equally policy-makers have begun to shift their focus from a universal concern with welfare-orientated family-centred programmes that assume motherhood as the most important role for women in the development process, to a diversity of programmes that emphasize the productive role of women. The so-called Women in Development (WID) approach, with its underlying rationale that women are an untapped resource who can provide an economic contribution to development, has had an important influence in popularizing income-generating projects for women. The objectives behind such projects now vary considerably: these range from an anti-poverty approach, with its focus on very poor women (particularly those who head households), to those designed to empower women and give them economic independence from men. All income-generating projects, nevertheless, are primarily concerned with women's work in paid employment.[2] This concern has meant that until recently far less attention has been devoted to women and their needs in human settlements. Very broadly, research on issues relating to women, housing, and human settlements can be equated with the geopolitical division between the First and the Third World. While a diversity of studies have provided empirical evidence of the severe housing problems facing low-income women in Third World cities (especially women who head households), the primary concern of this policy-orientated research has been to bring to the attention of national governments and international agencies the extent to which women have been 'left out' in housing provision. Following the WID approach, as with employment, the focus has been to negate the hypothesis and show that the specific needs of women have been excluded from current housing policy and programmes.[3]

Recent work in the First World on gender, the built environment, and industrial society has been largely concerned with the domestic labour debate and the nature of housework, and its implications for the relationship between women, design, and the organization of space. While feminists in the USA have written about women in ideal communities in the eighteenth and nineteenth centuries, recent work in the UK has examined the implications for women of recent urban and suburban planning and the growth of suburbs, as well as the effect of homelessness for women. Lastly, recent anthropological work has focused on issues relating to women as mediators of space.[4]

THIRD WORLD HOUSING POLICY DEBATES

While this recent First World research has provided an important feminist critique of the gendered use of space, it has not been primarily policy-orientated.[5] Nor has it focused specifically on the more fundamental issue of the role of women in the *provision* of housing and basic services, particularly self-help housing solutions. Given the magnitude of the 'housing problem' in the Third World, it is not a coincidence that some of the most important alternative housing solutions have occurred there. This is particularly so in Latin America. Therefore any examination of the needs of women and housing in the Third World must be understood not only within the context of its urbanization processes but also within the context of its housing solutions.

The debate about the 'housing problem' in Third World countries and the ensuing fundamental changes in housing policy stems from the fact that for the past twenty years conventional government housing programmes have failed to satisfy low-income housing demand (Moser 1982). The direct consequence of this failure has been the proliferation of squatter and shanty settlements. In the 1950s and 1960s these were viewed as a temporary phenomenon: a consequence of extremely rapid urbanization. Newly established, makeshift settlements were identified as reception areas for migrants who were still 'unintegrated' into the city. Illegal land occupation and the failure to pay rent or to compensate the 'owner' meant that squatters were seen as existing outside the capitalist land and housing market. Policy-makers regarded squatter settlements as zones of social breakdown, and equated the problem of marginality with that of substandard housing. Marginality was considered as something to be physically eradicated, a manifestation that had a simple cure (Perlman 1976).

Government interventions based on these assumptions often involved the bulldozing and clearance of whole settlements. Such action was justified on the grounds that the settlements constituted 'public eye-sores', were 'insanitary', or represented a form of urban 'cancer'. Demolition occurred in cities as far apart as Hong Kong, Nairobi, and Rio de Janeiro, with displaced squatters sometimes being relocated in new, more distant, and usually inappropriate housing areas. Rarely did governments consider whether the housing was compatible with the occupations and incomes of the resettled population; usually the result was that public housing was too expensive for the 'target group' for which it was intended.

By the late 1960s it was widely recognized that 'self-help' housing was a rational response by the expanding low-income population to the growing shortage of conventional housing. In particular the formative work in Lima, Peru, of Turner (1968, 1970) and Mangin (1967) led to 'self-help' squatter settlements being viewed as a sensible alternative to the housing shortage; it allowed the low-income population to build their own homes; incrementally to relate their investments to their income level; and to give them 'freedom' to decide on size, standard, and style of home according to individual family needs. Although the consolidation process could take at least ten years, subletting and informal sector activities were seen as mechanisms that could be used to increase the home-owner's income.

Widespread acceptance on the part of international agencies and national governments that the process of 'self-help' does not represent a problem and might even be a solution to the housing situation has had significant policy implications. Governments have come to realize that 'self-help' housing is functional to the city's economy, and a benefit to the government since as they are largely self-organized, self-built, and self-managed, this reduces the responsibility of the state to provide adequate conventional housing for the large labour pool within the city. A large number of Third World governments shifted during the late 1960s and early 1970s from conventional formal housing policies to 'self-help' alternatives, of which the most important types were 'site and service' housing projects and then 'upgrading' schemes. It is now recognized that the self-help solution offers a cheaper alternative housing policy, benefiting a larger proportion of the urban population than before, but without major increases in the proportion of investment allocated to housing. Since 1974 self-help has been officially endorsed by the World Bank, which has meant that funds and loans for the financing for such schemes have increased considerably.

While governments have enthusiastically adopted self-help housing solutions, criticisms of these policies have increased not only over the practice and internal contradictions of self-help housing, but also and more importantly because of the ideological implications of self-help housing as an instrument of policy-making. Among the most articulate criticisms are those that argue that self-help allows labour to be doubly exploited (at work and in self-help house construction), which in turn subsidizes wages since access to low-cost shelter reduces the wage level required for subsistence. What Turner definitively called 'freedom to build' (Turner and Fichter 1972), such critics as Burgess (1978) have argued was the only housing alternative which the majority of low-income groups had, involving pathetic suffering and appalling living conditions. Above all self-help releases government from its responsibility to provide adequate housing as a basic need for its low-income population.[6]

The fact that the case studies in this book are concerned primarily with site and service and upgrading projects is a reflection of the reality that most Third World governments in the past decade have shifted from top-down public housing projects to a diversity of assisted self-help solutions. Nor is it a coincidence that the case studies are mainly from Central and South America. To date most research, especially in relation to women and human settlements, has been undertaken in this region. It is important, however, to recognize that the Third World housing debate still lacks a fundamental feminist perspective. Emphasis has been almost entirely on the economic relations of housing with the focus on such issues as urban housing markets, land tenure, and the role of the state in housing provision. Far less attention has been paid to the social relations of housing. Thus, through the examination of the relationship between gender and housing, the purpose of this book is also to contribute to the debate on the importance of housing and human settlements not only as an economic relation but also as a social relation (Saunders and Williams 1986).

WOMEN AND HUMAN SETTLEMENTS OR GENDER AND HUMAN SETTLEMENTS?

Literature on Third World housing shows that little attention has been given to explaining the important reasons for focusing on the particular problems and needs of women. But is it necessary to plan for the needs of women in their own right, rather than planning for the needs of families and households? To answer this question it is necessary at the outset to understand the distinction between sex and gender, and in this way to make clear that the overall concern in this book is not so much with women and human settlements as with gender and human settlements.

The term 'gender' was originally developed by feminists, who were concerned about the overtly biological overtones of the word 'sex' (see Whitehead 1979). For while sex is a biological concept, used to identify what is biologically important but different between men and women, gender is a social concept, used to identify the differences between men and women as social beings, and the social meaning of what is important to being men and women. In other words gender refers to men and women not as 'natural' sexual categories, but to the relationship between them, and the way these relationships are socially constructed. Men and women play different roles in society with gender differences shaped by ideological, historical, religious, ethnic, cultural, and economic determinants. These roles show both similarities and differences across and between classes as well as societies. An understanding of the social construction of gender relations also recognizes that because men and women play different roles in society they often have different needs. Planning at the level of the household or family does not necessarily accommodate these needs. Therefore in the examination of gender and human settlements, and the planning of housing policy, it becomes important to disaggregate within families and communities on the basis of gender.

Contributions to the book

The first chapter of the book provides a conceptual framework for the analysis of women's needs in human settlements and housing, and for the development of more appropriate policies to meet their needs. In it Caroline Moser identifies the extent to

which low-income women in developing countries have particular housing needs, on the basis of gender, by examining the
reality of their lives in terms of present assumptions underlying
government and international housing policy. She shows how
stereotypes, concerning both the structure of the family and the
divisions of labour within it, result in a failure to recognize
either the triple role of women (as reproducers, producers, and
community managers) or the increasing number of households
headed by women. She examines the consequences of these
fundamental misrepresentations in terms of current practice,
and concludes by indicating the importance of understanding
the distinction between practical and strategic gender needs of
low-income women in future housing policy. This provides the
background for the case studies that follow, in which the diversity of recent experience of women and human settlements is
examined.

While the review presented in the first chapter is critical of
housing policy and practice for failing to address the needs of
women, by contrast, the case studies are intended largely to
show the ways in which low-income women, despite differences in cultural contexts, are increasingly participating in
human settlement and housing projects and making their needs
heard by policy-makers and planners. The case studies reflect
experience from Asia, Africa, and Central and South America,
describing both the experiences of women in self-help 'bottom-
up' slum settlements, as well as with 'top-down' site and
service and upgrading projects. Lastly, they illustrate stages in
the project cycle with progression from project formulation
through implementation to issues of maintenance.

The project cycle, in fact, provides the rationale for the order
in which the case studies are presented. First is the issue of
resources for housing and the relationship between income and
decisions about housing in low-income households. That
women who head households are likely to be amongst the most
disadvantaged suggests that their housing conditions in
squatter settlements are likely to be amongst the worst. Sylvia
Chant, in a case study from Querétaro, Mexico, examines the
way in which various types of households make decisions about
housing consolidation. She shows that household structure is
an important determinant of willingness to invest in housing.
Her study reveals that, contrary to the stereotype view, in man-
headed nuclear units there is no significant correlation between
income and house type, while in non-nuclear units, woman-

headed, and extended, each improved category of house is related to an increase of income. She concludes household structure rather than income is the critical determinant of housing consolidation.

Although women may be primarily concerned to allocate resources to housing, in many contexts women who head households are frequently excluded even from access to new housing in government-sponsored projects because of lack of gender-awareness in project design. This problem is identified by Leda Machado in a case study from São Paulo, Brazil, where up to 30 per cent of low-income households are headed by women. Her appraisal of the Brazilian Housing Bank's Profilurb programme shows that in a number of site and service projects targeted for low-income families, women who headed households were excluded by various eligibility criteria. This chapter highlights the severity of the problem faced by low-income woman-headed households in their attempts to secure access to housing. As the next case study by Paula Nimpuno-Parente reveals, these difficulties continue throughout the project cycle. Her study of the World Bank funded Dandora housing project in Nairobi, Kenya, illustrates that even when women who head households meet eligibility criteria, they face problems at the implementation stage. In this study particular focus is given to the different strategies adopted by these women in the consolidation phase.

While women can play a crucial role in the building and consolidation of housing, this is not always recognized by planning authorities, or necessarily considered desirable by sections of the community. That this attitude is now changing is exemplified by a case study of women's participation in both the planning and implementation phases of a low-income housing project implemented by a non-governmental organization. Marina Fernando examines the experiences of local women in a US Save the Children Fund upgrading project in Kirillapone, a squatter settlement in Sri Lanka. Here women were recruited alongside men as members of a housing construction work-force in a 'top-down' community-based self-help project. She describes how the project initially did not focus specifically on the needs of women but identified itself as working with the community generally. Over time, as the particular problems faced by women became obvious, the project began to facilitate the participation of women in a wider range of activities relating to housing. These resulted in new skills, more confidence, and autonomy among women and new leadership within the community.

Two additional housing solutions are discussed by Linda Peake, in her chapter on the effects of government housing policy on low-income women in Guyana. In the Georgetown area, as in so many urban contexts, rental housing provides one of the most important solutions for low-income women. The case study identifies the problems women face in attempting to enter this sector. In addition it examines the government's official housing solution of co-operatives, and documents the constraints and setbacks at different stages of the project cycle experienced by an all-woman co-operative. Many of the difficulties arise from a lack of awareness by officials, of the problems faced by women involved in self-building. She concludes by analysing the extent to which the housing needs of low-income women in Guyana are met.

The last two case studies examine participatory experiences of low-income women in different human settlements. In her case study from Managua, Nicaragua, Irene Vance describes women's participation in the San Judas self-building housing project. This started as a 'bottom-up' initiative generated largely by the women, which then received government recognition of its participatory approach to house construction. Building groups, of both men and women, succeeded in constructing new houses. Nevertheless in the process of working together various conflicts occurred, both between the community and the authorities, and between men and women. Irene Vance assesses the extent to which these conflicts were gender-based, and identifies how gender-ascriptive roles affected both the form and degree of women's participation in different phases of the project. As the final case study shows, not only do women participate in projects to build houses or improve existing housing, but also in their community-managing role they participate in popular mobilizations which pressurize governments to allocate the basic infrastructure required for survival. Caroline Moser in her case study from Guayaquil, Ecuador, discusses the critical role women play in the formation, organization, and success of local-level groups. She focuses on the fact that protest around collective consumption issues is seen as 'naturally' women's work, and shows that this has implications both for women themselves, in terms of the development of their consciousness, as well as for the nature of struggle at the point of residence.

In their conclusion, Caroline Moser and Linda Peake highlight further important work for those involved in human settlements and housing, whether as activists or researchers. A comparison of the case studies in terms of which practical and strategic gender needs are met, indicates the extent to which current housing policy is feminist in practice. In the same way assessment of the objectives of including women's participation in the implementation phases of different projects indicates the extent to which this is motivated by principles of efficiency rather than equity. Lastly, and of fundamental significance is the question of consciousness, and the extent to which the experience of participation leads women to challenge further the nature of their living conditions, if not their own subordinate position.

Notes

1 Throughout this book the term 'productive' work is used to indicate paid work, in other words work, both in the formal and informal sectors, with an exchange value (even if, as is sometimes the case in family enterprises, this may not be perceived of as paid work with a salary given directly for work undertaken). It is critical, however, to acknowledge that reproductive work is also productive, but because it is the production of use values under non-wage relations it often fails to be acknowledged as productive work. For further discussion of this debate see for instance Gardiner (1977), CSE (1976), Barrett (1980). It is recognized, therefore, that the use of the term 'productive' work as paid work in this text is an oversimplification of reality. The purpose of simplifying is not to undervalue or ignore the importance of production for use value, but is based on the necessity for the conceptual rationale of gender planning to recognize that women, unlike men, have a triple role as producer, reproducer, and community manager, as discussed further in Chapter 1.

2 One of the staunchest proponents of the Women in Development approach has been USAID with its Office of Women in Development. Together with the Harvard Institute of International Development they have been responsible for developing a case study based methodology for identifying how women have been left out of development, on the premise that,

> Although there has been much activity, development planning efforts still fail to recognize fully women's actual and potential contribution to the development process or the effect of the development process on them. Women are key actors in the economic system, yet their neglect in development plans

has left untapped a potentially large economic contribution.

(Overholt *et al.* 1984: 3)

Critics of this approach argue that low-income women have always been integrated into development, their problem is one of inequality not only in class terms but also on the basis of gender, with their subordinate relationship to men their real problem. Thus the objective of women's projects should be to empower women, and to reduce the inequality between men and women (Moser and Levy 1986).

3 Much of the US work written about women and housing in the Third World has been written by, or commissioned for, USAID: see for instance Lycette and Jaramillo (1984) and Sorock *et al.* (1984).

4 Matrix (1984) has summarized these issues. Kaluzynska (1980) has provided a useful account of the domestic labour debate. For writing by US feminists see for instance Wekerle, Peterson, and Morley (1980); Wright (1980); and Hayden (1981). For recent work on the effects of urban planning on women see Davidoff (1979); McDowell (1983); and the Women and Geography Study Group (1984). Austerberry and Watson (1983) have provided a detailed examination of the effects of homelessness on women in the UK, while Ardener (1981) has examined issues of gender and space from an anthropological perspective.

5 An important exception to this is provided by Dutch feminist groups. See for example van Wijk (1986).

6 A succinct introduction to the debates about self-help housing has been provided by Ward (1982), from whose work these issues are summarized. In addition to Ward, probably the most rigorous critiques of the concept of self-help are those provided by Pradilla (1976) and Burgess (1978).

CHAPTER 1

Women, human settlements, and housing: a conceptual framework for analysis and policy-making

CAROLINE O.N. MOSER

Do women have particular housing needs that differ from those of men? Are there specific constraints that limit the access of low-income women in Third World countries to housing projects such as squatter upgrading and site and service schemes? In addressing these two questions the purpose of this chapter is to provide a conceptual framework of women's needs in housing and human settlements, both for analysis and policy-making. Examination of the assumptions that underlie government and international agency housing policy shows why it is necessary to distinguish housing needs not only on the basis of *income*, now commonly accepted, but also on the basis of *gender*, by which is meant a recognition and understanding of the different needs of women and men in low-income communities. The chapter concludes by highlighting the importance of distinguishing between practical and strategic gender needs, in order that future housing policy may be more appropriate for low income women in Third World countries.[1]

Housing policy and the needs of women

To identify the extent to which women have particular housing needs on the basis of gender, it is important to start by understanding the assumptions underlying housing policy relating to both the structure of low-income families and the division of labour within the family. Policy-makers, planners, architects, and designers both within governments and international agencies, all perceive themselves as planning for people. But regardless of the reality of the particular planning context there is an almost universal tendency to make two assumptions: first, that the *household consists of a nuclear family of husband, wife, and two or three children* and, second, that *within the family there is a clear sexual division of labour* in which the man of the family as the 'breadwinner' is primarily involved in productive work outside the home, while the woman, as housewife and 'homemaker', takes overall responsibility for the reproductive and domestic work involved in the organization of the household. Implicit in this is also the assumption that within the household there is equal control over resources and power of decision-making between the man and the woman in matters affecting the household's livelihood. In most societies this sexual division of labour is seen to reflect the 'natural' order and is ideologically reinforced (M. Mackintosh 1981; Scott and Tilly 1982).

Housing policies based on these unacknowledged assumptions are well known and widespread. For instance policy-makers tend to identify target groups in terms of the income of the male breadwinner; project authorities design eligibility criteria for participating in site and service projects in terms of the income of men and evidence of regular employment; and architects design houses to meet the needs of nuclear families, in which all productive work is undertaken by men outside the home.

THE 'TRIPLE ROLE' OF WOMEN

In most Third World contexts there are problems with this abstract stereotype model of society and the division of labour within it. First, it fails to recognize the *triple* role of women. In most low-income households 'women's work' includes not only *reproductive* work (the childbearing and rearing responsibilities) required to guarantee the maintenance and reproduction of the labour force, but also *productive* work, as primary or secondary income-earners, in rural areas in agriculture, in urban areas in informal sector enterprises located either in the home (in subcontracting or piece-rate work) or at the neighbourhood level (Moser 1981; Roldan 1985; Afshar 1985).

In addition, particularly in urban areas, women are increasingly involved in *community managing*, organizing at the community level in relation to the provision of items of *collective consumption*. With the inadequate provision by the state of housing and basic services, it is women who not only suffer most, but also are forced to take responsibility for allocating limited basic resources to ensure the survival of their households. In those instances where there is open confrontation between community-level organizations and local authorities over allocation of resources for infrastructure, it is women who, as an extension of their domestic work, take primary responsibility for the formation, organization, and success of local-level protest groups. In their gender-ascribed roles as wives and mothers, women struggle to manage their neighbourhoods and in so doing show their acceptance of the sexual division of labour and the nature of their gender subordination.

Because the triple role of women is not recognized, so neither is the fact that women, unlike men, are severely constrained by the burden of simultaneously balancing the three roles of *productive, reproductive, and community-managing work*. In addition only productive work, because it has an exchange value, is recognized as work. Reproductive and managing work, because they are both seen as 'natural' and non-productive, are not valued. This has serious consequences for women. It means that most of their work fails to be recognized as such, either by men in the community or by those planners whose responsibility it is to assess different needs within low-income communities. While the tendency is to see the needs of women and men as similar, the reality of women's lives is very different.

WOMAN-HEADED HOUSEHOLDS
The second problem is that this model fails to recognize that low-income households are heterogeneous in structure. The most important type of household, apart from nuclear families, are *de facto* and *de jure* woman-headed households in which the male partner is absent, either temporarily (for instance because of migration or refugee status) or permanently (because of separation or death). It is estimated that one-third of the world's households are now headed by women (Buvinic, Youssef, with von Elm 1978). In urban areas, especially in Latin America and parts of Africa, the figure exceeds 50 per cent, while in the refugee camps of Central America, it is nearer 90 per cent. Globally this is a growing rather than declining phenomenon.

The economic condition of these households varies considerably, depending on the marital status of the woman, the social context of female leadership, her access to productive resources and income, and lastly the composition of the household. It is important to recognize, therefore, that while women who head households do not constitute a separate category, nevertheless because they are also the primary income-earners the triple burden is likely to be exacerbated for them.

GENDER AND PARTICIPATION IN SELF-HELP HOUSING PROJECTS

Because of the self-help nature of so many settlement and housing policies in the Third World, the discussion of stereotype housing target groups must also include the issue of women's participation in self-help housing projects. Again it is necessary to identify the implications of present assumptions relating to the structure of the family and division of labour within it, in terms of the planning of community participation in human settlement projects.

The importance of community participation in human settlement projects is now widely recognized in terms of the role that intended beneficiaries and local organizations can and do play, not simply in the implementation and management phases of development projects, but also in decision-making about the design and allocation of resources.[2] Although participation is universally considered a 'good thing', because the implication is that the community influences the direction and execution of development projects rather than merely receiving a share of project benefits, the motives and objectives behind it are not always clear. As recently defined by Paul, these can range from empowerment and capacity building to increasing project effectiveness, improving project efficiency, and project cost-sharing (Paul 1986). The important distinction, however, is between projects that include an element of empowerment and those that do not. One 'measurement' of empowerment in projects has been through the distinction between participation as a means and participation as an end (Oakley and Marsden 1984). Where participation is a means it generally becomes a form of mobilization to get things done. This can equally be state-directed, top-down mobilization (sometimes enforced) to achieve specific objectives, or bottom-up 'voluntary' community -based mobilization to obtain a larger share of resources. Where participation is identified as an end the objective is not a fixed quantifiable development goal but a process where the outcome is an increasingly 'meaningful' participation in the development process (UNRISD 1979; Moser 1981).

Whatever the objectives of participation, ultimately it is a question of who is participating and the accessibility of a project to a target population, that determines the extent to which real participation occurs. At the policy level the tendency has been to conceptualize at the level of the family, with further disaggregation within the household not considered necessary. Above all this means that the important role that women play in community participation is only rarely mentioned at the policy level, despite the constant comments from those working on the ground that 'without the women the project would not have worked'. The fact that disaggregation on the basis of gender, which recognizes that men and women play different roles in society and consequently in community participation, is not considered important in many projects can have serious implications. Cultural variations and regional differences with regard to the role of women in society and in the household limit the participation of women. Nevertheless there are particular reasons for recognizing the role all women can play in community participation.

Three reasons have been advocated for incorporating women's participation in human settlement projects.[3] First, the participation of women is an end in itself. Women as much as men have the right and duty to participate in the execution of projects which profoundly affect their lives. Since women accept primary responsibility for childbearing and rearing, they are most affected by housing and settlement projects. They should, therefore, be involved in the planning and decision-making as well as the implementation and management of such projects. The objective identified here could be said to relate to both empowering and capacity building.

Second, the participation of women is a means to improve project results. Since women have particular responsibility for the welfare of the household, they are more aware than men of the needs for infrastructure and services and are also more committed to the success of a project that improves living conditions. The exclusion of women can negatively affect the outcome of a project, while their active involvement can often help its success. In this case the objectives relate to efficiency, effectiveness, and cost recovery.

Third, participation in housing activities stimulates the participation of women in other spheres of life. Through active involvement in housing projects women may be encouraged to participate fully in the community. Participation in projects has been seen as an important mechanism to 'overcome apathy' and 'lack of confidence'. It can show women the potential of self-help solutions and may raise awareness that women can play an important role in solving problems in the community. The objectives here reflect a welfarist concern to 'integrate women into the development process' or an anti-poverty preoccupation to assist low-income women (Moser and Levy 1986).

Consequences of household stereotypes for human settlement and housing policy

What then are the consequences of these fundamental misrepresentations in terms of the stereotyping of housing target groups? How does this widespread tendency to assume the abstract ideal world described above affect current human settlement and housing policy? In order to answer this question it is necessary to examine some of the problems that women experience in present housing practice, because of the lack of recognition of their triple role.

In reality the three different roles that women perform cannot be seen as separate from each other, since it is their very interdependence that is the critical determinant in identifying their needs. Thus for instance, while reproductive and domestic work often determine a woman's ability to participate in the labour force, this may well determine the extent to which she has free time to participate in managing work at the community level. Nevertheless since many needs are specific to the different roles of women these are discussed separately.

WOMEN AS REPRODUCERS
Women, in their roles as wives and mothers, are the primary users of space both in their houses and in the local community. Yet their particular needs are often ignored or not recognized in both *settlement planning and house design*, and they are rarely consulted at this stage of human settlement projects.

In settlement planning the most critical issue for all women is *rights to tenure*. These are usually given to men on the assumption that they head households, even where women have primary *de facto* responsibility for their families. Obviously this problem is most extreme in those countries where women, by virtue of their legal standing, do not have rights of ownership. This has several important implications for them: without rights to land, women are often unable to protect themselves and their children from unstable or violent domestic situations; property rights tend to reinforce the control that the man, as primary income-earner, already has over the household and its dependants; without land rights women are often unable to provide collateral to gain access to credit; finally, ownership of land represents a form of saving, as it appreciates over time. Thus where women have no title to land they may end up without capital in the event of marital separation.

17

Where land is a scarce and expensive resource, decisions about land-use are made primarily with reference to technical and financial criteria, and often without consideration of the culture and life-styles of future residents, especially women. Land-use planning involves trade-offs between the allocation of space for public and private use, and between different uses. In many countries women are restricted by the physical boundaries of the house or the community, and therefore the *settlement layout* affect them profoundly. Their needs in terms of plot arrangements may be quite different from those of men. For example they may prefer plots to be grouped around services so that domestic work can be increasingly communal.

Where plots are arranged with a communal orientation the work of women can be eased by mutual help. However since it is most often cheaper and more efficient to lay out services on a grid basis, this type of pattern is not often implemented. For example in the settlement planning of George, an upgrading project in Lusaka, Zambia, roads and plots were laid out on a grid pattern. The traditional layout had been circular with women able to carry out housework within sight of each other. The new layout forced them to work in more isolated conditions; they were no longer able to leave their houses unlocked or their children playing under the watchful eye of neighbours (Schlyter 1984).

Because of their low-paying capacity residents can generally afford only a limited provision of services: public water taps, pit latrines, simple roads, and open drains. Where the priorities of women are not taken into account this can cause severe problems for two reasons. First, women have first-hand experience of domestic labour without services, and therefore can best order the *provision of different services*. Second, women's work can be adversely affected by the introduction of services totally inappropriate to their needs, as a result of lack of prior consultation. This is frequently the case in the *design and planning of community facilities*. For example water pumps, introduced to provide clean water, have broken down because handles were designed for use by men, and women and children (the principal waterbearers in the community) broke them through their inability to operate them correctly (IWTC 1982). Women are very rarely consulted about the design of sanitation they will use. In a project in El Salvador, for instance, women would not use the toilets designed by male engineers because a gap left at the bottom of the door exposed their feet, and offended notions of privacy (IWTC 1982).

In some countries the provision of sanitation is a low-priority issue because men, unlike women, do not require the same privacy to perform ablutions. For example in many Middle Eastern countries, because of the purdah system, women can defecate only on rooftops. Case studies from Bangladesh have shown that without adequate private toilets, women can relieve themselves only before sunrise or after sunset, causing severe medical problems. In the slums of Bombay, women without private toilets have to perform their ablutions in isolated locations where they are particularly vulnerable to rape and molestation (Agarwal and Anand 1982). Rubbish collection is another service where the opinions of women are important. In Lusaka project authorities found that most households threw rubbish away in such small quantities that they budgeted for shared dustbins to improve efficiency of emptying. Dustbins were returned, however, because people insisted on individual household ones, a situation that might have been avoided had women, the principal domestic users, been consulted.

Although women are the primary users of space within the house they are infrequently consulted in *house design*. This can become a problem for women when 'modernization' or 'developmentalism' results in radical changes from traditional to modern house design. For instance in Tanzania, the 'Better Housing Campaign' was initiated to persuade people to replace traditional houses, built with local materials, with more durable dwellings. This required people to use imported materials, which raised costs. As a result the establishment of new houses was impeded. This threatened tradition because it prevented the normal practice of separate accommodation for different family members. Where men were required to stay with their families the traditional autonomy of women was undermined as they were redefined as dependants (Caplan 1981).

The detrimental effects of insensitive house design often affect Muslim women who, because their social life is almost entirely confined to the home, have special needs for internal space. For instance in two low-income settlements in Tunis, Mellassine, a squatter upgrading project, and Ibn Khalkdoun, a planned community (with a wide range of units from basic core-housing to comparatively elaborate three-bedroom dwellings), women were dissatisfied with house design, because of the small size of the inner courtyard. Most houses were a compromise between the traditional dwelling with several rooms around a spacious internal courtyard, and a modern European-style house, with a space around the outer walls. Pressure on land, insensitivity to women's needs, and middle-class aspirations to European architecture, had resulted in a reduction of inner courtyard area, in some cases leading to psychological depression, neuroses, and even suicide among women (Resources for Action 1982).

Because women accept primary responsibility for household budgeting, the *financing of housing and repayment of loans* is often also their responsibility. While husbands often agree to loan conditions wives have to balance household budgets to pay this back. Investment in housing may be linked to potentially disposable income within the household, but women do not usually control this. Where the household is committed to self-build their house to a certain standard in a certain time this can have an impact on other aspects of household finance; if house finance is made available at the expense of the domestic budget, women may end up cutting back on food and working much harder in the home to compensate for the drop in resources and to save money.

WOMEN AS PRODUCERS

Lack of recognition that women have productive income-earning roles means that their economic functions are not identified. As a consequence, in the planning of settlements and the design of houses, planners and architects fail to appreciate that the pattern of women's work differs from those of men both spatially and in the type of employment they undertake.

A critical element in the decision-making over the *location* of a settlement, of either a new site and service project or a squatter resettlement, relates to the location of work of the target group. When a new community is located near an industrial zone there is often male bias in location, despite the fact that women have to combine economic and domestic roles. For example in Delhi, between 1975 and 1977, there was a massive relocation of 700,000 squatters to seventeen resettlement colonies on the outskirts of the city. In Dakshinpuri, one such settlement with 60,000 residents, it was found that women were far more affected than men by the move. Relocated some distance from their former place of employment, many women could no longer combine domestic and productive work adequately, and with the cost of public transport cutting deeply into their meagre earnings, working was no longer feasible. Thus while the rate of male employment fell by 5 per cent the employment of

20

women declined by 27 per cent (Singh 1980).

Although central city locations are often desirable for plot location, high land prices generally force low-income housing projects to the periphery of the city. While trade-offs are made between land and transport costs these rarely take account of the needs of women, for whom there are often opportunity costs in terms of time spent fulfilling their triple role. In Belo Horizonte, Brazil, for instance, it was found that urban transport services were organized in favour of men's employment needs. Buses ran from the periphery to the centre at peak morning and evening periods to take the male work-force to their jobs. Although women needed to use public transport for activities such as taking children to and from school, shopping, making health-related trips, and above all getting to their own part-time jobs, many buses were withdrawn during the daytime making the average daily travel time for women three times longer than that of men (Schmink 1982).

Zoning legislation, which separates residential and business activities, may prohibit the development of income-earning activities in the home or locally in the residential areas. This is problematical for women who are involved in informal sector activities in their homes. The only solution very often for women making goods in their kitchen or selling products from their front room is to do so illegally. In the same way zoning legislation that prohibits subletting of space within homes often prevents women from their only possible independent source of income, as well as preventing families from increasing their total income.

The assumption that women are involved only in childcare and childrearing means that settlement planning does not usually allocate resources for *childcare provision.* Lack of such provision at the work-place often results in children being left on their own, or in women having to work from home, either in less remunerative retailing activities or more exploitative subcontracting or outwork. Even where provision is made for childcare, problems often arise because of lack of credit facilities. In the Dakshinpuri resettlement project in Delhi, for instance, several women wished to be self-employed in income-generating activities such as sewing and knitting. Consequently a large 'industrial shed' was established in the community by the government. However the scheme bypassed women completely because it failed to recognize their lack of necessary skills and finance to set up production units. As a result the benefits

21

of the income-generating component went mainly to skilled male residents or to outside entrepreneurs who took advantage of subsidized work space and the abundance of cheap labour (Singh 1980).

In *designing houses* architects rarely pay attention to the need for women to generate an income in the home. Lack of consultation with women means that the designs of dwelling structures are inappropriate for cottage industry or renting. Space and design requirements for commercial activities obviously vary according to cultural context. In some circumstances women may wish to run a shop from their front room, in which case a large room with plenty of storage space and several power points for electrical items such as refrigerators would be desirable. In other cases, especially in hot climates, women may need a large verandah, in order to combine income-generating activities such as sewing, small-scale production, or retailing undertaken simultaneously with childminding.

Although in the design and planning phases of housing projects the productive role of women is often ignored, in the implementation phase of both site and service and upgrading projects, women often play an important part in *house construction*. Women are involved in house-building in a number of different ways (individually, as members of a family, or in community building groups) depending on the type of project and the cultural context. However, major obstacles such as lack of time, skill, and confidence, as well as culturally specific reasons may prevent women from participating. Rigid notions about the sexual division of labour, upheld by both women and men, mean that in many contexts the involvement of women in construction represents an invasion of what has traditionally been seen as men's work. Sometimes if wives are seen to work, men may be exposed to public humiliation and derision from friends. In other situations women are present but in a supportive role providing unskilled labour, which is often not recognized. Where housing project authorities build on local traditions and assume only men are capable of house construction, they may find they are reinforcing gender inequalities. On the other hand through involving women equally in house construction they may be able to effect changes in terms of the work relationships between women and men.

Constraints relating to the composition and organization of self-help building groups affect women in different ways, again depending on the cultural context. Frequently project authorities recruit male members of households on the basis that it is 'natural' to train men in construction skills. However many building projects recognizing the skills of women have been highly successful. In a women's self-help construction project in Panama, for example, 91 of the 105 women members were provided with training in order to construct 100 houses: two-month courses provided training in carpentry, masonry, or plumbing. They then worked in building groups of eight to ten members supervised by an instructor. Construction was completed in ten months, only three months longer than anticipated. As each set of houses was finished the women decided amongst themselves who should receive the dwelling, using criteria of who had worked the hardest and who was in greatest need. This mutual construction was not conflictive, but provided the basis for a sense of self-reliance and employability (Girling, Lycette, and Youssef 1983).

In the Panamanian project the self-help building groups were women only. Not all groups are so harmonious, however, and in those contexts where men work alongside women in mixed building groups the potential for disagreement appears to increase. For example in the overspill area of an upgrading project in Lusaka, Zambia, where construction teams were based on the block, problems arose through differential contributions. Despite the greater constraints on women's time, the evidence showed that while men attended most of the meetings, the women ended up doing most of the work (Rakodi 1983).

WOMEN AS COMMUNITY MANAGERS

In their role as community managers women are often involved in vital but largely unrecognized work. This includes mobilizing for community facilities, maintaining such facilities once obtained, and organizing reproductive activities such as cooking and childcare at a community level. After plot allocation and house construction the provision of services is the next important stage in the formation of settlements. Basic infrastructural services such as water, electricity, sanitation, and roads are required, as well as social services such as schools, clinics, community, and religious centres. The extent to which these services are obtained through community action varies according to the type of settlement and the manner in which it was established.

Frequently it is to obtain basic infrastructural services in squatter settlements that community organizations are first formed. Although women do not necessarily see themselves as natural leaders they play an important role in the formation of such organizations. In many societies both men and women consider it an extension of a woman's domestic role that she obtains services for the community. Therefore in the long process of struggle to persuade the authorities to allocate the desired services women are often particularly effective in lobbying and organizing community participation, despite the time-consuming nature of their domestic duties and planners' lack of awareness of their roles and preference to negotiate with men.

Community involvement in the *maintenance of infrastructure* is important not only in squatter settlements but also in self-help housing projects, where it reduces additional expenses during the cost recovery period. This involves learning how to use infrastructure such as public water taps and latrines. As the primary users of infrastructure in settlements women have a vested interest in keeping them as hygienic and habitable as possible even in the face of extreme hardship, while in many community-level projects maintenance is seen as the 'natural' responsibility of women because of their involvement in domestic labour. When women are effectively involved in the decision-making, training, and construction phases of projects the tendency is for them to assume responsibility for maintenance. Problems arise, for instance, when they are unwilling to maintain new equipment because of lack of training. In addition old customs are frequently difficult to break especially when the new technology is not aimed at women. Therefore the combination of inappropriate design and inadequate discussion with women as to how to use the new infrastructure can result in a lack of commitment on their part. A comparison between two Mexican projects where new waste management systems were introduced showed that more effective results were achieved in the settlement where the role of local women was recognized, than in the other where the engineers and government officials ignored women (Schmink 1984).

In many Third World countries the problems of day-to-day subsistence have been exacerbated in recent years, by the effect of the debt crisis on the lives of the low-income population. In efforts to provide community-level solutions women play a significant role, in taking responsibility for the allocation of limited basic resources to ensure the survival of their households

For example in Lima, Peru, one response to the high cost of food and rising incidence of tuberculosis and deficiency diseases has been the development of the communal kitchen movement using donated foodstuffs. In a society where cooking by a woman for a man is the public sign of their having initiated marital life together, the socialization of this reproductive activity has had important consequences. For men, community kitchens undermine their position in the household, whereas for women they offer a means of alleviating poverty (Sara-Lafosse 1986).

PARTICULAR CONSTRAINTS ON WOMAN-HEADED HOUSEHOLDS
In describing some of the problems women experience in Third World housing practice reference has been made throughout to low-income women generally, without specific reference to their marital status or position within the household. For the vast majority of low-income women in the Third World have a triple role, regardless of whether they live with a spouse or partner. However, those women who head households experience additional constraints, not only because their triple burden is exacerbated but also because of the assumption in planning that the man-headed nuclear family is the 'normal' household type. Since *de facto* woman-headed households are an increasing global phenomenon it is important to identify in greater detail the particular housing problems they experience.

The most important consequence of the man-headed nuclear family stereotype is that women who head households are frequently excluded from low-income housing projects because of a lack of gender awareness in the eligibility criteria, especially in terms of income level. Women usually predominate in unskilled non-unionized occupations, earn lower wages than men, and are not protected by social services. To be eligible for housing projects, usually families need to have an income greater than the lowest 10 per cent of the population. That estimates of household income are based on earnings alone means that 'transfer' income is discounted. Yet this often makes an appreciable difference to the total income of households headed by women. For example, in the Solanda site and service project in Quito, Ecuador, woman-headed households made up 30 per cent of the total applicants, but 46 per cent of them did not qualify for access to the scheme because their incomes were too low. In addition the requirement for a down payment, of between 5 and 15 per cent of total housing costs was prohibitive for women unable to save money or gain access to credit (Lycette and Jaramillo 1984).

Because women are usually in jobs without legal status or protection, secondary criteria requesting proof of stability of employment discriminate against women who head households. Another common problem occurs when it is assumed that the head of household is not only a man but also married. Sensitivity to this problem was shown in a site and service scheme in Mexico City, organized by a low-income co-operative (USCOVI) which drew up eligibility criteria specifying that applicants had to have a partner, although not necessarily married to them (Arredondo, Kusnir, and Largaespada 1984).

Methods of recruiting beneficiaries, including means of announcing the scheme, applications procedures, and down payment requirements often inadvertently discriminate against or exclude women. When project authorities assume that everyone reads newspapers or public notices, with information distributed in written form, women are often missed. In many parts of the world women's access to education is considerably less than that of men. In addition women are less likely to be exposed to information because of their lack of daily mobility. Responsibilities in the home mean that they are often unable to participate in activities where information is likely to be available. In two low-cost housing projects in a squatter settlement in Paraguay, nearly 50 per cent of the women interviewed complained that lack of information about shelter was a major obstacle to improving their housing conditions, whereas only 16 per cent of the men complained of a similar problem (Sorock *et al.* 1984). However, even where more direct methods of advertising are used by project authorities, such as a meeting where eligible applicants are likely to live, women are often prevented from attending by domestic responsibilities, with house-to-house visits ultimately the only guaranteed way of reaching them.

Application and selection procedures often present problems for women when they involve complex forms that require documental substantiation, such as proof of identity and an employer's reference. Women are less likely than men to have been previously involved in formal dealings with public agencies and may have difficulties in filling in application forms. In the Solanda project in Quito, Eduador, some 30 per cent of the original women applicants dropped out of the project before the selection ever began, due to their inability to get together all the necessary documents (Lycette and Jaramillo 1984).

Women who head households often require special assistance not only to acquire a plot in housing projects, but also for financing house-building. They have particular disadvantages in securing loans because of such problems as lack of information about credit programmes, low and irregular incomes, lack of collateral, complicated loan application procedures, discrimination on the part of men bureaucrats, high interest rates, and women's lack of legal standing in certain areas. Project authorities may attempt to compensate for the exclusion of women from formal credit facilities, first through the stimulation of informal women-only saving co-operatives, and second, through establishing a project loans fund for the specific purpose of house-building. A number of successful credit programmes for women have been established, but oriented towards employment rather than housing. Examples include SEWA (the Self-Employed Women's Association) in India with over 13,000 members, 90 per cent of whom are illiterate (IWTC 1981; Singh 1980); the Women in Development Loan Fund in Barbados (where 42 per cent of all households are headed by women); and the African Co-operative Savings and Credit Association (ACOSCA) in Nairobi, Kenya, which attempts to pressurize government bodies to promote the participation of women in credit unions (IWTC 1981).

Financial hardship during building affects all households, but is particularly severe for women who head households since they are often the only income-earner. The most effective way to ensure that they continue in housing projects is to support them directly during the building phase. In the Women's Self-Help Construction Project in Panama 100 houses were built by women, 45 per cent of whom were heads of household. The project included a stipend for women during the construction phase, the purpose of which was to free them from routine economic responsibilities during that time. Together with the cost of building materials the grant was not required to be repaid until the building was completed and the women housed. Although the stipend solved the immediate economic problem of finding time to build, it nevertheless necessitated financial strain for many years afterwards, since the agreement specified that the loan should be repaid over a twenty-five-year period (Girling, Lycette, and Youssef 1983).

Cost recovery is one of the most difficult aspects of low-income housing projects and women who head households are especially disadvantaged if project authorities calculate 'feasible' cost-recovery payments on the basis of average household earnings for the community as a whole. Because most women are in self-employment they are often unable to pay fixed sums every month. However, despite greater economic difficulties, women are nevertheless more responsible in repaying loans. A survey of the National Housing Trust in Jamaica (where 40 per cent of households are headed by women, and unemployment rates for women are twice as high as for men) found that relatively greater numbers of men were in arrears. Furthermore women appeared more responsible about their debts, personally visiting the Trust's office to discuss their problems when unable to repay. There were also instances of women in households headed by men making personal payments on mortgage loans to ensure that they protected the shelter for their children and themselves (Population Council 1983).

Women who head households also have special problems in house construction. Frequently they lack both skills and time to self-build but are often required to do so in the absence of funds for professional labour. However where minimal housing standards are required, with specific time limits the process becomes both more expensive and more time-consuming. The World Bank funded housing programme in El Salvador, for instance, showed the special dilemma of women who had insufficient time or income either to buy or to complete shelter units or to hire skilled labour. Loss of time at work implied a loss of earnings to which there was no satisfactory solution without radically restructuring project plans to incorporate awareness of gender, such as paying women a stipend during the construction phase (Lycette and Jaramillo 1984).

The training of women in construction skills is important, especially for those who head households. This is being recognized within the organization of women-only projects. In Jamaica, for instance, the Western Kingston Women's Construction Collective originated from a plan for women to enter construction through a training and employment programme. To a certain extent it represented a break with traditional gender-ascribed roles for many women. Over 90 per cent of those trained have since found work, repaying the investment made in their training. Employers, pleased with female performance, have requested more women workers because of their high productivity and low rates of petty theft and violence (Schmink 1984).

Meeting the housing needs of women: the question of practical and strategic gender needs

The fact that women, because of their triple role, have particular needs in housing that differ from those of men, or low-income families generally, indicates that women's needs will not be achieved by simply 'grafting' on 'women' as a category to existing housing policy. Fundamental changes in attitude towards traditional stereotypes are required before a gender-aware approach can be reached: this is an approach capable of acknowledging that women have different housing needs from those of men, by virtue of their gendered position, and that in many societies there are specific constraints that limit women's access to housing on the basis of gender, regardless of income.

Ultimately, however, it is also important to identify how far planning for the housing needs of low-income women is necessarily 'feminist' in content. The distinction between practical and strategic gender needs may be useful in the clarification of this issue.[4] Practical gender needs are those needs which arise from the concrete conditions of women's positioning, by virtue of their gender, within the sexual division of labour. Within these positions, needs are formulated by women themselves, in response to the living conditions which they face daily. Therefore in many contexts needs such as adequate housing, clean water supply, or community crèche facilities are identified as the practical gender needs of low-income women, both by planners as well as by women themselves. In reality practical needs such as these are required by all the family, especially children, and their identification as 'women's needs' serves to preserve and reinforce the sexual division of labour. At the same time it is important to recognize that such needs are in no sense 'feminist' in content.

By contrast, strategic gender needs are those needs identified from the analysis of women's subordination, and, deriving out of this, the formulation of an alternative more satisfactory organization of society to those which exist at present, in terms of the structure and nature of relationships between men and women. A diversity of ethical and theoretical criteria, many of which are culturally specific, assist in the formulation of strategic objectives to overcome women's subordination. Depending on the particular socio-political context, strategic gender needs may include the abolition of the sexual division of labour, the alleviation of the burden of domestic labour and childcare, and of particular relevance to housing, the removal of institutional forms of discrimination by creating equal rights to land ownership or to access to credit. Strategic gender needs are generally considered 'feminist', as is the level of consciousness required to struggle effectively for them.

Although the provision of housing is meeting family needs these are frequently identified as meeting the practical gender needs of women because in their domestic roles women are the principal users of housing. However this does not mean that they automatically become the owners of either the house or land. In many housing projects tenure has been increasingly identified as a significant issue with rights to land generally given to men on the assumption that they are household heads. It is only where housing projects have been designed to provide for ownership regardless of the sex of the household head that women have been able to achieve equal right to own property. In such cases the project can certainly be evaluated as 'feminist' in content, if not in design.

The distinction between practical and strategic gender needs is useful to correct the assumption that meeting women's practical needs automatically furthers women's strategic needs. In addition it highlights the constraints encountered by those who seek to challenge existing policy and practice in human settlements and housing. In many contexts there is resistance to changing the existing sexual division of labour within the household, and the division of responsibility between men and women in issues relating to human settlements.

This opposition may derive equally from two sources. First, it may derive from 'integrationalists' who want better conditions and the incorporation of women into policy frameworks, but within the existing structures, accepting the triple role and endorsing what for many is an inequitable status quo. This may include not only policy-makers but often the majority of low-income women, whose power derives from their gender-ascriptive roles as wives and mothers. Second, opposition may derive from policy-makers who conveniently base their work on inappropriate abstract models of society.

Thus the specific circumstances by which conventional assumptions can be challenged and restructured may be dependent on the development of consciousness at two levels. It may depend as much on the 'bottom-up' emergence of women's consciousness through the experience of participation in human settlement, as it does on the 'top-down' opening up of political space. Ultimately it may be the conjuncture of the two that is necessary for any fundamental change in the nature of gender relations and housing to occur.

Notes

1 This chapter draws substantially on four articles all of which are concerned with different aspects of the needs of low-income women (Moser and Levy 1986), with the importance of women's participation in urban housing projects (Moser and Chant 1985; Moser 1986), and with housing policy and its attitude to women (Moser 1985a).

2 No clear consensus exists as to what is meant by participation with the diversity of definitions reflecting the ideological range of interpretations of development and different approaches to planning which have themselves changed over time as is shown by three United Nations definitions. At one end of the continuum the UN in 1955 identified community participation as synonymous with community development when it stated that 'community development is a process designed to create conditions of economic and social progress for the whole community with its active participation'. At the other end of the continuum UNRISD in 1979 identified the real objective of participation as 'to increase control over resources and regulative institutions in given social situations, on the part of groups and movements of those hitherto excluded from such control' (UNRISD 1979:8). More specifically in the field of human settlements UNCHS in 1984 defined community participation, referring to it as 'the voluntary and democrative involvement of the urban poor in carrying out these project activities' (UNCHS 1984a: 1; Moser 1986).

3 These three arguments follow the same format as UNCHS's three arguments employed to advocate the incorporation of people's participation in the execution of projects (UNCHS 1984a: 1). These were first identified by Moser and Chant (1985) and have now been included into the UNCHS training manual on the participation of women in the execution of housing projects (UNCHS 1986). Moser (1986) has further elaborated on these issues.

4 The development of this terminology is derived originally from Molyneux (1985a) who distinguished between practical and strategic gender interests, which were translated into planning terms as strategic and practical gender needs. Thus Molyneux wrote:

> Gender interests are those that women (or men for that matter) may develop by virtue of their social positioning through gender attributes. Gender interests can be either strategic or practical each

being derived in a different way and involving differing implications for women's subjectivity.

(Molyneux 1985: 232)

Practical and strategic gender needs are discussed in further detail in Moser and Levy (1986).

© *1987 Caroline O.N. Moser*

CHAPTER 2

Domestic labour, decision-making, and dwelling construction: the experience of women in Querétaro, Mexico

SYLVIA CHANT

Introduction

This chapter examines the role of women in the production and consumption of self-help housing in irregular settlements in Querétaro, Mexico.[1] The aim is to show that the participation of women in the housing process is a critical determinant of dwelling standards and that participation is often conditioned by the type of household to which women belong. Particular consideration is given, therefore, to the ways in which women's involvement in decision-making and dwelling construction varies with household composition. The type of household to which women belong not only affects the extent to which women are included in the housing process, but also has considerable implications for the kinds of dwellings produced by self-help methods. Generally speaking, in households where women participate in decisions affecting housing priorities, as well as in the organization and building of their homes, proportionally more time and income are allocated to housing than in households where women have only limited authority over household budgeting and expenditure.

The chapter is divided into six sections. The first reviews the factors influencing the construction and improvement of dwellings and indicates how women and household structure have been ignored in the analysis of self-help construction. The second section describes the study area and considers the political economy of low-income housing in both Mexico and Querétaro. The third section briefly examines women's role in

33

household survival strategies in the study settlements, particularly in terms of their involvement in domestic labour, while the fourth section looks at the extent of women's participation in housing decisions in various types of households. The fifth section considers the organization of house-building by low-income households paying particular attention to the economic constraints created by the construction industry. The final section traces the implications of differential participation by women in housing for the design and quality of self-help dwellings.[2]

The determinants of dwelling construction: an overview

Studies of Third World housing have rarely considered the role of women in either the production or the consumption of self-help dwellings. To an extent this is due to the nature and scale of the issues addressed. For example many analyses have tended to focus on the broad economic and political implications of irregular settlement development. However, even in micro-level household or community studies, women have not been a specific focus of attention. The literature on house construction and improvement *per se* is particularly notable for its omission of women since, in most parts of the world, women play a crucial role in the process of home-building (Nimpuno-Parente 1985; Moser and Chant 1985; Vance 1985). The literature falls into two main groups. The first deals with the problem of house-building in irregular settlements 'from above' stressing the importance of structural economic factors such as inflation in the cost of construction materials or land prices as a major determinant of the potential levels of house consolidation by low-income groups. (Consolidation refers to the gradual improvement in dwelling standards – Connolly 1982; Herner and Ziss 1980.) The second approach deals with the problem 'from below' emphasizing the influence on the consolidation process of factors operating at the level of the household (Turner 1972, 1976; Sudra 1976; Ward 1976). Studies in the latter category have not concerned themselves with the issue of gender. Instead they have emphasized the significance of the following factors in the self-construction process. First, security of land tenure is seen as a *sine qua non* of housing improvement (Clarke and Ward 1980; Doebele 1983; Dwyer 1975; Sudra 1976; Turner 1976; Angel *et al.* 1983). While people live under the threat of eviction, they will not use scarce and expensive resources building permanent homes. Rather they construct houses out of lightweight, easy-to-assemble materials that may be easily dismantled and rebuilt in another area should an eviction be ordered. Beyond the prerequisite of secure tenure for house construction, studies have also stressed the importance of a series of 'quantitative' variables such as length of residence, levels of education of the occupants, employment of the household head, and most significantly income, in influencing willingness and ability to invest in housing (Turner 1972, 1976; Ward 1976; Angel *et al.* 1983). Literature that deals with the impact of more 'qualitative' aspects of home construction, let alone the issue of gender, is very scant.

One of the few works on the relationship between households and the housing market in Latin America was that of John Turner in the early 1970s. In his article 'Housing as a verb', he maintained that housing is not so important for what it *is*, as for what it *does* for people: 'The worth of the physical product cannot be assumed to lie in its physical qualities, but rather in the relationship between the object and the user' (Turner 1972: 159). Turner developed a schema of residential patterns embodying the idea that there are three existential needs operating for low-income households in their search for shelter: these needs were termed 'opportunity', 'security', and 'status'. The search for 'opportunity' (economic opportunities or jobs) is the principal need and is reflected in the desire for a central location near to sources of employment. 'Security' refers to the need for legal tenure which translates into a shift of tenure from renting to ownership. Finally, in the latter stages of the life cycle, households may begin to think about the material quality of their homes. This last priority is termed 'status' to convey an idea of house consolidation as an outward manifestation of the household's desire to demonstrate their improved economic condition.

While there have been numerous critiques of Turner's work (Burgess 1978, 1982; Harms 1982) in relation to its political and economic implications, none have focused attention on its androcentric nature. In particular the priorities outlined above are not necessarily indicative of the needs of individual members other than the heads, who are assumed to be men. The priorities of women and children as the most direct 'users' of housing are ignored. In addition, given that women's work in particular is greatly affected by the material condition of the house, the use of the term 'status' to describe the desire to improve the physical quality of one's dwelling is inappropriate. It implies that concern lies with the external appearance of the home and not with the quality of housing, which affects the work and daily living experiences of those who spend a great deal of their time within the home. Thus Turner's work exemplifies a gender-blind approach, characteristic of most of the literature on self-help housing. Not only does this literature ignore the fact that household members other than the head (assumed to be male) may have different priorities for housing, but also it remains silent about the role, however limited, that women and children may have in housing improvement. Nor does it take into account the way in which households headed by women operate.

In the light of these gaps in the literature on the impact of household composition on decision-making, the remainder of this chapter demonstrates how both the structure of the household, and the division of labour within it, are of vital importance to house construction. In fact these may be of far greater importance than quantitative variables such as income and length of residence which have been emphasized as the major determinants of housing improvement.

The settlements in the study

Since the Second World War Mexico has undergone a rapid and intense process of economic transformation and development, marked by an average annual economic growth rate of 6 per cent. Post-war development has been concentrated in the manufacturing sector and has led to heavy investment in urban areas and a concomitant rise in migration and urbanization. Thus whereas in 1940 only one-third of the Mexican population lived in urban areas, by the 1980s two-thirds of the national population were classified as urban dwellers. Prior to the 1970s most migration was directed to the major industrial centres of the country, namely Mexico City (the capital), Guadalajara, and Monterey. However, from the 1970s onwards successive government administrations have attempted to encourage decentralization of industry and population towards smaller urban centres, both to forestall problems arising from over-concentration of manufacturing activity, and to spread the benefits of economic growth to other parts of the country.

Querétaro is one of the cities designated as a priority area for decentralized industrial production.

One major problem caused by large-scale migration from rural areas to cities has been pressure on the limited, 'formal' housing supply. The problem of housing shortage has been compounded by the fact that urbanization has often outstripped the capacity of the industrial sector to provide jobs. Multinational firms in particular tend to use capital-intensive production methods resulting in comparatively low labour requirements. Because many migrants are unable to find jobs in the manufacturing sector conventional housing supply is not only scarce, but also too expensive for most urban residents. Consequently the majority of the low-income population have been forced to occupy land illegally and to build their own shelter in irregular settlements.

There are three main types of irregular settlements containing self-help housing in Mexico. The first type is that of the squatter settlement in which public or private land is invaded. The second comprises clandestine subdivision in which land is bought at low cost from private owners who have no authorization to sell for residential development. These settlements are illegal because the owners lack planning permission to sell for the purposes of residential development, and also because the settlements do not usually comply with minimum official norms for services and infrastructure. The third type of settlement, perhaps peculiar to Mexico, is the *ejidal* urban settlement. The Mexican *ejido* is an area of land handed over by the state to a specific agricultural community. Despite the fact that this land may not be sold, or in any other way alienated, many *ejidal* communities sell lots illegally for urban development.

In all these cases, title to land for urban settlers is initially nonexistent. However, if the authorities allow the settlement to remain, land is eventually regularized and the residents pay to obtain a title deed. The Mexican government have had to accept that irregular settlements constitute the only way in which low-income groups can obtain housing and, therefore, usually have condoned their existence. Irregular settlements, then, are the most common form of low-income housing in most Mexican cities undergoing industrialization and Querétaro is no exception.

Querétaro lies about 200 kilometres north of the capital, Mexico City. The city was originally founded in 1531 and remained distinctly colonial until the mid-1950s when the first multinational manufacturing firm was established, attracted by abundant space and cheap land. Since then Querétaro has received many industries under the nationwide programme of industrial decentralization. Its relative proximity to Mexico City and its abundant natural resources have made it a zone of high priority for decentralized investment. Thus over the last twenty years Querétaro has grown more than fivefold and currently has a population of about 400,000. Much of this population growth has resulted from in-migration of rural people in search of industrial employment.

Given the rapidity of Querétaro's development, there has been great pressure on housing and irregular settlements have proliferated. In 1980 it was estimated that 38 per cent of Querétaro's population were accommodated in ten major irregular settlements on the outskirts of the city (Chant 1984a). Most of these settlements grew out of illegal land sales by *ejidatarios* (the members of *ejidal* communities). Although a government agency, CORETT (la Comision para la Regulariza- cion de la Tenencia de la Tierra) has now, in most cases, expropriated land acquired illegally in the settlements on the outskirts of Querétaro and regularized the property rights of the inhabitants, large areas remain poorly serviced, lacking water, sewerage, paved roads, and rubbish collection.[3] Indeed one community waited eight years to receive electricity, which is the cheapest service to provide.

Three communities in Querétaro were selected for study on the basis of age, origins, and service levels. The first settlement, Bolaños, is one of Querétaro's oldest irregular settlements with a population of approximately 3,000 people. The first families arrived in 1970 and bought their plots, most of which have now been regularized, from the *ejidatarios* of the agricultural community of Bolaños. The settlement is located on a hillside to the north-east of the city where the land surface is rough, rock- strewn, and littered with broken glass, tin cans, and decompos- ing rubbish. Its topography poses major difficulties for the provision of services. Apart from electricity, two elementary schools, and a bus service, Bolaños lacks all other services.

Los Andadores, the second settlement, dates from 1976 and is much better serviced than Bolaños. It is one of two settlements in the city to result from an illegal promotion of lot sales by government officials on land designated for services. Situated in the south of the city on the margins of the largest irregular settled area in Querétaro, Lomas de Casa Blanca, it is on flat land with regularly laid-out plots. About 3,500 people live in this densely populated settlement, which is provided with electricity, rubbish collection, paved roads, and pavements, in addition to access to a range of amenities installed in nearby Lomas de Casa Blanca. Furthermore, most people have legal title to their land in Los Andadores.

The third study area is Las Américas, one of the most recent settlements in the city. It is another *ejidal* urban zone, which still remains unregularized and like Bolaños is very poorly serviced. Although its formation began in 1978, most people did not arrive until 1980 and currently it has a population of around 2,500 people. On a hillside in the northern part of the city, it overlooks the Industrial Zone, and has electricity, a few public standpipes for water, and a daytime bus service. Most of the population in the community are owner-occupiers, as in the other two communities, although legal title has not yet been awarded.

A total of 244 households in owner-occupation in the three settlements were interviewed with a structured questionnaire. These households represented around 30 per cent of the owner-occupiers in each settlement.[4] Nuclear units, all of which were headed by men and consisted of a married couple with children, constituted two-thirds of the sample (see Table 1). Households headed by unmarried, separated, or divorced women living alone with children accounted for 10 per cent of the sample. Extended units, where one or more relatives of the head of household reside in the same house, sharing all domestic functions and finances, and living as full members of the household made up the remaining one-quarter of the sample (four-fifths of these were headed by men and one-fifth by women).[5]

Table 1 *Household composition in three irregular settlements in Querétaro*

Household composition	Settlement		
	Bolaños %	*Los Andadores* %	*Las Americas* %
Nuclear	72.0 (72)[1]	63.0 (58)	71.2 (37)
Woman-headed	10.0 (10)	8.7 (8)	7.7 (4)
Man-headed extended	13.0 (13)	22.8 (21)	19.2 (10)
Woman-headed extended	5.0 (5)	5.5 (5)	1.9 (1)
Total	100.0 (100)	100.0 (92)	100.0 (52)

Source: Chant 1984a.
Note: [1]Number of cases

It is important to note that household structure is not static; over half the units in the study settlements had experienced the loss or gain of members between 1976 and 1982. These changes in composition are most likely to occur when household heads are a little older than the average of 35 years or when a woman head or spouse is about 40 years old, that is at a stage when sons or daughters are likely to get married and in-laws come to live in the house, or when a parent dies.

The role of women in household survival strategies

Before discussing how household composition affects the role of women in decision-making over housing, a brief outline of women's role in household survival strategies is necessary, to clarify how and why women's participation may affect dwelling standards.

Most women in the survey (two-thirds) were full-time house-wives and even for those who took on income-generating activities, housework and childcare still occupied a great deal of their time. Since management of domestic labour was seen to be the primary responsibility of women they had a substantial interest in what happened to their homes. Not only is a woman's domestic labour affected by the quality of housing, but also it is women who are most knowledgeable about the ways in which housing might be best improved to increase their efficiency. If women are not included in decision-making, it is possible that the improvements or extensions to housing might not benefit them particularly.

Housing in the settlements varies greatly. Approximately one quarter of those in the survey lived in shacks of flimsy building materials such as tin-can or corrugated cardboard with dirt floors. Another quarter lived in houses that were a mixture of brick and board, and although the remaining half lived in brick-built dwellings with concrete floors and roofs, these 'finished' houses often lacked glass in the windows, solid doors, plastered interiors, and easy-to-clean vinyl or wood floors.

When people in low-income communities without basic services, such as water, paved roads, sewerage, and rubbish collection also lack soundly built housing, women have to work harder in order to ensure minimum levels of hygiene. For example the lack of a concrete floor posed may difficulties. Dirt floors are often responsible for parasitic infections in children such as hookworms, which can enter their bare feet, so that young children have to be constantly supervised in their play. As there was a considerable amount of dust generated by earth floors, household utensils, clothes, and furniture stored in wooden crates or cardboard boxes got dirty very quickly. In the dry season, women regularly had to sprinkle water to stop the dust from rising and, in the wet season, when rainfall may be torrential, people could find themselves up to their knees in mud, so that women had to rewash everything. Lack of glass in windows also resulted in dust being blown in from unpaved roads and open lots. Another problem with shack dwellings was the lack of space: twice daily women rearranged bedding and furniture. Furthermore, there was little security in this housing, and many women felt worried about leaving their shacks unguarded. The quality of housing, therefore, obviously affected women greatly.

The need for women to be included in decisions about the housing process also stems from the fact that women in Querétaro appeared to be more concerned about the quality of family life, in which the nature of housing plays an important part. Since the home was the area in which the majority of family interaction occurred, women tried to ensure that their homes were as pleasant and comfortable as possible. If they were denied the right to make full use of the resources available, they understandably felt a great sense of disillusionment and frustration.

The study showed that there was often no correlation between household income and house quality. For example sometimes two households of similar size, age, structure, income, and length of residence would be living in very different types of dwellings. The most significant factor accounting for difference appeared to be the nature of the relationship between husband and wife and the freedom of the woman to earn money and exert authority over the allocation of the household income. Women tended to have a more dominant position in the households if they had paid employment, which was usually associated with the amount of freedom and responsibility their husbands allowed them. This comparatively greater investment in housing was reflected in higher dwelling standards than households of similar income levels in which the woman was severely constrained by her husband. In this latter group not only would women be prevented from sharing in the control of household expenditure or going out to work, but also they would have to contend with living in poorer-quality dwellings, since their husbands did not consider the quality of housing to be of great importance.

The hypothesis that male control over women's involvement in household budgeting and housing decisions was a crucial factor determining quality of dwelling was substantiated by the fact that many women who headed households began to improve their housing only after their husbands had died or deserted them. Contrary to the stereotype, households headed by men were living in inferior dwellings to those headed by women, despite having higher earnings.

The evidence suggested that income may be managed and distributed very differently in different households, and that higher incomes were not necessarily related to better housing standards. Thus while the possibility of generating a financial surplus for home improvements was an important factor, it is suggested here that it is a dependent rather than an independent variable in determining housing strategies and investment. Of greater importance was the composition and cohesiveness of the household unit, and especially the degree of involvement of women in economic matters.

Household structure and decision-making

Having outlined the rationale for women's involvement in housing decisions and having argued that their inclusion in decision-making may be a key determinant of dwelling standards, the possibilities of women becoming involved in housing are explored in relation to different household structures.

NUCLEAR UNITS
These units, which constituted the majority of owner-occupier households in the settlements studied, offered women least scope to participate in decision-making. This was partly because of the sharp demarcation between the roles of men and women in these households. A couple with children had to find the best way in which to combine the paid (income-earning) and unpaid (domestic labour/childcare) aspects of survival. The sexual division of labour meant that women spent time not only bearing but also rearing children, thus interrupting their employment. This, plus the fact that men were likely to earn twice as much as women doing the same jobs, favoured men as breadwinners

(Selby *et al.* 1981). Furthermore, men often did not wish their wives to work because this could threaten their authority in the family, undermining their role, which may already be precarious if wages were low and employment insecure (Bridges 1980): in the nuclear units in the survey two-thirds of the women were full-time housewives, few being allowed by their husbands to engage in paid work. Their subordinate position to men was thus reinforced not only by the fact that their domestic labour was undervalued, but also by the fact that they had no independent source of income.

As the husband's wage was frequently the only wage, the household was dependent on one income, and the woman often had limited bargaining power in determining how these wages should be spent. As the man's economic situation was not dependent on co-operation with the rest of the household, the quality of life within it was often dependent on his whim, or the strength of emotional ties with his wife and children. While exenditure on housing was closely related to the extent to which men cared about and felt responsible for their dependents, poor and overcrowded housing itself may have encouraged men to spend more time away from their wives and children. In this situation relations progressively deteriorate, which in itself may further reduce male commitment to improving housing. This is important, because where people are living at subsistence level, with little job satisfaction and few rewards, the marital relationship may be subjected to a great deal of strain, with men looking for compensation in outside pursuits (Bridges 1980; Bromley 1982). As a result, there was often a great deal of 'secondary poverty' within nuclear households. Not only could male abuse go unchecked, but also men often spent a large portion of their wages on other women, drink, card games, and tobacco, and allocated only a little to the household. Therefore the standard of living of the male breadwinner was frequently higher than that of his dependants.

Within nuclear units, earning an income did not automatically increase a woman's decision-making power. In 60 per cent of the nuclear units in which women were earning, men still made decisions on such issues as spending on clothing and domestic items as well as daily expenditure on food, transport, schooling, and housing. Consequently the decision to invest in housing depended on the attitude of the male head. If he spent the greater part of his time at home rather than at the local bar then more money was allocated to housing.

In the remaining 40 per cent of nuclear units in which women were earning, decision-making was shared to a greater degree. In these units expenditure on housing was given a higher priority. The women cited housing as their first priority for investment, giving a number of reasons, including security in case of a death in the family or desertion by the husband, reducing time spent on housework enabling them to set up small businesses in the home, or enabling the household to enjoy being at home together with reasonable levels of space and comfort.

EXTENDED UNITS

In these the division of labour between men and women appeared less marked than in nuclear units. Why should this be so, and what implications does it have for decision-making and housing improvement? These units were composed of either an extended household headed by a man, or a single-parent household with additional relatives. The composition of extended units was often a consequence of a conscious strategy, especially in the case of households headed by women where the incorporation of additional adults into the household provided greater scope for managing both the paid and unpaid aspects of survival more efficiently (Blumberg 1978; Tienda and Ortega 1982; Winch 1978). When adult relatives moved into the home of a nuclear or single-parent unit they rarely remained for long unless they contributed substantially to the household. In the great majority of cases they participated both in waged and non-waged work for the household.

Three factors influenced the pattern of life in these units. First, there were at least two earners within the household and in many cases there were four or five if part-time workers are included. Second, the housewife's role, which in nuclear families was often burdensome and lonely, could be far more rewarding if the other members were women. Housework could then be shared which would increase efficiency through the division of tasks. Not only did this alleviate the domestic load of each worker, but also it provided company during otherwise menial and repetitive chores. Third, where the additional member was a woman, wives had a greater opportunity to take a job outside the home. This was due to the sharing of housework, which released women from the full-time role of wife and mother. Also the presence of other women in the household contributed to female solidarity and strength. Furthermore, the fact that household earnings were communal meant that to maximize income there was a vested interest for the household to send all possible members out to work.

In the survey almost half the women in extended units were involved in generating their own incomes. Decision-making patterns tended to be more 'democratic', because where there was more than one wage-earner in the household, co-operation and a common budget were required if the household was to function as a single unit. It was rare for one person's wage to be used for drink while another's was spent on housing or food. In turn, a common budget gave rise to the inclusion of a greater number of people in determining the allocation of resources, and the fact that women were frequently wage-earners resulted in women's priorities carrying as much weight as men's. Lastly, as paid and unpaid tasks were shared more equally between men and women, the work done by those who did not earn was valued more highly than it was in other households. Therefore non-earners' needs were also taken into account and given more priority in household decision-making. Extended households then, through their more collective and participative survival strategies, allowed women to be involved in decision-making to a greater degree than in nuclear households.

Women-headed units

Women heads of non-extended units had still more scope than women in extended households to participate in decision-making over housing. By virtue of being the head of their household, these women had more power and autonomy. For example they could decide whether or not to engage in paid work, although in some cases it was difficult for them to do so when they had young children. However, as the majority of these households formed when a mother was in her late thirties, they could often rely on both monetary and domestic help from their older children.

Although in the majority of cases it seemed that women became heads of household because their husbands died or abandoned them as they approached middle age, a substantial minority (about one-third) initiated separation from their partners, because of male abuse, especially if it was affecting their children. (There were no households headed by women who had never resided with a man.) This indicates that some women were prepared to contravene established social and cultural norms in order to gain control of their lives and protect their children. But whatever the reasons behind the formation of these households, as soon as they secured employment or access to income through their children's employment, the women concerned were in a position to control household decision-making and expenditure. Frequently older children participated in these decisions. As a result, housing often received far greater attention than it had when men had been in charge.

From this profile it is clear that women's involvement in housing decisions was often dependent upon the type of household unit to which they belonged. Women's participation was particularly high where they headed households (because there was no control by a husband); it was also moderately high within extended households where the authority of male heads was limited by other adults in the family; but it was low in nuclear households where women's lives were strongly conditioned by their husband. These variations in the position of women were expressed in housing standards. Before examining the implications of women's role and household structure for dwelling conditions, it is necessary to consider practical aspects of decisions about housing, particularly the organization of house-building.

The organization of house-building

In order to place the question of housing improvement in its economic context the effects of the current recession in Mexico on house-building must be examined. The role of household structure in housing consolidation and the participation of women in the self-help building are then discussed.

In the spring of 1983 a one-roomed house of 16 square metres, built of brick with a concrete floor and roof, one metal door, and one glass window, cost about 50,000 *pesos* (approximately £225) excluding land and labour. In terms of the legal minimum wage, this was equivalent to about five months' earnings. However, many women who headed households earned less than the minimum wage. In addition households were rarely able to save more than 5 per cent of weekly income, with at least half the population not saving anything on a regular basis. Therefore a one-roomed house was equivalent to about four or five years' savings for families with only one wage-earner. The financing of housing improvements has become increasingly difficult for several reasons. At the beginning of 1983, wages were increasing at a rate of 20 per cent, whereas the prices of many construction materials such as cement, wood, and iron were increasing at a rate of between 50 and 60 per cent. Labour costs were also rising steeply.

It is important to identify how inflation affects the households in the settlements studied by considering the extent to which the residents' labour can be substituted for professional skills and the scope for other methods of reducing costs. It has long been recognized that self-help housing is not necessarily self-built housing (Burgess 1978). In Querétaro 56 per cent of those surveyed hired paid labour for at least part of the construction tasks. However, at certain stages of housing improvement, some households had advantages relative to others. To elaborate, the process of housing consolidation must be examined in three stages: first pre-construction, which included lot clearance, laying the foundations, and erecting a temporary shack; second construction, which included bricklaying, flooring, and roofing; and third finishing, which included plastering, painting, and electrical wiring.

Pre-construction tasks such as lot clearance were relatively straightforward, although they could be long and arduous, especially in areas of difficult terrain. For example two of the communities were located on steep hillsides covered in cacti and rubbish, with a thin or patchy soil. To level the ground boulders had to be moved or broken. A lot of 200 square metres could take six months to clear with household members working in the evenings and at weekends. Tasks such as this were usually carried out with the help of friends and relatives, and occasionally paid labourers, who advised on the size of the foundations, the amount of cement needed, and so on. However, when households began to undertake building that involved specialized skills, they had to find the money not only for the building materials, but also for skilled labour, especially for flooring, roofing, and bricklaying. A few households did these jobs themselves, especially if there was a construction worker in the household, or if there was a close friend or relative who had worked in the building trade. However, because of the problem of wastage of materials it was often more cost-effective to hire professional help. The 'finishing' stages of housebuilding, involving such tasks as plastering and painting interior walls, and electrical wiring, were lighter and tended to be carried out by the households themselves.

In the survey, just over half of all households hired paid labour for at least one aspect of house construction. However, when different types of houses and tasks are examined, differences emerge. The first point to note is that poorer-quality homes tended to be self-built. Thus while 90 per cent of all shacks were built by households themselves, only one-quarter of the brick and concrete dwellings had been built entirely by household labour. Some households substituted their own labour for paid help to save money for other aspects of house improvement. For the less skilled tasks, such as painting or plastering, units in which there were many adults were more likely to be able to do the job themselves. Thus 59 per cent of extended households had homes with plastered walls, and of these, 77 per cent had carried out the job themselves. In contrast 52 per cent of nuclear households had homes with plastered walls, but only 30 per cent had carried out the task themselves. (The majority of these were households whose head was over 40 years old and had grown-up sons.)

Households headed by women tended to hire paid labour. Several remarked that 'women on their own could not build a home'. This was especially true of mothers, with dependent children, who had been abandoned. However, a substantial minority (one-third) built their houses with family labour, particularly if they were fortunate enough to have relatives living nearby who could help. Building was undertaken by these households either because they needed to save money on labour in order to purchase materials, or because it was known that workmen often took advantage of women. Labourers tried to capitalize on what they assumed was the greater gullibility and passivity of women.

Although there is wide discussion of the fact that people in the Third World have to build their own houses (Burgess 1978, 1982; Harms 1982; Ward 1982), there is little mention of women's involvement in house construction. However, it is very rare that women are not involved, even if this is merely an intensification of their routine domestic work, such as fetching and carrying water, clearing up after the labourers, or providing them with food and refreshment. Women's roles are supportive, and often remain unrecognized by other family members, or indeed themselves. Sometimes women were involved in supervision, particularly if labourers were hired, since they remained on site while their partners were at their place of work. However, when men were present, women tended to be relegated to the simpler or lighter chores. Male members of the household did not train women to carry out the heavier or more skilled tasks.

This division of labour was most marked in the nuclear units. For example in one-third of the nuclear units women had not taken any active role in building (although they had performed additional domestic chores) whereas this was the case in only 9 per cent of the households headed by women and 18 per cent of extended households. In most instances, however, women were involved in secondary or supportive roles, for example climbing ladders to pass on tools, mixing the materials, decorating the house interior, and clearing the lot. A small percentage of women, particularly if they headed households or belonged to extended households, were more involved in house construction and helped to carry out such tasks as bricklaying, roofing, and electrical wiring. When women were involved in these tasks not only was the household maximizing the use of its own labour resources, but also it was giving women a greater sense of worth, and a greater stake in the property. Although some construction work was very heavy women were capable of undertaking it; indeed what they did in house-building was only marginally more difficult than much of their domestic work. But what they often lacked was sensitive training and encouragement to do these heavier chores. As the sexual division of labour was so marked in nuclear families, young male boys were given construction jobs for which their mothers, by virtue of their greater size and strength, were better suited. This implies that the tasks women performed in construction were still identified as domestic activities and therefore undervalued as work for house-building *per se*. Despite the help of women, men often claimed that they had built their houses entirely on their own.

The fact that in certain households women were not encouraged, or sometimes allowed to participate to a greater extent in house-building, meant that construction proceeded only if men were present. Consequently jobs took longer, work often being limited to weekends, although women might have been able to finish certain tasks during weekdays when there was sufficient light. Thus women's greater participation in construction might not only have reduced costs by saving on hired labour or favours to male kin, but also have improved the speed and efficiency of construction.

Housing standards and household composition

Having discussed the ways in which different household types make decisions about the building of their homes, and the extent to which they involve women, the relationship between household composition and dwelling standards is now examined. In the survey, house standards were assessed quant-itatively using an index of dwelling consolidation developed for a housing study carried out in Mexico City in the early 1970s (Ward 1976). The index was modified to suit local circum-stances. Numerical scores were given to three aspects of the dwelling condition: the level of services, the quality of materials used in various parts of house, and the amount and type of consumer goods possessed by the family. For example a composite score was obtained for the second aspect, from the materials used in the roof, walls, and floor. If the walls were constructed of debris a score of one was recorded; if built of corrugated cardboard or wood, two; if of unplastered brick or stone, three; and if of plastered brick or cemented stone, four, and so on. The composite scores for the three aspects of the dwelling services were summed to give an overall score. A brick and board house with a legal electricity supply and a latrine and consumer goods such as a radio and a television would score eighteen. (Scores ranged from 7 to 27.) Table 2 shows that extended households headed by men had the highest mean score, followed by nuclear households, then extended house-holds headed by women, with non-extended households headed by women having the lowest score.

Holding sex of the head of household constant, extended households (headed by women or men) scored higher than nuclear households. This may reflect the ability of extended households to make savings on labour costs that did not require specialized knowledge. When household structure is held constant, the relationship between income and house type becomes clearer, except in the case of nuclear households, as is shown in Table 3. Furthermore, it appears that non-nuclear households lived in better housing than their nuclear counter-parts on the same per capita income. For example an average nuclear unit had 6.2 persons, meaning that the weekly per capita income was 499.3 *pesos* in a shack, 491.0 *pesos* in a brick and board house, and 686.3 *pesos* in a brick and concrete struc-ture. Extended families contained an average of 10.6 persons, meaning that in a shack the weekly per capita income was 263.1

Table 2 *House scores and household structure*

Household structure	House score	Scores		
		Standard deviation of house score	Range of scores	
			Lowest score	Highest score
Nuclear	18.3	4.5	7.0	27.0
Single-parent	15.4	3.5	8.0	20.0
Man-headed extended	18.7	3.7	8.0	25.0
Woman-headed extended	16.1	3.6	9.0	21.0
Mean	18.0			

Source: Chant 1984a.

Table 3 *Average weekly household incomes to household structure and house type*

Household structure	House type			Average income
	Shack	Brick and board	Brick and concrete	
Nuclear	3,095.8[1] (35)[2]	3,044.2 (53)	4,255.4 (79)	3,630.0 (167)
Single-parent	2,647.2 (12)	3,545.0 (7)	4,100.0 (3)	3,131.0 (22)
Man-headed extended	4,124.7 (9)	4,458.0 (11)	4,752.5 (24)	4,548.5 (44)
Woman-headed extended	2,789.0 (3)	4,462.0 (6)	4,896.0 (2)	4,082.0 (11)

Source: Chant 1984a.
Note: [1]All incomes quoted in Mexican *pesos* (1983)
Note: [2]Numbers in brackets refer to numbers of cases

pesos, in a brick and board dwelling 420.9 *pesos*, and in a brick and concrete structure 461.8 *pesos*. Therefore, although factors such as the labour market, the price of construction materials, and earning differences were important, household structure also had a great effect on the willingness to invest in housing. This in turn was related to the degree to which women were allowed to participate in housing decisions and dwelling construction. Provided a surplus could be generated in non-nuclear households, where women tended to have far greater authority, then more disposable income would be allocated to home improvements. While the correlation between income and consolidation levels was not direct in non-nuclear households, the figures do show a broadly positive relationship, which was not the case for nuclear households.

It is also important to draw attention to housing design, particularly of kitchens. There was a higher incidence of separate kitchens in extended households and those headed by women. Most of the women attached importance to a private kitchen area, arguing that it was easier for them to cook in a separate space, but one from which they could supervise their children; they also felt that a separate structure was more hygienic. Hygiene was further improved by brick-built structures, which helped to reduce dust and insects. Proportionally more women in nuclear households were confined to makeshift, lean-to kitchens or were forced to cook in one corner of the bedroom or living-room. This was particularly the case in nuclear households where women did not have an independent source of income. Lastly many households thought that the quality and appearance of their homes reflected the relative happiness of the people inside it, with a solid, well-kept house symbolizing a stable and happy family life. This finding suggests that care should be taken not to over-emphasize 'quantitative' variables such as income in determining levels of house consolidation.

Conclusion

In this chapter it has been argued that women's involvement in the production and consumption of self-help dwellings is important in the understanding of house-building and improvement of irregular settlements. It is also pertinent because previous studies of the determinants of dwelling consolidation have been limited in their power to explain how households of similar income levels and length of residence in a settlement occupy markedly different types of housing. Further, the approach adopted in this chapter combines the conventional, quantitative approach with qualitative material and observations, such as the issue of household composition and dynamics.

The survey has shown that women are likely to wish to invest surplus household income in the improvement of dwellings, not only because better-consolidated housing alleviates the hardship associated with domestic labour in the complete or partial absence of urban services, but also because women are concerned with making their homes as pleasant and comfortable as possible. Consequently in households where women are allowed to exercise a considerable influence over the allocation of household finance, a greater amount of disposable income is spent on the improvement of dwellings. Women's participation in housing decisions has been shown to be greatest in households headed by women and in extended households.

From the data presented here, a case may be made for the need to incorporate household decision-making, and particularly women's role within it, into more general analyses of house construction and improvements in irregular settlements. The study has emphasized that housing is a commodity that affects all household members. Decisions about investment in housing and in design and construction should therefore involve all household members. Where such decisions rest with one male member households may face the prospect of living in sub-standard shelters.

Notes

An earlier draft version of this chapter was published as Chant (1985) 'Family composition and household consolidation: the case of Querétaro, Mexico', *DPU Gender and Planning Working Paper* no 2, University College, London.

1 The word 'irregular' instead of squatter settlement is used because in the Mexican context squatter settlements refer to only one of three settlement types. This is discussed in greater detail in the text on p. 37.
2 This chapter is based on fieldwork in Mexico carried out between June 1982 and June 1983. It was financed by the Social Science Research Council of Great Britain (now the Economic and Social

Research Council) under the supervision of Drs A.G. Gilbert and P.M. Ward in connection with their research project sponsored by the Overseas Development Administration, entitled 'Public intervention, housing and land use in Latin American cities'.

3 CORETT was established by the government in 1974 to regularize tenure of irregular urban settlements in Mexico.

4 The term 'household' here is used to describe a group of individuals who live under the same roof and who participate in and benefit from the collective survival strategy and experience of the residential unit. All households in the survey were family-households, consisting of kin. Kinship relationships are of two types: consanguine and affine. Consanguine relationships involve blood ties between people, for example between a parent and children, brothers and sisters, cousins, and so on. An affine relationship describes a formalized or legalized affective relationship such as that between husband and wife, in-laws, and so on.

5 There were also a few 'nuclear-compound' households where two or more nuclear families lived on the same plot of land, but had separate financial and domestic arrangements. They were excluded from the sample population on the basis that the degree of 'living apart' on the same land plot varied greatly, making generalization impossible.

CHAPTER 3

The problems for woman-headed households in a low-income housing programme in Brazil

LEDA M.V. MACHADO

Introduction

Housing policy for low-income groups has tended to treat women as invisible such that their needs have not been taken into consideration. If programmes are to increase low-income groups' access to services and infrastructure without excluding women and children, there is a need for gender-aware interventions. The relevance of studying woman-headed households in Brazil, as in many other developing societies, is that this group is increasing in size. Moreover, households headed by women are usually dependent upon the earnings of women and children. Thus because of wage differentials between male and female workers, woman-headed households are in a more disadvantaged position than those headed by men of the same social class. Although woman-headed households may be found in high-income groups in Third World countries they are more frequent in the lower-income groups, in other words, groups that are normally employed in the informal sector of the economy. It is the latter that form the focus of this study.

This chapter examines the extent to which a government housing programme in Brazil has considered the specific needs of women who head households. Profilurb (*Programa de Financiamento de Lotes Urbanizados*) was created in 1975 as a programme of site and services schemes. It was the first programme of its kind in Brazil. Before appraising this programme a review is given of the economic development of Brazil and the associated changes in women's employment structure with specific reference to the 1970s. This is followed by a discussion of the material conditions and the economic characteristics of woman-headed households. The Profilurb Programme and the position of woman-headed households within the programme are then examined. The conclusion highlights issues that could lead to the incorporation of gender issues on to the planning agenda.

Brazil's economic development and changes in women's employment structure

The objective of outlining changes in women's employment structure is to understand better women's employment structure in the 1970s, the period of the Profilub programme, and the implications for women's capacity to generate income for the household, especially households headed by women.

Madeira and Singer (1975) identified three phases in the evolution of women's participation in the work-force in a developing country. First, at commencement of industrialization, the greatest number of people employed are in the agricultural sector and there are many small-scale home-based enterprises (both manufacture and commerce) in which women's participation is high. Second, with the reduction of small enterprises at a domestic level and the expansion of industrial production the level of female participation tends to diminish. Third, female participation rises owing to the growth of job opportunities in the tertiary sector that is now able to absorb women who have been squeezed out of other sectors. (It should be noted that the economic participation of women is underestimated in official sources. Neither domestic work nor work in the informal sector is included in the census. Few women, therefore, have all their economic activity taken into consideration. Thus statistics used in the following section are only approximations.)

These three phases will now be applied to an overview of women's employment in Brazil. Although industrial manufacturing production began in the nineteenth century (Singer 1968), until the beginning of the twentieth century, the Brazilian economy was essentially agriculture-based (Furtado 1971). According to the 1872 census 45 per cent of the work-force were women mostly employed in agriculture and domestic service (Saffioti 1978).[1] In the twentieth century women continued to comprise a large part of the work-force. This first (pre-industrial) phase ended with the start of the First World War when internal demand for products from the major industries (mainly the textile and food industries) increased as a result of the difficulty of importing goods. Expansion of industry coincided with a decline in female labour force participation rates. By 1920 the proportion of women in the working population had fallen to 15 per cent. Merrick and Schmink (1983) consider that this decline may relate to changes in the compiling of employment statistics but it also undoubtedly relates to the fact that, as industrial production expanded, female workers were being replaced by male workers (Saffioti 1978).

Industrial production continued through the first half of the twentieth century. During the Second World War import sub-stitution policies caused a further increase in the rate of industrialization while the post-war period was marked by the penetration of foreign investment, mainly from the USA. This internationalization of the Brazilian economy introduced multinational industries which were large-scale, using sophisticated technologies and skilled workers, invariably male. Merrick and Schmink (1983) point out that between 1950 and 1970 the textile industry reduced the number of female workers by one-quarter while in the same period it nearly doubled the number of its male workers. This resulted in the absorption of the rest of the labour force into other economic sectors: the majority of urban workers have swelled the services and commerce sectors, particularly those characterized as the 'informal sector'. 'These workers, *many of them women*, have more erratic earnings and less stable employment patterns' (Schmink 1982: 4, my italics). Thus the 1950s and 1960s ushered in the third phase. During this period women worked in agriculture, essentially as unpaid family workers in subsistence production (Saffioti 1978), but were primarily concentrated into what were seen as suitable 'female' occupations in the service and commerce sector such as primary-school teachers, seamstresses, and domestics (Abreu 1977). By 1970 women comprised 20 per cent of the working population. Their numbers continued to increase throughout the 1970s, and by 1979 had reached 32 per cent. Of these 24 per cent were employed in the primary sector, 13 per cent in the secondary sector, and 63 per cent in the tertiary sector (IBGE 1981).

According to Paiva, in the occupations that women dominate, for example teachers and domestic servants, their wages were lower than, often only half, those for men (Paiva, quoted in Barroso 1982). Furthermore, in relation to wage levels, women have been concentrated in the lowest category. From the (monthly) half minimum wage category up to the maximum category of more than 20 minimum wages (in 1978) the proportion of women decreases steadily from 60 per cent down to only 7 per cent.[2] Another important consideration is that the lowest paid workers, among whom women predominate, do not have their work cards signed, which is a necessary precondition for access to National Social Welfare (INPS).[3] This lack of signed work cards pertains to both male and female workers; however, the percentage of female workers without signed work cards is higher than for male workers. In 1976, for example, 89 per cent of female agricultural workers and 44 per cent of female non-agricultural workers did not have their work card signed. The corresponding percentages for male workers were 81 for agricultural workers and 23 for non-agricultural workers (Barroso 1982). This brief examination of women's employment in the 1970s indicates that women are disadvantaged in relation to men in terms of access to housing programmes that specify an income level of greater than one monthly minimum wage. The following section illustrates the heterogeneity that exists amongst women and focuses on the particular problems faced by woman-headed households.

Woman-headed households: trends and characteristics

Information on woman-headed households in Brazil as in many other countries is limited, and the number of woman-headed households is probably underestimated. This is because the concept of the 'head' of the household is defined in a misleading manner in both the Brazilian Census and in the National Household Sample Survey (PNAD): 'The head would be the person considered responsible for the family. In principle the head should be the husband. The woman was only considered head if she was not married or did not live in a stable consensual relationship' (translated from IBGE/UNICEF 1982: 88).

Bearing in mind these problems the census data still provide some useful information. The period 1950–70 saw a growth in the number of woman-headed households, with absolute numbers doubling from 1,219,000 in 1950 to 2,416,600 in 1970 (corresponding to total numbers of households of 10,046,200 to 18,554,400); this represents a rise from 12.1 per cent to 13 per cent of all households. For urban areas, in which woman-headed households are geographically concentrated, the corresponding percentage for 1970 was 16 per cent as against 9 per cent for rural areas. These figures by 1977 had risen to 18 per cent and 11 per cent respectively. Furthermore, the largest percentage increase in woman-headed households is found in the poorest regions of the country (the north and north-east). According to Barroso (1982), in 1973 the north-east region had the highest percentage of woman-headed households (16 per cent). The lowest percentage (10 per cent) was in the prosperous south. By 1977 these percentages had risen to 18 per cent in the north-east region and to 11 per cent in the south.

The economic characteristics of woman-headed households are important for the assessment of the Profilurb programme. Data for the 1970s from IBGE/UNICEF (1982) show that the income of households headed by women was lower than for those headed by men, and that 20 per cent of the households headed by women in 1970 did not have any income. (The percentage of households headed by men in the same category was only 1.3 per cent.) This percentage fell to 7 per cent by 1977, but still meant that 244,389 households were without an income. In addition 5 per cent of woman-headed households fell in the lowest minimum wage category with an income equivalent to no more than half the minimum wage.

These low household incomes may be explained by the fact that woman-headed households are likely to have a low level of access to the INPS and that households headed by women generally comprise children, old people, and other women (IBGE/UNICEF 1982). As the greatest increase in woman-headed households has come from an increase in separated and divorced women they usually lack a male secondary worker, making them dependent upon the earnings of other women and children. Possible explanations of the way in which these households survive is through child work, or through a system of interchange of favours with neighbours or extended family, or through work in the informal sector (Barroso 1982; IBGE/UNICEF 1982). Low-income woman-headed households, for example, generally have fewer children or no children at all registered in school, compared with man-headed households. This may be explained by the need for children to earn. However, the situation is worse for girls than for boys. In one study of woman-headed households, it was found that 30 per cent more girls missed school than boys. Of these girls, 80 per cent missed school owing to domestic responsibilities, in order to allow other household members, usually their mothers, to work (Machado Neto, quoted in Schmink 1982). In order to eliminate the cost of their upbringing, girls often work outside the home as domestic servants, rarely receiving money for their labour (Merrick and Schmink 1983).

If woman-headed households lack adequate access to housing, it is more difficult for them to secure the conditions necessary for their maintenance and reproduction. Given the constraints which many women who head households have to face such as having a low income, lack of access to the National Social Welfare system, and the need for their children to work, adequate housing is crucial for their survival. These groups should therefore be a priority in the provision of housing by the government. The success of one such programme in meeting the needs of women-headed households is now appraised.

The Profilurb programme

The Brazilian Housing Bank (BNH) was founded in 1964 after a right-wing military coup in Brazil which brought about a bureaucratic and authoritarian regime. Although the BNH was recently abolished (in November 1986) it played a major role in the provision of housing in Brazil. State intervention at the national level on the housing question had occurred prior to the existence of the BNH. The first institution created was the Popular Housing Foundation, which failed to solve the housing problem primarily due to the fact that it was a low priority for the populist government of the day, therefore, in 1953 the government proposed the creation of the Mortgage Bank. This was never implemented, and in 1961 the government created the Brazilian Housing Institute. But, as a result of administrative problems and lack of finance this did not function effectively. Thus the government created the BNH to 'direct, discipline and control the Financial Housing System, which aims at promoting home ownership for Brazilian families, especially among low-income groups (up to three minimum wages)' (BNH, nd).[4]

At this time the country was facing economic recession, and construction of housing was considered as a way of stimulating the economy and creating employment as well as giving the possibility of home ownership to the low-income sectors of the population (which was an important ideological component of this programme) (Bolaffi 1979). There was a need for the government to gain popular support in order to legitimize the new regime, and home ownership provided an opportunity to reduce dissatisfaction. A great deal of emphasis, for example, was given to the statement that every Brazilian family should own a house (Dos Santos 1979). So the BNH was founded, not only as a mechanism to ameliorate the housing situation, but also to stimulate the economy and to legitimize the new regime.

The BNH lent money to private housing agents, in charge of middle-class housing provision, and to the Housing Companies (COHABS). The COHABS can be constituted either by the municipal or the state government; their objective is to deal with the provision of housing to low-income sectors of the population, that is those with three or fewer minimum wages. The COHABS receive and administer funds from the BNH and contract the promoting agents (building companies) to carry out the work (De Azevedo and De Andrade 1982).

In 1973 the National Popular Housing Plan (PLANHAP) was drawn up. It aimed to provide housing, infrastructure, and community facilities for families with an income of between one and three times the minimum wage, living in medium-sized cities of 50,000 inhabitants or more, or in towns with fewer than 50,000, growing at the rate of at least 7 per cent per annum (BNH 1978). The Profilurb programme was created in 1975 with the goal of increasing the sections of the population serviced by the PLANHAP (Fundacão Joao Pinheiro 1980). The objectives of Profilurb were to produce plots that would (eventually) be owned by low-income families and to develop a programme to improve their housing conditions.

The owners of the plots were responsible for the building of their own dwellings, in accordance with their financial resources. Loans were made available subject to repayment within fifteen years at an interest rate of 1 to 3 per cent a year in instalments of no more than 9 per cent of the minimum wage. In some cases the repayment time was extended to twenty-five years (BNH 1980). The state was to finance the plots as well as providing access to building materials and technical advice. However, the programme was primarily one of self-help, following Turner's (1976) concept of 'user-participation', and emphasizing the role of the users in producing their housing.

Five projects were implemented within Profilurb of which three are considered here. The data come from a survey commissioned by the BNH programme, and implemented in 1979 by the Fundacão Joao Pinheiro (BNH 1980).

BOA VISTA PROJECT

Boa Vista settlement is located in the southern part of the city of Vila Velha in the south-east region of Brazil. The Boa Vista project was the result of the evacuation of 137 families from a slum, called Salamin, only 800 metres from the project site. The total area of Boa Vista comprises 224,139 square metres, and is divided into two parts, the higher ground designated for 1,542 flats and the lower part for 446 plots. These plots ranged in size from 90 square metres to 180 square metres (Fundacão Joao Pinheiro 1980). An area was also reserved for the building of a social centre, a first grade school, and a number of commercial establishments. Each plot was supplied with a high standard of fittings for the installation of water, electricity, and sewerage systems, along with a brick-built sanitary unit.

The candidates with priority for plots in Boa Vista were those evacuated from Salamin, together with squatters from nearby areas such as Ilha dos Ayres, Cophabsol, and Alfredo Copolito, plus a group of forty people from a nearby *cortico* (a group of slum dwellings around a common courtyard). Because a considerable number of people, some 700 families, contacted the COHAB to buy a plot in Boa Vista, a system of permanent registration (SIP) was established (Fundacão Joao Pinheiro 1980). Through the SIP, 200 families were able to buy plots. Three different criteria were used to determine their eligibility. First, the candidate should have a family income of one to three minimum wages and should live and work in Vila Velha, or second, that the candidate should be a pensioner with an income of one minimum wage living in a rented shack in Vila Velha, or third, that the candidate should be employed or self-employed in Vila Velha and be the father [sic] of at least two children.

The process of building was undertaken at first using an individualized form of self-help. Problems with this sytem led to the use of *mutirão* ('collective work of all for the benefit of the one who, on that day, has to foot the bills'). The COHABS also became involved in this process. After conducting a survey that confirmed the interest of people in financial aid for the buying of building materials, loans were made available late in 1977. The COHAB drew up plans for the construction of the houses through *mutirão* on the basis of the following rules. The COHAB would provide finance for building materials only for those residents who agreed to take part in the process of *mutirão*, and this finance was to be related to family income. The building materials would be delivered to the dwellers in fixed quantities according to house type, at appropriate intervals during construction, and material for the subsequent phases of construction would be delivered only when the whole *mutirão* group had finished the preceding phase.

The COHAB aimed to cater for 150 families organized in twenty-two *mutirão* groups. Of these families twenty were classified as having a high income, sixty-five were in the middle income bracket, and the remaining sixty-five had low incomes. These figures indicate that Profilurb was not merely a project for low-income groups; a survey conducted for the BNH confirmed this. In 1979 88 per cent of the interviewed heads of household received up to three minimum wages (Fundacão Joao Pinheiro 1980). (The value of the minimum wage in the south-east region in 1979 was about US $50 or £22.50. Figures calculated by the author based on data from IBGE 1981.) However, it was also estimated that approximately one-third of the sample, in order to supplement their income, had an extra job. The average price of the plots in 1979 in Boa Vista was estimated to be approximately US $606. Again, this price may appear beyond the reach of those on low incomes but the survey revealed that 99 out of 102 households paid in instalments that were not more than 8 per cent of their income.

NOVA ALVORADA – IMBITUBA PROJECT
This project is located in the city of Imbituba, in the southern region of Brazil. The implementation of the Profilurb programme in Imbituba was an attempt to find a solution to the problem created, in 1976, by the clearance of a low-income residential area of approximately 4,000 people, for the purpose of creating an industrial complex. The expropriation of the area was the responsibility of CODISC (Company of Industrial Districts of Santa Catarina State) who in 1976 proposed a project for the construction of 488 housing plots on an alternative site. After the BNH's approval of this plan the phases of expropriation, compensation, the division of the land into plots, and the building on these plots were undertaken by CODISC. In early 1977 the COHAB commercialized the plots and in July 1977 the first residents arrived.

The new settlement covered an area of 316, 247 square metres, with plots accounting for 57 per cent of the total land area. All plots have a high level of provision of fittings including a water-meter, a tank, a sanitary unit, fittings for electricity, water, a concrete cesspit, and a drainage system (Fundacão Joao Pinheiro

1980). The settlement also has a health centre, a commercial centre, a community centre, a first grade school, a police station, and a sports ground.

Selection criteria were very straightforward in Nova Alvorada. In order to qualify for a plot it was merely necessary for the family to have a home in the expropriated area. The majority of the families simply moved their houses to Nova Alvorada, which was possible because they were made of wood. Only 18 per cent of the families built new houses in Nova Alvorada, although 43 per cent made some modifications or improvements to their houses, usually employing contract labour. Families did not, however, receive any financial help or technical support for these modifications.

In the BNH's survey of families in Nova Alvorada 22 per cent received no more than the minimum wage, 34 per cent received between one and two times the minimum wage, another 34 per cent received between two and three times the minimum wage, and 11 per cent received over three times the minimum wage. In order to make it possible for all families to buy a plot, five types of plots with different prices were defined, the average price of which was approximately US $260 (Fundacão Joao Pinheiro 1980).

ACUDE I – VOLTA REDONDA PROJECT

The project Acude I is located in the city of Volta Redonda in the south-east region of Brazil. The project resulted from the invasion by sixty families of an area of land owned by the BNH. The Profilurb project to rehouse these people commenced in 1975, its implementation surviving stoppages and financial setbacks. The project area has 516 plots which cover only 25 per cent of the total area (Fundacão Joao Pinheiro 1980). Each plot has a sanitary unit with fittings for water, electricity, sewerage, and a water tank. The settlement also includes a first grade school, a health centre, and a community centre.

Candidates were selected according to three criteria: those already living in the immediate area (27 per cent); people removed from the invasion area (46 per cent); and those who were registered in the local COHAB (22 per cent) (Fundacão Joao Pinheiro 1980). The criteria for the selection of those registered in the COHAB were size of family income and number of dependants. As in Nova Alvorada the majority of the families (67 per cent) transferred their old houses to the new plots. Of the remainder, 30 per cent built new houses, 2.5

per cent bought ready-made houses, and 1.5 per cent were already resident in the area. The COHAB helped in the demolition and rebuilding of the shacks that were transferred, and donated wood to enable the dwellers to repair damage incurred during the move. The other changes were undertaken with the resources of the residents themselves: self-help accounted for 80 per cent of the changes and 12 per cent were implemented using a contracted labour-force (Fundacão Joao Pinheiro 1980). Unlike the other two projects the dwellings are in poor condition: half of them do not have electricity, 60 per cent do not have water, and just under half do not have an internal lavatory.

The majority (52 per cent) of the families have an income ranging between one and two minimum wages, and 27 per cent have a wage of less than the minimum. Although the price of plots varied according to the income of the family (the cheapest, in 1978, being approximately US $922) the majority of families were not in a position to buy their plot. The COHAB, therefore, decided to concede the right of tenure. The dweller would be charged monthly for the occupancy of the plot (at the same rate they would have paid instalments on the plot). However, because of the transfer of plots without the knowledge of the COHAB, payment of the occupancy charge was suspended in August 1979.

Factors affecting woman-headed households' access to the Profilurb programme

It is important to make clear that in this appraisal not all issues are specific to woman-headed households: some are applicable to all low-income households. The main factor excluding woman-headed households from gaining access to the Profilurb programme was that of income. The programme stated that it would assist families with an income of between one and three minimum wages. However, in 1977 approximately one-half of woman-headed households had an income of less than half the minimum wage (Barroso 1982). This actually made them ineligible for the programme. Also important is the source of earned income. Eligibility for the programme required proof of income through documents demonstrating formal employment. As Keare and Parris stress this criterion often precludes selection of woman-headed households:

If selection is based just on earned income rather than total income from all sources, projects may exclude large numbers of households which, by virtue of the combined resources of their extended families, can afford the programmes. Furthermore the criterion will be biased against female-headed households as they rely more on transfer payments from kin than do male-headed households.

(Keare and Parris 1982: 72)

The repayment time for plots on the Profilurb programme was initially fifteen years and later extended to twenty-five years. To assume a debt for fifteen to twenty-five years implies a stable and regular source of income. Similarly instalments of a fixed per cent of the minimum wage imply a stable income. Neither a minimum wage nor a stable income are characteristic of many woman-headed households.

In the case of the Nova Alvorada project another condition laid down for the would-be candidate was that they should already have been the owner of a dwelling. Given the disadvantaged economic conditions of women who head households, it was unlikely that they would have owned a dwelling.

When referring to the target group that the programme intended to assist, the reference to 'families' appears to refer to all types of family. However, in the Boa Vista project it was a requirement that the candidates should be the *father* of at least two children. If the intention was not to exclude woman-headed households reference should have been to a person responsible for two children. Even if this was only a problem of semantics, other requirements relating to the status of the applicants also tended to exclude women who head households. Pensioners were eligible for plots at Boa Vista. However, they were required to have paid INPS contributions. This is normal for formal sector employees. However, many women who head households work in the informal sector. Even if they want to pay their INPS as a self-employed person, they probably cannot afford to do so. Consequently, they lose access to the project.

The processes used in the Profilurb programme included self-help, *mutirão*, and the contracting of skilled labour. Since women who head households are responsible for the management of the household and the care of the children, sometimes also caring for small animals and cultivating garden crops in addition to involvement in income-generating work, little time is left for building their houses or taking part in a *mutirão*. Those women who do take part in the process of construction have to work very long hours. Furthermore, problems faced by women who head households are often aggravated by the lack of help from other household members, themselves too old or too young to assist.

Access to employment for residents was not a consideration of the Profilurb programme. As most women who head households are engaged in work in the informal sector, it is convenient for mothers to operate an informal business from home, enabling them to look after their children at the same time. However, this advantage should not be overstated, as difficulty in getting to sites of formal employment restricts the range of job options for women. Only in the Boa Vista project was the new settlement located nearby the original residences of the participants, enabling them to continue working in the same places of employment. Besides access to employment and marketing of goods made at home, women who head households need access to other services such as health centres, nurseries, and transport. In the Profilurb programme all settlements have health centres and schools but none have nurseries. While in the Boa Vista project the residents were largely satisfied with the transport facilities they had and with access to work and other facilities, in the case of the Acude I project the residents complained about the distance to the city centre (approximately forty minutes by bus), as did the settlers of the Nova Alvorada project.

Conclusion

This chapter has shown that the Profilurb programme did not define woman-headed households as a target group. In defining its target only in terms of income not gender, it neglected the Brazilian reality in which a considerable number of households are headed by women. Furthermore, since Profilurb did not define woman-headed households as a target group within the low-income population it may be concluded that this was due to the fact that this group is viewed as being responsible for its own poverty. Woman-headed households tend to have lower incomes than those headed by men, since low-income women have more limited access to skilled and well-paid jobs, particularly in the formal sector. The economic situation of these households lies in the absence of male earners, forcing many to rely primarily upon the work of children and women. This highlights the need to consider different subgroups among the low-income population which is clearly not a homogeneous group: 'differentiation and heterogeneity are essential characteristics of the urban poor' (Moser 1977: 470). Projects and programmes designed to ameliorate poverty affect households headed by women in different ways. This chapter shows that a considerable number of households depend on the income of women and that these households are among the poorest in the country. This strongly suggests the necessity for policies sensitive to the needs of households headed by women.

In designing housing programmes to reach these households the following should be considered. First, women who are heads of households frequently take longer to build and/or complete housing because of other responsibilities for their household: thus they prefer completed units to be offered. Second, because their income is lower than that of men who are heads of households they tend to have problems in securing and repaying loans and in meeting service charges. Third, the lack of infrastructure has more immediate consequences for women than men because of their responsibilities for domestic work. Fourth, woman-headed households tend to have lower levels of access to essential services than do households headed by men. Thus if the intention is to help women, housing policies sensitive to gender roles and divisions are required.

Notes

This chapter is based on work for an MSc. dissertation submitted in 1983 in partial requirement for an MSc. in Economics at the Development Planning Unit, University College, London. This was sponsored by the *Conselho Nacional De Desenvolvimento Cientifico E Tecnologilo* of the Brazilian Ministry of Planning.

1 The first census in Brazil was carried out in 1872 (thereafter in 1890, 1900, and 1920). From 1940 censuses were conducted every decade. The last census in 1980 added data on the building industry, insurance, water and sewage supply, and garbage collection.

2 The minimum wage in Brazil was established in April 1938. The minimum wage was the

minimum income owed to every adult worker, with no distinction of sex, according to a normal day's work, able to satisfy at a certain point in time and in a certain region of the country the normal food, housing, clothing, hygiene and transport needs of that worker.

(translated from Saboia 1985: 2)

Thus it was established at different levels for different regions of the country and did not include expenses relating to education and leisure. (It is important to note that the minimum wage decree was in flagrant conflict with the 1934 constitution, in which it was determined that the minimum wage should be calculated for a family of four.) Since 1964 the real minimum wage has been losing its purchase power owing to government economic policies and recession. In May 1984 the minimum wage was unified for the country as a whole (DIEESE 1984). Before this the minimum wage varied from region to region. In 1978/79 the lowest was about US $53 or £26 and the highest was about US $74.5 or £36.5. (Figures calculated by the author based on data from IBGE 1981.)

3 Although social welfare can be said to have commenced in 1923 with the *'Eloy Chaves'* Law, it was not until the creation of the *Instituto Nacional de Previdencia Social* (INPS) in 1966 that urban workers qualified for assistance. Offering financial help for pensions, health care, and disabled people, workers have to be in regular employment to qualify. Employees pay 8 per cent of their wages to the INPS and the self-employed pay 16 per cent.

4 All the financial transactions of the BNH are made using UPC, that is the Unidade Padrao de Consumo (the Established Unit of Consumption). It has a certain capital value which is readjusted with inflation every three months. The average value of the UPC unit in 1979 was Cr $374.06. This is the equivalent of US $1,402 (Banco Central do Brasil 1983).

© *1987 Leda M.V. Machado*

CHAPTER 4

The struggle for shelter: women in a site and service project in Nairobi, Kenya

PAULA NIMPUNO-PARENTE

Introduction

Since women bear primary responsibility for reproductive activities, such as childbearing, child-rearing, and domestic work, they are also the main users of housing, infrastructure, and community services. Consequently a better understanding of women's lives is important for urban planning. The experiences in African cities, however, is that planning specific to the needs of women has not been undertaken, even though women usually constitute more than half of the applicants in low-income housing projects and they also contribute 80 per cent of the labour input into self-help projects (CBS/UNICEF 1984). In addition women's access to resources continues to be determined by their relationship to men. Yet married women often have to engage in paid work because their spouses are unable to earn enough to support their families. Rising unemployment and the still prevalent practice of polygamy intensify this phenomenon. And because the instability of marriage is increasing a great number of women bear sole responsibility for their own and their children's survival. Data on the number of women heads of household in Kenya are limited. However, Clark (1984) estimated that 29 per cent of the 1.7 million households in Kenya are headed by women. These households are the most impoverished and it is therefore not surprising that they predominate in low-income housing projects.

This chapter examines the efforts of women in one such project, namely the Dandora Site and Services Project in Kenya.

The project was initiated in the 1970s, funded by the Nairobi City Council (NCC), the Kenyan Government, and the World Bank. The scheme is to be implemented in five phases, and when completed 6,000 serviced plots will have been provided. The evaluation focuses on Phase I in which 1,029 serviced plots were to be completed for a population of 6,000–10,000. The aim is to examine the difficulties that women faced both in fulfilling the selection criteria and as project beneficiaries. The project is considered to have successfully included women, who made up 49 per cent of the beneficiaries of Phase I. However, this evaluation demonstrates how project assumptions about both self-help and finance can be detrimental to women.[1]

The Dandora site and services project

The current population of Nairobi is estimated to be well over 1 million and is expected to increase to about 3 million by the year 2000. The rapid population growth in urban areas, about 7 per cent per annum, and the corresponding demands on housing and infrastructure became an issue of concern for the NCC in the early 1970s. Squatter settlements were erected by low-income households, and in response the NCC abandoned its policy of constructing conventional low-cost houses for rent and resorted instead to a more cost-effective site and services approach (Chana 1979).

In the mid-1970s, in its attempts to provide housing and services to the urban population the NCC established the Nairobi Urban Study Group (NUSG), which was to define and co-ordinate strategies for both low- and middle-income groups in the Nairobi area for the period 1979 to 1985. At the same time the International Bank for Reconstruction and Development (IBRD) at the World Bank expressed an interest in financing urban projects that would upgrade urban infrastructure and housing in underdeveloped countries. Drawing on this source the NUSG proposed that Dandora, an area 10 kilometres east of Nairobi, was suitable for the development of a community of 60,000 people. It was to be a model for urban development in Kenya. The project area covers 350 hectares and was chosen mainly because it was the only substantial and uncommitted parcel of land owned by either the government or the NCC. The site was also adjacent to existing housing areas and was within easy reach of the city centre and two industrial areas.[2]

The Housing Development Department (HDD) was established by the NCC to oversee the Dandora project. The HDD has three divisions, each with distinct responsibilities: the Finance Division, which is responsible for financial arrangements; the Technical Division, which is responsible for monitoring construction; and the Community Development Division (CDD), which is responsible for the selection of beneficiaries and for extending social support to those with the lowest incomes. The HDD was required to prepare and service 6,000 residential plots. The following rules governed its activities. First, it was to confine itself to the provision of infrastructural services and sanitary facilities. The construction of houses was the responsibility of those allocated plots. Construction was to take place by the process of self-help, which secured a reduction in production costs through the utilization of the participants' unpaid labour. (This is the main rationale for site and service projects.) Second, it was to administer a materials loan and provide technical guidance and supervision during the period of construction. Third, it was to apply specified criteria in the selection of project participants (see p. 73).

The HDD also provided social and commercial facilities such as schools, markets, workshops, and community centres. The infrastructure facilities in the project were conventional: sewerage, access and circulation roads, domestic plumbing, street lights, municipal refuse collection, and storm-water drainage. These facilities were contractor-built and were to be operated and maintained by the NCC. Public stand-pipes or ablution blocks and a limited-access road system could have been delivered at much lower cost. However, low-cost infrastructure would have constituted a sharp break with the existing practice of the NCC and was considered too controversial.

Most women who applied to the project were heads of household. A 10 per cent sample of (forty-three) women revealed that 89 per cent were heads of household with an average of five dependants. They came from different areas in Nairobi, where most had lived in rented rooms or shacks. They originally came to Nairobi as migrants from rural areas, looking for jobs in the city, following their husbands, or escaping failed marriages. Their housing conditions were often precarious, aggravated by the instability of illegal housing, resulting in frequent shifts from place to place. Housing insecurity and job insecurity tended to reinforce each other. Dandora appeared, therefore, to offer a solution through security of tenure. It promised legality, improved housing conditions, and title to land. This was a great change from traditional practice in which women could not inherit land (Barnes 1975). It is not surprising therefore, that the project attracted so many women.

What are the difficulties that women had to face in the stages of project design and implementation? The remainder of this chapter assesses the impact on women of both the selection criteria made during the project design process and the assumptions made by planners during the implementation process relating to self-help and finance.

The project design process: selection criteria

Urban housing projects are intended to benefit those whose limited earning capacity precludes access to conventional housing. However, projects such as Dandora are also designed to recover a substantial proportion of the costs. Consequently the criteria for selecting participants often deny access to the lowest income groups. This section examines how criteria for selection at Dandora, outlined below, affected women participants. Applicants

- had to have a monthly income in the range of Ksh. 280–560 (US $15–30);
- had to pay a down payment of Ksh. 600;
- had to be heads of household;
- could not own other property in Nairobi;
- had to have lived for more than two years in Nairobi; and
- needed supporting documents.

These criteria adversely affected women applicants in a number of ways.

Applicants were asked to provide information about their income in the form of a cash flow statement. In order to reach those on low incomes charges were linked to 20–25 per cent of household income (Development Plan 1979–83). The cost of the project plots was based on this assumption (Chana 1984). However, this assumption proved to be inadequate. A baseline survey carried out soon after plot allocation (Senga, Ndeti, and Associates 1977) reported that 63 per cent of the applicants worked in the informal sector and therefore had irregular incomes. Of the women in the survey fewer than a fifth worked as cleaners, messengers, and teachers in the formal sector (with an average income of Ksh. 1,235 per annum). About one-half were self-employed, with an average income of Ksh. 970, which came from selling vegetables and charcoal either from their houses or in the market. The remaining third's source of income was from subletting rooms and this averaged Ksh. 695. These women with no declared employment also included those who were too old to work or who had lost their source of income when they moved to the project area. Thus, many of the women heads of household did not have a cash income to report when they applied for the project. They relied on income transfers from relatives and existing social networks. The assumption, therefore, that 20–25 per cent of the household income can be spent on housing is unrealistic owing to the irregularity of earnings of most women. However, the number of women heads of households who were selected suggests that project staff frequently relaxed the income criteria.

The down payment requirement of Ksh. 600 to cover the costs of water connection and loans for building materials proved to be too high for the vast majority of the women applicants. Many women were forced to secure loans from informal money-lenders and relatives in order to meet it since they had no savings of their own and, therefore, they incurred extra debts.

Applicants also had to be heads of households. Western perceptions of the ideal household as a nuclear family headed by a man abounded, despite the large number of households in Kenya headed by women. Moreover, women whose husbands had left them were often reluctant to change their title because of the status attached to being married. But married women were widely assumed not to be heads of households, so this criterion was often detrimental to women.

Women applicants had to prove that they were separated, widowed, or single, and that they supported children, in order to be considered for the Dandora project. (Single women with no children were not considered.) In the sample nine women were separated, four were widowed, nineteen were single, and eleven were married. But of the latter group only five lived with their husbands on the plot. The other six were part of poly-gamous households, two of whom had not seen their husbands for ten years, but still reported themselves as married.

Those who owned property elsewhere in Nairobi were not eligible for plots at Dandora. This criterion excluded many women whose husbands owned property. Moreover, control of property at Dandora was often an issue for women. For example, they complained that their husbands had sold their plot in Dandora without the family's consent. Husbands would sell the house secretly and disappear with the money. The situation became clear to the wives only when the new owner came to the house to declare his ownership and evict the resident family. At the time of this research (in 1984) project staff were considering adding the wife's name as co-owner to prevent this.

Residency in Nairobi was another requirement that was often difficult for women to confirm. If they came to Nairobi with their husbands it was usually only the husband who registered as resident. Moreover, because married women were economically insecure in urban areas they often returned to their rural homes at harvest times or to help their families in time of economic pressure. Thus the length of their residency in the urban areas was open to dispute.

The requirement of supporting documents assumed that project applicants had regular employment; however, 63 per cent of the applicants worked in the informal sector, in small family enterprises or in self-employment. Women were the majority in these categories. Although a hawker's licence (a licence for the informal sector vendors issued by the municipality) was also accepted as evidence of employment, few women were able to comply because they were not officially registered.

The completion of application forms also merits attention. The project staff were to check and help applicants who either did not know how to or did not feel confident enough to fill in the forms. This was particularly important for the 33 per cent of applicants who were illiterate. Women constituted a high percentage of the illiterate applicants (67 per cent of the sample), and although many gained access to the project, others may not have applied because of the administrative demands this procedure made on their time.

Project implementation

Women who passed the selection criteria were subject to further discrimination because of assumptions about self-help and because of the methods of financing house construction. These problems are examined in this section.

The participation of women in the house construction phase was assumed to be crucial for the viability and success of the project. All the women in the sample had been involved in building their own houses. Although the degree of involvement varied with each household, they cleared the plot, carried stones, mixed concrete, and cleared the debris after construction. However, this unskilled work was not acknowledged by their male relatives or by the project planners who viewed it merely as an extension of women's domestic work. Construction in the urban areas is a male-dominated profession while in the rural areas it is carried out jointly between men and women. Thus ideological assumptions in the urban areas about construction prevented women from building, although they were more strongly reinforced in households headed by a man than in those headed by women. There was a definite division of tasks when a husband was present in the household. Women tended not to do manual work on site but spent their time on supervisory work, cleaning, and cooking. Men and women remained bound by their conventional roles: men's domain was the building site and women provided support.

The plot sizes in the project ranged from 100 to 160 square metres. Plot beneficiaries could choose from three plot types. First, type A plots which provided only a 'wet core' (a lavatory and shower). Plot beneficiaries were given a loan of Ksh. 5,760 for building materials, with a repayment period of thirty years. They had to comply with the lease agreement of building two extra rooms within eighteen months. Of the women in the survey 95 per cent chose this option and the majority of households to take up this option were headed by women, that is fifty-eight compared to forty-six man-headed households (Baseline survey 1977). Second, type B plots which consisted of a 'wet core', a kitchen, and a store. A loan of Ksh. 2,880 was available with a twenty-year repayment period and beneficiaries had to build one extra room on to the house. The 1977 Baseline survey revealed that only six woman-headed households took up this option, compared to thirty-five households headed by men. Third, type C plots which were built complete with a wet core, kitchen, a store, and one room. These were sold at the market rate for cross-subsidization purposes in order to establish the material loans fund used to enable the type A and B plot tenants to borrow money for building materials. Sixty-four woman-headed households and eighty-one man-headed households took up this option. Only participants who had been allocated type A plots needed to build temporary shelters for residence during construction or for storage of building materials. They were supposed to be demolished after the eighteen-month construction period although keeping the temporary shelters enabled women to let rooms, providing them with an extra income. Demolition of this shelter was, however, reinforced by project staff.

FORMS OF SELF-HELP

During the building process, beneficiaries used three forms of self-help: self-help by the beneficiaries, contractual self-help, and self-help within building groups.

Beneficiaries' self-help is the true form of self-help and was most popular with woman-headed households. The beneficiary is the main decision-maker in planning, construction, and managing the building process. The building materials used are often of a cheap and temporary nature in order to maximize savings and the labour (unskilled) is not paid for in cash. The efforts of friends and relatives are very important. The use of such social networks can, however, be difficult in a new settlement. For example some women claimed they had left all their contacts in their previous settlement. By contrast those who moved jointly with previous neighbours continued to have the co-operation of others, receiving and giving advice on building materials and on the availability of good labourers.

Many women were unable to be on site all the time because of their responsibilities for earning a living, childcare, and domestic work. But greater site supervision and construction work was possible for those working in the informal rather than the formal sector. Because the self-employed had more flexibility in organizing their time they were able to contribute more to construction than the formal sector workers. However, house-building may conflict with earning money. This was particularly the case for self-employed women because men usually had a wife or other relatives to contribute or supervise the site, and therefore did not have to choose between earning a living and building. For these reasons many women relied on contractual forms of self-help. Although the project assumed that beneficiaries would use their own labour, many participants did not understand this. In particular, women misunderstood the meaning of self-help and their role in the implementation process. They expected to get completed dwellings and to have no role in construction. This confusion resulted in participants having to hire skilled or semi-skilled labour. Furthermore, women were unable to utilize their own skills, given the need to conform to the high building standards. The division of labour was distinct: while the skilled labourers performed more complicated tasks, such as advising on technical issues, quality of building materials, and the organization of the construction team, the participants performed the unskilled work, endorsed the decisions of the craftsman, supervised the construction team, and looked after financial matters.

Women used twice as many craftsmen and labourers as men. Despite the high costs of construction by contractors, 89 per cent of the women in the sample (all of them heads of households) opted for this method. This caused them to exceed the materials loan and incur heavy debts. The problems faced by women beneficiaries are well illustrated by the case of Wanjiku, who has five children and was allocated a type A plot. She had to employ a builder as she lacked construction skills and she did not have a male adult in her household. During the construction phase she was earning Ksh. 450 monthly by selling vegetables; this income was barely enough for her family's survival. As she could not build a temporary shelter because of lack of time and skills, she had to live in her previous residence and visit the site daily to supervise the labourers to ensure she was not subject to shoddy work and cheating by the craftsmen. As another woman claimed:

> I could not take leave during construction, neither had I another adult person in my household. Therefore the construction and supervision was left in the hands of the craftsman and labourers. During my absence he mixed less cement than required and sold the remainder together with my building materials. Apart from having to hire more unskilled labour I had to meet extra costs from the lost building materials.

Thus the combination of being the head of household and not having other adults in the household exposed women to abuses by craftsmen. As another woman recounted: 'I bought three window frames and all of them were stolen by the craftsman. He would not fix them to the wall, so it was easy to come in my absence and steal the frames'.

Technical assistance was provided by the HDD in order to ensure that building standards and by-laws were followed and orientation meetings and field visits were made by the project staff (social workers and building foremen). However, the ratio between the number of plots to be supervised and the number of technicians (500:1) was far from ideal: 23 per cent of women reported mistakes during construction because of the infrequency of visits by project foremen. However, a parallel survey of men revealed that only 1.8 per cent had reported cases of theft and breaking-off of contractual agreements.

Building groups combined self-help with mutual assistance. The majority of the beneficiaries who joined building groups were women, particularly those on the lowest incomes. The building groups were organized by the project agency for those who were not able to raise finance and labour to start construction. In Phase I there were fifteen groups. Each had ten to fifteen members and elected at least three officers (chair, secretary, and treasurer) whose main duties were to organize the construction, either through one of the group members or through a building foreman, to organize meetings, and to keep records and minutes of meetings (Senga, Ndeti, and Associates 1979). The groups were assisted and supervised by Community Development Assistants. Group membership was not based on prior social contacts nor on ethnic links, but for the sole purpose of building together. The prominent positions in the groups were usually taken by the better-educated people, who tended to be men and who sometimes used their positions to favour construction work on their own plots.

Group members had to pay dues according to their means. The construction schedule for the individual rooms of the group members was decided by a lottery. The digging of foundation trenches was usually carried out by mutual assistance; thereafter a building contractor would often be engaged to organize and lead the work of the group. This enabled group members to contribute more labour to the construction of their houses than other beneficiaries could. After completion of one or two rooms, subletting would provide income to finance the building of the next room to be built by the group. This process would continue until the completion of the entire building programme. The building groups worked more slowly than contractors, but there was little difference in cost between rooms built by contractors and by building groups. Moreover, raising the large amounts of money needed for construction, which would have been impossible for individuals, was possible within the building groups. The hiring of contractors would also have been very difficult for individuals but was possible collectively, as was the setting of wages for workers and controlling the quality of work.

The main difficulty for the building groups was to maintain group cohesion and to ensure all members could afford to stay in the group. A lack of trust among previously unacquainted members, for whom the only common interest was the construction of plots, further impeded the cohesion of groups. These factors resulted in a high drop-out rate which adversely affected the performance of the groups. Moreover, some members left as soon as their own rooms were completed, causing delays and loss of resources to the remaining members. Only one building group survived beyond the completion of the basic programme of constructing a unit for each member.[3] Of the ten women in the survey belonging to building groups, only five had their rooms built by the groups, while the other five complained of failure of the group to build for them. Despite these problems the groups were important for women, if the groups were cohesive enough to negotiate for their members at the planning stage and keep together until the last member had his or her own rooms built. Moreover, in one of the groups, women allottees living close together were reported to have shared food during the construction time when the household budgets were under stress (Senga, Ndeti, and Associates 1979).

HOUSING FINANCE

The prices of the plots in the Dandora scheme were based on the following assumptions: that people could afford to allocate 20–25 per cent of their income for housing purposes; that there would be provision of infrastructure including sewerage; and that letting rooms would provide them with an additional source of housing finance. The main financial provision was the loan for building materials. Problems soon emerged because this loan, which was paid in cash, was not linked to inflation although the costs of building materials were rising sharply. Further, procurement and transport of the small quantities needed by individuals was much more costly than if this had been organized centrally. In addition to the 8.5 per cent loan charges, beneficiaries had to finance their cost over-runs, usually at higher interest rates. For those who could not do all the work themselves, including most of the women, labour costs were also incurred. The financial provisions within the project, therefore, were inadequate to ensure the completion of the house and additional finance arrangements were necessary for all plot owners. The average cost of building one room during the period 1977–83 was Ksh. 7,650, while the material loan for type B plots amounted to Ksh. 2,880 (UNCHS 1983). The solutions adopted to meet these costs shed light on the conditions low-income women have to endure in order to obtain secure homes and demonstrate flaws in the assumptions of project planners.

The most widely used methods of obtaining finance adopted by the sample of women were borrowing from relatives and friends, and joining a building group. Private loans, savings schemes, and subletting were also used. Contributions in the form of cash and building materials from friends and relatives were common, as was their physical support in the building of the house. Although no money changed hands the labour of friends was not free but in most cases had to be repaid in kind. Accommodation in exchange for labour costs was also used: one woman in the sample reported having housed a craftsman and his family in two rooms of her house for a period of five years as payment for his services in building the whole house. He had accommodation valued at Ksh. 30,000, which represented three years' wages for work that probably took no more than eight months.

Without friends and neighbours to rely on some women had to resort to private loans. Beneficiaries could receive their title deed only after full repayment of the material loan, and without the title deed they could not use the property as collateral for loans. Official mechanisms were also denied them because of their low income, lack of savings for down payments, and the impossibility of following rigid payment schedules which did not take into account the irregularity of their employment and earnings. Furthermore, women disliked the risks attached to large loans. They preferred small and successive loans which banks do not find cost effective. It was also found that access to bank loans was dependent on ethnic and political affiliation.

Women working in the formal sector had more options for housing finance than the self-employed, in the form of loans from co-operatives in their place of work and loans from their employers. Although in some cases these loans were substantial, women in these categories also made use of informal sources. The extra interest caused by multiple loans was a heavy burden on household budgets; 14 per cent of the women in the survey had loans from co-operatives in their place of work. These women worked as messengers and cleaners in the NCC; only one woman had a loan from a credit institution, under special conditions that did not require collateral or guarantors. Although she chose not to disclose these conditions she developed her plot and built more rooms than most. More typical was a woman on an income of Ksh. 1,400 per month, who had two loans, one of Ksh. 9,000 from a work-based co-operative and the other from informal lenders. From 1977 to 1984 she was repaying the co-operative loan with deductions from her salary. She was also paying the loan to the informal lenders with 25 per cent interest. Since she could not meet her payments and was the sole breadwinner, she had to send three of her six children to be taken care of by relatives in the rural areas.

Saving schemes in which collective savings are allocated to each participant in turn for the purchase of building materials were also used. The collective nature of the saving provides an incentive to make regular contributions. It requires, however, both administration and a level of trust, neither of which may be available. In Dandora six women reported belonging to such groups either at their places of work or within the residential area. This latter, however, was less common, because of lack of familiarity among beneficiaries.

From the outset, partial subletting was planned by the HDD, not only as a source of income for home-owners but also to provide shelter for people who were not eligible as project beneficiaries. Income from subletting was often the main source of finance for plot development: 60 per cent of the women in the survey had used rental income for further construction. The success of this strategy was difficult to assess. Total subletting (the letting of an entire plot) was not allowed under the regulations of Dandora, but it occurred frequently as a means of both continuing the development of plots and repaying loans. However, it was difficult to distinguish between subletting to eliminate debts and speculative subletting. The high level of mobility of beneficiaries prevented the detection of speculators, who operated as absentee landlords. Absenteeism has been estimated to account for up to half the plots (UNCHS 1983). In the survey about one-quarter of the women lived elsewhere in order to sublet their completed rooms, but only one had sold her plot.

Women in Dandora were less likely than men to sell their plot for three reasons. First, the project gave women the opportunity to own property in an urban area, which they had not pre-viously had. Second, while both women and men tend to consider the house as an economic asset, women also emphas-ized the social value of the house and plot to their families. Third, the subletting of rooms was important for many women because it was often their main source of income. Thus among women, absenteeism was a temporary phenomenon arising from economic and family responsibilities.

Plots that were still undeveloped usually belonged to women who had not utilized the option of subletting and who still resided on their plot. They were often women heads of households with many dependants, unable to proceed with plot development according to the planned schedule. Among the women who did sublet (about half the sample) competition for tenants was high and several had had rooms empty for most of a year before reducing rents to attract tenants. The average rent which yielded between Ksh. 250–300 in 1980 had dropped to Ksh. 180 in 1984, barely adequate to meet plot charges. Subletting appears to have become still more difficult since 1984 and there are many unoccupied rooms in the area. The deterioration of the infrastructure services, with blocked sewerage, uncollected garbage, broken street lights, and lack of security has enabled lodgers to choose only the best-maintained plots. However, some of the lowest income households did not use available empty rooms for their children, keeping them empty for possible future tenants. This is quite interesting in view of the relative overcrowding in Dandora.[4]

In mid-1986 the Project Administrator decided to make use of remaining funds by supplementing loans to beneficiaries at the same interest rate. These loans would be limited to those who had not consolidated their houses. However, due to the lack of time to administer the loans properly, as well as organizational constraints within the HDD, they became available to all allottees resulting in a new phase of construction work. One result of the loan supplement, however, has been overbuilding within plot boundaries. Open yards are making space for new rooms which will yield long-term income from subletting. The loans are also being used to connect electricity. Unfortunately, the rapid disbursement of the loan resulted in widespread corruption and embezzlement which especially affected women.

Cost recovery is essential in site and services projects. Of the forty-three women in the survey only two paid their debts regularly. These two had well-developed plots and lived on income from subletting and from small-scale businesses. Both were heads of households containing other adults who contributed financially to the household. Among the other women it was found that arrears were related to income from subletting as well as from employment. When asked how they intended to pay their arrears, seventeen of the women indicated that they would be able to pay when the plot was fully developed and six answered after harvesting. The payment of school fees was a considerable burden for women with children of school age, six women claiming that they would otherwise have been able to pay their arrears. Building regulations such as zoning, which prohibits the use of residential space for business, have reduced the scope of many women to generate income. Seven women were waiting for their or their husband's job opportunities to improve in order to pay rent arrears.

The HDD takes action on arrears only after six months, when warning notices are sent. By early 1985 the first notices had been sent to twenty defaulters, six of whom were women. An influx of payments ensued, some from those only one month in arrears (personal communication with Assistant Director, Financial Division). Some of the women in default were considered welfare cases and therefore were not evicted. According to the Financial Division women are less indebted than men. Absentee landlords, most of whom are men, often went heavily into arrears, partly because they had little identification with the community and therefore felt little obligation to pay. However, they were able to pay off debts with a lump sum after collecting rents from their tenants.

Conclusion

As the above discussion has shown, the participation of women in the Dandora project was impeded by both the criteria for selection and the implementation process. Moreover, the significance of the activities of women was underestimated by planners. The design of the project revealed the lack of awareness of the sexual division of labour and of the triple role of women, as producers, reproducers, and community managers. Such policy blindness has serious implications for women when low-income housing programmes are designed to include the participation of their beneficiaries in order to reduce costs. In cases where women are project beneficiaries, this also has consequences for the success of the project. To conclude this chapter these limitations, and potential solutions for their removal, are discussed.

Design specifications meant that many beneficiaries had to hire labour for skilled construction work. Women in particular were unable to use their traditional skills; this in turn reduced the ability of beneficiaries to keep up with repayments. Future housing projects could make provision of building materials optional to the beneficiaries. Women could also be trained in construction skills as a number of projects elsewhere have demonstrated (see Girling, Lycette, and Youssef 1983; Fernando 1985). These projects also serve to counter the argument that the provision of building skills to women beneficiaries would result in high costs for the project agency. Further, the view that 'women do not build in Kenya' and that they just 'help out' the skilled and semi-skilled workers on site runs contrary to the traditional division of labour in rural areas where the construction of the house is an equal and joint effort between men and women. Training of women in construction skills not only would provide them with a skill for future employment, but also would mean they would not have to hire labour. Many women heads of households who had hired labour had suffered a deterioration in their diet and living standards as a result. However, when asked if they would use building skills in the future if they could acquire them, women between the ages of twenty-one and fifty responded affirmatively but added 'only to build my own house'. These responses appear to reflect an acceptance of conventional gender roles in the new urban setting.

The municipality has not been able to maintain the project area to minimum standards because of inadequate resources. Plot maintenance depends instead upon the presence of the beneficiaries. As the number of absentee landlords is high the level of maintenance is low. Given that the rate of absenteeism is higher for men than for women, this problem could be reduced by encouraging more women to participate. The ability of beneficiaries to invest in housing is related to the income of the household and to other demands such as for food and school charges. The assumptions about unpaid labour and about the level of income contributions have been shown to be incorrect. Credit arrangements have also been shown to be inappropriate for women. Creative financing techniques, with flexible repayment schedules tailored to individual income patterns, could usefully be adopted by planners and policy-makers. Women's access to credit could also be improved by redefining acceptable forms of collateral. For example Non-Governmental Organisations (NGOs) could retain the title deeds and act as guarantors for women borrowers. Credit should be provided to cover the cost of hired labour required to finish houses, as well as for building materials. Short-term seed loans with flexible repayments would enable women to obtain successively larger loans. Income criteria should also take into account income in kind and gifts, as these constitute a large portion of the household budgets of woman-headed households. Lastly project staff could visit women working in the formal and informal sectors to assess their type of work and income, eliminating the need for formal proof of employment.

The project correctly recognized the significance of subletting. For many beneficiaries this became the only stable source of income. Most other schemes for generating income offered by NGOs and other organizations focused on domestic activities. Further, the zoning regulations in Dandora limited the opportunities available to women, many of whom are restricted to the vicinity of their homes because of responsibilities for children. When the HDD staff commenced the preparation and plot allocation for a new scheme at Kayole, illegal informal sector activities (metaphorically) exploded in Dandora and many women subsequently operated businesses from their plots and street corners.

The inclusion of women as project beneficiaries obviously met a need by giving them tenure of the plot, but it proved to be insufficient. In order to consolidate their plots women require specific interventions to ensure they acquire extra credit and training in building skills, which would eventually give them more control over their resources and lives. Women's participation is clearly crucial for the successful implementation of housing projects, and discriminatory practices against them, both in financial arrangements, in access to economic resources and in training must be removed.

Notes

This chapter is based on an earlier draft, Nimpuno-Parente (1985) 'Gender issues in project planning and implementation: the case of Dandora site and service project, Kenya', *DPU Gender and Planning Working Paper* no 13, University College, London.

1 The data presented in this chapter are based on research carried out in 1984, six years after the first phase of plot allocation. Beneficiaries were supposed by this time to have completed their houses. The

research used several methods of data collection including interviews with a 10 per cent sample of women beneficiaries, case studies of women beneficiaries, and participant observation. Secondary data, in particular the results of a baseline survey (Senga, Ndeti, and Associates 1977), were also employed.

2 The project was not conceived solely as a housing project but had wider social and economic objectives, the funding of which involved several non-governmental organizations (NGOs). These included the Ford Foundation, which funds the Welfare Fund; UNICEF, which provides tools and capital for income-generation projects; and church organizations such as the National Council of Churches of Kenya (NCCK) and the Holy Cross Fathers.

3 In this case members were known to each other prior to allocation. They all lived in Mathare Valley (a squatter settlement in Nairobi) and when in Dandora, they asked to form their own group.

4 The building code defines overcrowding as more than two people per room (40 square feet) (Senga, Ndeti, and Associates 1977).

CHAPTER 5

New skills for women: a community development project in Colombo, Sri Lanka

MARINA FERNANDO

Introduction

Housing projects worldwide have accommodated the needs of politicians and planners, and where popular participation is acknowledged the 'head of household' is usually assumed to be a man. Although women are the major users of housing, they are frequently excluded from the planning, design, and construction of housing. Their participation is usually identified with the implementation phase of the housing project and with the maintenance of housing stock. This situation arises because housing is seldom integrated with other aspects of community life. The inherent links between, for example, housing and health, housing and income-generation, housing and community cohesion, are overlooked by architects and planners who tend to view housing as a discrete activity that takes place between the drawing-board and the construction site.

This chapter is concerned with a community development project undertaken in the late 1970s and early 1980s by US Save the Children (SAVE) in Kirillapone, Colombo, Sri Lanka, in which housing was one component of an integrated plan. Interest in housing was generated by the importance of that activity in a number of areas: these included meeting the needs of the community; its potential for generating income within the community; its contribution towards improving health in general; and the possibility of maximizing community participation. The chapter describes how a project which initially took no special account of the needs of women, was forced to change its approach in the implementation process, and the consequences this had both for the project and for women. SAVE programmes are implemented internationally in rural villages, and deprived urban areas. All projects have a common approach, addressing children's needs through integrated, multidisciplinary planning. SAVE works in partnership with communities, identifying problems and long-term solutions and attempting to transfer skills to local people to ensure that programmes are sustainable. Although women are included in SAVE's projects it is not the policy of the organization to focus specifically on the needs of women. It seeks, rather, to include women among its target beneficiaries as an underprivileged group. Since the major concern of SAVE is the livelihood of children, women as the providers of children are the most legitimate vehicle by which child welfare objectives may be achieved. Traditionally SAVE has viewed women from a welfare perspective, but over time has moved towards an anti-poverty approach. Thus SAVE not only targets women in their reproductive roles through health and nutrition education, but also acknowledges the productive role of women and therefore their need for income.

At the beginning the Kirillapone project assumed that the involvement of women in community participation was a national and automatic process with self-reliance of all the community's members its end result. Early experience, however, showed that while considerable self-reliance was demonstrated by the women within the confines of their physical and social environment, their participation in activities organized through formal associations was limited and their needs seldom articulated. SAVE recognized that the basic need in the community was to strengthen the women in the numerous roles they played within it. The agency therefore addressed itself to the need to give them training, skills, and confidence. Thus empowered, it was hoped that the women might participate more effectively in community life and begin to exert more control over their lives and those of their families.

In order to ensure this process of empowerment the Community Development project radically changed its course. From a bottom-up attempt at 'grassroots development' SAVE, as the implementing agency, turned to top-down intervention in order to favour women. The housing project not only was used to provide women with marketable skills and income, but also in a wider context it embraced health, childcare, better household management, and control of the environment, combined with providing the opportunity for women to organize and negotiate for better control of their lives and develop their potential for community leadership. For implementation, SAVE built on existing participation by women in traditional areas of work such as self-help and *shramadana* (donation of labour). In this way, the known propensity of women for self-reliance was used to wean the community from a dependency on handouts which had been generated by over fifty years of welfare policies in Sri Lanka. It was evident that women were inhibited by formal organizations, which tended to be dominated by men. SAVE relied instead on informal activities in the fields of housing, health, nutrition, domestic production, and childcare to give women the opportunity to associate with each other and articulate their concerns, develop new skills, and eventually manage activities. Training and placement in jobs, particularly in non-traditional areas of work, gave them better access to the economic opportunities available in the urban sector.

The experience provided valuable lessons for SAVE itself. The staff learned more about women through the experience of attempting to make community participation more effective. The project demonstrated the dangers of placing women in formal structures where most of them had little influence. It raised issues that related to replicability and the need to insure the community against indifference and abeyance when the implementing agency withdrew. Furthermore, the project demonstrated the urgent need to establish linkages between women in the community and outside institutions, which affected the quality of their lives.

The national context

The welfare ethic in Sri Lankan politics and policy-making has a history that pre-dates the country's independence. In 1931 a new constitution, drafted by the British for implementation during the transition to full independence, granted universal suffrage to men and women over the age of 21 and gave legislative power to a popularly elected assembly and its Board of Ministers, but left financial control in the hands of the British-appointed financial secretary. The Board of Ministers, determined to demonstrate the bankruptcy of British constitutional reform, legislated free education, free health, and a host of subsidies. By the 1950s state-sponsored welfare had become a deeply rooted tradition and one that no politician has since wanted to tamper with.

Although housing was a low priority in the list of subsidies, it was none the less regarded as the responsibility of the state. This was demonstrated by the construction of houses for civil servants by the British colonial government; by resettlement schemes and the building of flats in urban areas under successive post-Independence governments; and by the commitment to a more equitable housing policy by the socialist government of Madame Bandaranaike in the early 1970s. A change of government in 1977 gave a new focus to housing when the housing portfolio was added to the responsibilities of Prime Minister R. Premadasa.

The population at this time was about 14 million, while the number of occupied dwellings was around 2 million. Although the number of housing units had kept pace with the increase in population since Independence, congestion and overcrowding, inadequate construction, and the lack of basic amenities have contributed to an inadequacy in most of the housing stock. In 1978 the prime minister announced that 100,000 new houses were to be built over a five-year period. Planned initially with an emphasis on direct construction by the state, the scheme was soon amended to incorporate aided self-help. By 1983 75 per cent of this target had been achieved through the initiative of the National Housing Development Authority (NHDA) and the remainder through the Mahaweli River Diversion Programme. At the end of this period the prime minister announced a new target of 1 million new houses by 1988. This plan introduced a new approach, in that it was based on a system of state support rather than state intervention. The state would provide seed money to beneficiaries who had already made some minimal investment in their own housing, for example through land development or improvements in services. The scheme would be decentralized to function through community organizations. Of the earlier 100,000 houses target 64 per cent have been constructed in rural areas. However, the 'million houses programme' included for the first time a commitment to large-scale improvement of low-income urban housing. Half the population of the city of Colombo lived in slums and shanties (Robson 1983). In 1981, of the 509,000 houses listed in urban areas, 70,000 were slums, and almost half of these were in Colombo. In addition, one fifth of all Sri Lanka's temporary dwellings were in urban areas. Robson (1983) revealed that 31 per cent of urban houses comprised only one room, 36 per cent used a communal source of water, 24 per cent shared a lavatory, and 20 per cent had no toilet facilities.

Also within urban areas the spontaneous development of squatter settlements has been unwittingly consolidated by state action over the years. During the 1950s the government attempted to solve the problem of low-income housing by building high-rise flats in the cities. The flats, although intended for the squatters, were too expensive so they moved elsewhere to create new squatter settlements. In the 1960s and early 1970s successive governments relocated these squatters on the outskirts of the city, freeing valuable inner city land for commercial development. In the process, the governments legalized the settlements, allocating plots (though without title) to the people they settled while providing them with basic amenities such as water and sanitation.

The cumulative effect of these moves, both planned and spontaneous, has been to create considerable confusion in the tenurial status of squatters. A squatter settlement may house the following settlers: owner-occupiers – those who have bought a plot of land from the original owner in an informal transaction where no deeds were exchanged; private tenants – those renting a dwelling; subtenants – those to whom the private tenant sublets a room or part of the house; public tenants – those allocated a plot by the government in a resettlement scheme; part-owner squatters – those who have settled and are now in the process of 'buying' the plot by instalments; and outright squatters – those who have erected their dwelling on an adjacent site.

Despite the problem of low-income urban housing it has received only cursory attention. It was not until 1979 that the new government established a Slum and Shanty Unit (SSU) under the aegis of the Urban Development Authority (UDA) in the Ministry of Local Government, Housing and Construction (MLGHC). The goal of the SSU was to co-ordinate all low-income housing programmes. However, this was at variance with the UDA, which was bound by economic considerations. By 1984 SSU housing activities still extended to only eight projects, while its sites and services functions duplicated those of its ministry's Common Amenities Board. In 1985 the unit was merged with the NHDA, bringing it in line with the objectives and activities of the 'million houses programme'.

During this period, however, a small number of urban development projects had been undertaken by international non-
governmental organizations (NGOs) in slums and shanties in
Colombo. In 1978 the MLGHC had drawn up a Master Plan for
the city of Colombo which included the improvement of slum
housing by building more high-rise flats. Later, the MLGHC
welcomed other solutions proposed by the international NGOs,
including the community-based housing projects of the
Norwegian and US Save the Children Funds. The UDA/SSU
worked closely with the NGOs in designing surveys, house
plans, and household amenities. Initially some co-ordination of
agencies involved was undertaken by the MLGHC but meetings
did not continue beyond the first six months. Thereafter the
UDA/SSU was the sole co-ordinator of NGO efforts. Lack of
influence within its ministry reduced the effectiveness of
UDA/SSU. By default, the initiative in conducting household
surveys, ironing out the complexities of land tenure and housing finance, and devising new technologies for low-cost water,
sanitation, and housing was left to the NGOs. This gave them
considerable freedom in seeking solutions to the many problems
they encountered among the slum and shanty communities.

The project site: Kirillapone

Kirillapone is one of the larger collections of squatter settlements
that have mushroomed in Colombo since the 1950s. The earliest
squatter settlements were the result of rural–urban drift and of
intra-urban migration. Migrants found shelter in the gardens of
derelict houses, putting up makeshift housing which they
consolidated with structures that were often sublet to new
tenants. These instant 'neighbourhoods' came to be called
'gardens' by virtue of their location (Adamson 1983). While all
squatter settlements in Sri Lanka may be identified by their
location in a district or municipal ward, within each squatter
settlement there are distinct subdivisions, identified by a
'garden' name.[1]

Kirillapone is composed of five separate 'gardens', and was
originally settled in 1953 along the banks of a canal and on
adjacent grass fields. The earliest 'garden' came to be known as
Elakandiya, deriving its name from the canal bank. One enter-
prising owner-occupier then began erecting small shacks on the
grassland, subletting them to new migrants. This second

'garden' came to be known as Assanarwatta or Assanar's Garden, after the owner-occupier. This land was later appropriated by the state during the implementation of a policy of land reform in the 1970s and used to relocate squatters from the vicinity of the city's Conference Hall prior to the Non-Aligned Conference of 1976. These new settlements comprised two gardens named Kumbikelle (ant-forest) and Paspatiya (bed of earth), after their original squatter settlements. A year later, as the Municipal Council began to clear the land on either side of the main road in Kirillapone to erect a market, twenty or thirty shanty structures were moved to create a 'fifth garden', Kirula (from the ward name, Kirillapone or Kirulapone).

The immediate outcome of these relocations of the 1970s was violent conflict between the residents of the 'gardens'. The new settlements were pillaged by the older settlers who resented the intrusion into their territory. The residents of Elakandiya had thus far plied a lucrative trade in illicit liquor and gambling; their armed gangs were considered a threat to the municipal ward of Kirillapone. The new settlers of Kumbikelle and Paspatiya dared not venture from the safety of their gardens after dark, and their own thugs and thieves were soon subdued by the gangs of Elakandiya. The conflict eventually left three surviving gangs based on shifting alliances. Subservience to all three was a necessary element of daily life for the ordinary squatter.

In 1979 Kirillapone had a population of 1,661, almost 50 per cent of whom were below 17 years of age. The people were a mixture of Sinhalese (55 per cent), Tamil (37 per cent), and Moor/Malay (8 per cent). The residents survived on casual employment in the city, the men finding work as unskilled labourers or semi-skilled artisans (such as shoemakers, tinkers, bicycle repairers, and gardeners) while the women were mainly engaged in domestic service in the city's more affluent homes. Opportunities for self-employment were provided by the open market on the shanty's frontage where home-made snacks were sold or vegetables and groceries retailed at competitive prices. Of the population of working age in the shanty, 52 per cent were employed.[2] Of these, 40 per cent were in permanent employment, the majority labourers, messengers, sales assistants, masons, tailors, and gardeners. Approximately 50 per cent were in casual employment as unskilled labourers and only a very small number, 10 per cent, were self-employed. This relatively pessimistic picture is confirmed by the fact that 66 per cent of the shanty households were living below the poverty line, which

94

in 1979 was determined by the government at Rs 300 (£10 per month).[3]

A state hospital, municipal health clinic, and state dispensary are situated within 2 kilometres of the shanty but for many residents use of these facilities was constrained both by lack of information and self-confidence. Similarly, although a number of schools are located within the 3 kilometre radius defined as the residence qualification for admission to school, in 1979 24 per cent of Kirillapone's children of school age were not enrolled in school. Furthermore, although education to university level has been free for over fifty years in Sri Lanka, educational standards in the shanty were low: 11 per cent of the population were illiterate: only 48 per cent had completed primary school, while only 8 per cent continued to GCE ordinary level examination, which is the minimum qualification for white-collar employment.

A random sample of fifty-one households (thereafter termed the baseline survey) was conducted by the Marga Institute to gain a better idea of living conditions in Kirillapone. The sample showed that only 11 per cent of households were owners or public tenants, whilst the remainder were squatters.[4] There had been a high turnover in occupancy over the previous two years. Some settlers had returned to the site of their previous settlement when the Non-Aligned Conference was over. Others had 'sold' their allocated plots and now lived in other squatter settlements. Some acted as absentee landlords, having sublet the houses they had built on the allocated plots. The claims to ownership of the houses were later settled, in consultation with the UDA, in favour of the current occupant.

Government policy precludes the provision of amenities such as water and sanitation to squatter settlements because they are illegal and therefore regarded as temporary. In resettlement schemes initiated by the government, services were provided by the government as part of the sites and services arrangement. Thus when squatters were resettled by the government in Kumbikelle, Paspatiya, and Kirula, the Common Amenities Board of the MLGHC provided four water taps and two bucket-latrine complexes with separate units for men and women. These were located in the newly settled 'gardens'. Residents of the older 'gardens' dared not use them and used a public lavatory located about 700 metres away. Investigators in the baseline survey found that the residents of the newly settled 'gardens' did not fare much better. Over a hundred families in

Kumbikelle used only two taps; the tap serving sixty families in Paspatiya was in a bad state of repair, while the other in Kirula could not be shut off.

Arrangements made with the municipal council for the daily emptying of the bucket latrines had broken down because the labourer who came once a week carried only two buckets in a handcart: if the effluent exceeded the capacity of the buckets it was dumped into an open pit behind the latrines. The pit was a seething green mass, infested by flies. Many residents had made their own sanitation arrangements in preference to using the municipal lavatories. These makeshift latrines usually drained into the canal in which children often immersed themselves at play. The settlement was situated on low-lying, marshy grass fields, which made it susceptible to flooding. During the rainy season access paths became impassable. Children told the investigators that during these periods they could not get to the main road safely and were therefore absent from school.

The baseline survey classified 77 per cent of all houses as makeshift or temporary, being made of mud, plank, cadjan, or cardboard walls, with mud floors, and roofs of either cadjan thatch or galvanized iron sheets. The mud floors tended to be damp in the wet season, causing a high incidence of respiratory disease among the children. A few women would add a rendering of cow-dung to the floor, but this was both a time-consuming and infrequent occurrence because cow-dung was hard to obtain in urban areas. Few families had mats to sleep on, in contrast to houses in rural areas where local mat-weaving made bedding accessible even to the lowest income groups.

Half of the houses occupied a floor area of less than 18 square metres while 74 per cent of the houses had between four and nine occupants, with 41 per cent of households cooking, eating, and sleeping in the same room. The survey showed that 75 per cent of the households cooked only one meal a day. There was no electricity in the settlement and residents complained that the unlit access paths were a security problem. Patterns of health were closely related to the physical environment. Poor drainage, inadequate water supplies and waste disposal facilities, and the proximity to a sluggish canal that bred mosquitoes, all contributed to a high incidence of disease. Most common, particularly among children, were respiratory ailments and bowel disorders; 33 per cent of the children under 5 years of age suffered from chronic protein-energy undernutrition. On the other hand immunization against disease was available free of charge at state medical facilities. Only two households in the sample had not had their children inoculated.

The Save the Children project in Kirillapone

The arrival of SAVE in Sri Lanka coincided with an initiative by the newly elected government to move away from the welfare ethic. To some extent this move could be reconciled with SAVE's own ideology of self-reliance. However, the challenge lay in the response of the community in which SAVE would work. International agencies have long been considered 'an easy touch' in developing countries and Sri Lanka was no exception. The danger of being regarded as a donor rather than as a partner was more real in an urban squatter settlement than in a rural village. The proximity of squatters to affluent consumer-oriented, urban living, their regular exposure to advertising in the media, their awareness of politics and current events, all contributed to an undercurrent of cynicism.

SAVE encountered this cynicism very early. In the initial stages, when it was attempting to implement theories of bottom-up planning, it responded to 'felt needs' articulated by an elected community committee. These 'needs' were invariably goods and services. As SAVE developed experience, planning became more of an exercise to present a longer-term perspective to the community. SAVE considered this to be crucial if its goal of transferring the entire project to the community within a period of five to seven years was to be realized. Encouraging the community to participate and organize was an important aspect of the community development component of its programme; over time SAVE used three approaches to achieve these ends. The first was an evolutionary approach to community organization; the second used traditional forms of self-help to widen participation; and the third involved the training of community residents through implementation of projects.

COMMUNITY ORGANIZATION
Many of SAVE's early international programmes had developed formal community organizations, termed the community committee. As the elected representatives of a community, the community committee was an important link in the planning and implementation of a project. In Kirillapone, where no formal

organizations existed (except local branches of political parties), SAVE hoped to establish the same pattern. The Marga investigators, whose survey preceded the programme, were pleasantly surprised when, during the course of informal discussions on what was needed in the shanty, some of the more active participants in the discussions suggested forming a society to improve community conditions.[5] An election was organized and a constitution hastily drawn up. There was much wrangling over the election of office bearers between residents of different 'gardens'.

Anxious to eliminate rivalry, SAVE suggested a presidency to represent all 'gardens' with specific interests overseen by 'garden representatives'. SAVE also persuaded residents to represent women; this suggestion evoked considerable mirth, with one of the men hinting that 'they would soon need a representative for the man in the moon'. However, the suggestion was accepted. Despite this intervention, the women proved to be ineffective participants in the community committee. All posts were uncontested, probably by prior arrangement. The post of treasurer went to a woman whose husband was the moving force behind the local branch of the ruling political party. One woman was elected as a 'garden representative' but left for the Middle East a few months later. The women's representative, an elderly stalwart of the ruling political party, succeeded in getting re-elected every year although it was generally recognized in the community that she did not assume responsibility for any activity that improved the lives of her fellow women.

Early in 1979 when SAVE formally began work in the shanty, it was discovered that the community committee, far from facilitating community participation, actually discouraged many from participating in the programme. All but three community committee members had criminal records and a continual tug-of-war ensued between SAVE and the committee over supervision of programme funds. Misdemeanours such as misappropriation of finances, misbehaviour, and intimidation were uncovered. The majority of women would have nothing to do with a group that they considered to be a 'band of thugs' who had turned community leaders overnight. The SAVE personnel generally considered that the committee's perception of their role was as a pressure group for obtaining benefits. Thus school uniforms, books, jobs, and New Year festivities were high on their list of priorities, little attention was paid to health, training for employment, or long-term income generation.

The concept of community participation as a 'natural' and 'automatic' phenomenon lured SAVE in its first year into delivering services identified by the leadership and other groups in the community. The first and most important need identified in the community, expressed both by children and by importuning parents, was the opportunity to provide a formal education for the children. The community committee named the obstacles to school entry as the lack of birth certificates and the inability to negotiate with schools for admission. While the community committee identified the target group and collected lists of children, the investigators talked to school principals and were able to persuade one school to take in sixty-six children who had never been to school. SAVE provided uniforms while the community committee organized a *shramadana* in order to repair the school desks and chairs and level the playground by way of appreciation. In this example it is important to note that the problem, target, and strategy had been identified by the community committee; SAVE played merely a supporting role.

Within three months, however, shortcomings in the strategy became evident: 50 per cent of the new enrolment had dropped out of school. SAVE's field staff met with the community committee and evaluated the situation. It was concluded that non-enrolment in school was a symptom of more deeply rooted needs, that is lack of access to state services, malnutrition and hunger, lack of books and clothes, and instability and disruption in the family.

ESTABLISHMENT OF THE SELF-HELP ETHIC

The use of *shramadana*, as just described, was the second approach used by SAVE, who built on the tradition of self-help in the community. One positive feature of traditional Sri Lankan life that penetrates all segments of society, whether rural or urban, and reinforces the most fragile social fabric, is the practice of *shramadana*. Originating with labour donated in the king's service (*rajakariya*), the system was adapted by the British to build roads; by the Buddhist clergy to obtain agricultural services on temple lands; by local government institutions to maintain amenities in villages; and by politicians for rallying political support. *Shramadana* is a vital tool in social organization. Not only is it second nature for Sri Lankans to give their labour to a worthy cause, but also in the process of working together, it includes sharing meals and celebrating the achievements of the day. Thus *shramadana* is a social occasion. In fact very few women participated in the first *shramadana* the community committee organized, partly because the activity was organized by a committee who were known, individually, to round off such occasions with bouts of drinking. As project activities increased, however, women became the informal organizers of *shramadana* linked to their sectoral activities. Health auxiliaries would regularly round up the children to clean drains and collect garbage; access paths were levelled and tarred with male assistance; volunteer women ran a kitchen for malnourished children, and nurse aides who served as volunteers in state hospitals used their contacts to obtain specialized services for the children. Thus in a variety of ways, the women propagated the self-help ethic.

MULTI-SECTORAL PROJECTS
SAVE soon realized that it would have to bypass the community committee if it were to effectively reach the community. It noted that women were usually the most active people in day-to-day life in the community. As a result, long-term multi-sectoral planning was introduced by targeting women who were potentially the most effective agents of change. Through health auxiliaries, women masons, day-care attendants, nurse-aides, and trainees for industrial sewing, the circle of participation widened and interest in the programme increased rapidly. These areas had strong traditional associations for women. It was clear that women were more effective in project activities, through which they might organize themselves informally, than in formal organizations through which their interests were supposedly represented. The experience of the formal women's groups confirmed this, for while some loans were disbursed to individual women to assist in the generation of income, the groups did little more.

Basic needs identified by the community through the baseline survey provided the basis for multi-sectoral projects. These were various and included water supply, latrines, housing, roads, postal services, employment, and health. A general multi-sectoral plan was designed which was broadly divided into economic development, social development, community responsibility, health/nutrition, housing, and infrastructure. The survey did not focus primarily on the needs of women. Nevertheless, information recorded specifically from women provided reasonable guidelines for designing specific strategies

to support the participation of women in all sectors. At this
second stage SAVE took the decision to initiate three strategies
covering health, education, and women.

Health
Health rarely surfaced as a priority in the baseline survey.
Mothers preferred traditional remedies to standing in queues in
free government dispensaries. The community identified
hunger as a problem among children, but malnutrition had little
meaning for them. Housing was a community priority but the
connection between damp floors and respiratory diseases was
rarely made. Independently of the community committee,
SAVE decided in 1980 to select and train a cadre of community
health auxiliaries in preventive health and nutrition education.

Education
A second initiative focused on educational needs, both formal
and informal. In addition to enrolling children in school, a
carpentry training programme to service the housing project
was made available to men and women, but applicants could
not be found, due to the long three-year training period. The
carpentry unit became, instead, a rehabilitation unit for school
drop-outs and juvenile delinquents. Women were trained in
bookbinding and industrial sewing, and a cadre of nurse-aides
were enrolled as volunteers in state hospitals, all of whom eventually found employment in private hospitals. Other training
projects for women included nutrition-based home economics,
the construction of fuel-conserving stoves, domestic sewing,
and functional literacy.

Women
The development of programmes for women was seen as important for two reasons: women needed an income and they were
also the mainstay of the community, and therefore essential to
SAVE's project. In a sample questionnaire directed to the
people of working age within fifty-one households (sixty men
and sixty women) none of the women had studied beyond the
GCE ordinary level. The educational attainment of men and
women was comparable only at the lowest levels: 10 per cent of
the men and 17 per cent of the women were illiterate; 53 per cent
of the men and 67 per cent of the women had completed
primary school. Yet 67 per cent of the men in this latter group
had been able to find employment compared to only 25 per cent

of the women who were employed as unskilled labourers or domestic servants. SAVE's plans for generating employment and income focused particularly on women, not only because of the large numbers seeking employment but also because it was observed that much of the income earned by women was channelled to the family. This contrasted with men whose earnings were accounted for in good measure by individual needs, including cigarettes, alcohol, gambling, and the cinema.

It has to be recognized that part of the problem of access to employment lay in the women's own perception of their employment potential. Half of the women interviewed stated that they had no skills. Among the skills acknowledged by the other women were cooking, sewing, weaving, and laundering. No construction-related skills were recorded, although many of the unskilled women labourers worked on building sites. By contrast 12 per cent of the men interviewed professed to having masonry skills although, with one exception, they were all employed in similar construction tasks to those of the unskilled women labourers. The absence of knowledge about necessary skills for employment also hampered women in their search for employment. Again, half the women failed to respond to a question related to skills they would like to learn, whereas 12 per cent of the men specifically requested masonry training in response to this question. Yet there was no doubt that the women desired employment: 82 per cent of those women in the survey with neither permanent nor temporary employment expressed a desire to find paid employment. Among the constraints they identified were lack of training, lack of mobility to seek work, and the burdensome and time-consuming household tasks and childcare duties which were aggravated by inadequate water supply and sanitation; 42 per cent of the women were mothers who recalled that they had terminated their schooling in order to look after siblings. These constraints helped explain why the majority of women expressed a preference for work within the home.

Plans for generating employment for women were constrained by insufficient data on woman-headed households which hampered SAVE staff from identifying specific needs and possible solutions. As one initiative, SAVE devised a long-term strategy for training women in marketable skills such as industrial sewing and bookbinding. However, this required other support, such as travel costs, living costs during the training, and arrangements for childcare while women were away on courses. Although the training guaranteed employment to women who could complete the course, the high costs limited the number of beneficiaries. SAVE recognized the need for additional support for women engaged not only in training but also in employment. Young women were trained as day-care attendants and pre-school teachers and a project was planned to set up a day-care facility for children of working mothers. The lack of space to site the day-care centre delayed construction for a year and a half. Meanwhile, the urgent need continued to be large-scale, short-term training for employment.

Finally constraints at the community level made the task of training a delicate balancing act. On the one hand, the establishment of women's groups with independent funds for a credit programme provoked the hostility of the community committee, who complained that the women's groups did not keep them informed and tended to bypass them. On the other hand, conflicts among the women threatened to destroy the spirit of solidarity that SAVE was attempting to generate among the women. Health workers had been selected according to minimum educational levels, and, with access to influence and status in state hospitals, they came to be regarded as an elitist group.

The housing project: community-level projects

While field staff in SAVE's social development arm were grappling with the problem of women who headed households who had no income and were desperately in need of employment, plans for housing were being discussed by the SAVE's housing team and the elected community committee. The housing team acknowledged that participation by women in housing construction could meet the immediate need for large-scale, short-term training for employment. Misgivings were expressed in teams dominated by men. The social development team, however, urged that employment of women on site would solve the immediate problem of inadequate day-care facilities for working mothers. After some debate it was agreed that recruitment to all aspects of construction activity would be open to women.

It was inevitable that the capacity to generate an income should be linked with the housing project. The principle of cost-recovery, which had been stipulated by SAVE's funders, meant that incomes would have to be raised dramatically before the housing scheme could be affordable to a majority of the shanty residents. Although the government had agreed in principle to a forty-year leasehold right to 30 square metres of land per household, negotiations with the state bank for use of that right as collateral for loans had dragged on for so long that in the interim it was decided that borrowers should be required to find two permanently employed guarantors for their loans. SAVE decided that the housing scheme should be open to all households, and therefore agreed in principle to subsidize twenty of the lowest income households in which there were no employed adults. SAVE also decided against a sites and services project as a solution to the housing problem.

It was also recognized that while self-help housing in rural areas was facilitated by seasonal labour, in the urban areas time spent on self-help housing was time lost at work and consequent loss of income. SAVE's project therefore aimed to provide a combined solution to both unemployment and housing needs, by first training community residents as construction workers (with living costs paid during the period of training) and second, by using paid community labour in the construction of houses. To ensure that there was participation in the project SAVE used community labour, and provided sufficient training in skills to ensure that those trained could secure employment after the project was completed. SAVE introduced a scheme to produce most of the building materials on site. In this way construction expenditures were channelled into income for the community. This had significant implications for the choice of technologies. A production unit was set up to make roofing sheets using cement, sand, and coconut fibre. Six men were trained by a team of British consultants. This team also introduced laterite bricks, which required some strength in handling to ensure adequate compression. The strongest men in the shanty thus became the project's brickmakers. Within a year problems developed in both technologies. While SAVE undertook a costly revamping of the roof sheeting technology, the use of laterite bricks was abandoned, on the advice of the community committee. A subcommittee recommended a cement-sand brick in its place: this technology was simple, and SAVE was soon able to train a woman to take over supervision of the unit.

Selection of trainees for both house construction and the production of building materials was based on household income and need: the provision of employment to the lowest income households was necessary to ensure their ability to participate in the housing loan scheme arranged with the State People's Bank, which involved a monthly repayment of approximately Rs 54 (£2) over fifteen years.

In December 1979, five months after the housing project started, recruitment began for the trainees of the carpentry, masonry, roofing, and construction work-force. The initial response from the women in interviews for carpentry and masonry was discouraging, and SAVE had to schedule a second interview exclusively for women before they mustered sufficient confidence to apply: then fifty-eight women applied for the eight masonry training positions. In the selection priority was given to those women who headed households and those in desperate circumstances. It was agreed that the wages of the eight women selected would be on a par with those of the men. On the first working day after the interview only two women appeared to start their training. They stood outside the masonry training shed while the male trainer inside pretended not to notice them. It took the intervention of SAVE staff to persuade the trainer to find room for them in his overcrowded shed. However, once the training began male workers appeared to accept them without question. The fact that the women had had prior experience in house construction appeared to influence the male work-force more than the trainer's reservations about the suitability of women for construction work.

SAVE initially introduced a six-week period of formal training for new recruits to masonry. However, the continued demand for masonry skills among the women led SAVE to alter the method of training radically. It was decided to provide work to all women in desperate financial circumstances by absorbing them into the construction work-force as unskilled labourers. The work-force was divided into teams of eleven, usually made up of seven semi-skilled or skilled masons and four unskilled workers who dug foundations and transported bricks. The unskilled labourers would work alongside the skilled masons, learning the skill as they worked.

Since this first experiment SAVE has maintaned a waiting list of women applicants for the construction work-force, the majority of whom are from the lower income groups. They include women spouses as well as women who head households. In the baseline survey almost half the men interviewed had disapproved of their wives working. However, this appeared to be a relatively insignificant problem in the recruitment of women to the construction work-force since the process of recruitment was informal. A woman in need of work could register on the waiting list with a community health worker, a representative of the community committee, or she could speak directly to a member of SAVE's field staff. If the need for employment was urgent, she received priority on the waiting list. The system was not the most cost-effective, since the emergency response generated a heavy turnover. However, from the perspective of its objectives relating to childcare, family health, and domestic stability, SAVE believed that the trade-off was worthwhile.

SAVE also has had to address the long-term problem of the future prospects for employment of women masons and brickmakers. Although women are a common sight on construction sites in the city, they are usually employed as unskilled labourers, moving rubble and bricks on the ground. It is rare to see a woman ascend the scaffolding on a building. The average perception of a woman's role on a building site has little to do with modesty. Rather it is reflected in the SAVE foreman's response when the women were at work on the scaffolding of the high walls of their community centres: 'These women, from their natural foolishness, will lose their balance and fall and what a to-do we will have then!'

SAVE has consistently given a high profile to its women masons. They have volunteered to build community facilities in other shanties, demonstrating what it is possible for women to do, and there have been many interchange visits. The problem does not lie in women lacking skills for the construction industry; the barrier to employment is rather in the management of the construction industry. The key figure on a construction site is the foreman; his functions are not limited to quality control, but cover the prevention of pilfering and wastage, as well as maintaining tight discipline. Foremen usually list the latter duties as the most burdensome and at the same time the most important. The construction industry is not concerned with changing its social practices and considers that the addition of women to the regular work-force would result in the need to reorientate and widen the functions of management. In the housing project SAVE's management was undeniably more oriented in its emphasis. In the training, once the initial resistance by male supervisors was overcome, the management was intensive, informal, and personal.

Between March 1984 and January 1985 SAVE temporarily suspended housing construction and laid off the work-force as part of its strategy for pressurizing delinquent borrowers to pay up arrears on loan instalments. During the ten-month period the men masons in the project had no problem finding employment outside the shanty, but the women found it far more difficult. One woman found employment with a contractor who hired her to work on an extension to a middle-class home in the city as an unskilled worker, despite her protests that she was a skilled mason. As luck would have it, the contractor was absent from work one day and the woman took over the masonry work, much to the amazement of the owner-housewife who kept an eye on the construction. The result was a new contract, issued to the woman mason, at a lower rate of pay, but she had succeeded in breaking into a new area of work.

The incident raises an interesting issue: how far does intervention have to be gender-specific in order to ensure equality of opportunity for women in construction? Can women masons survive only as independent contractors, or can they find a permanent place in the labour force of the construction industry, given the relevant institutional support? If this is so, what kind of support is necessary to bring about this integration? One factor that is clear from the experience of the women masons of Kirillapone is the need for training to extend beyond women workers, to management who decide the allocation and selection of appropriate labour. Ironically prospects for future employment for the women masons have been found outside the construction industry, in the Middle East market for domestic servants. Women who joined the construction work-force found that as they acquired new skills so they also acquired increased confidence. Until this time female migration to the Middle East had been the preserve of literate women with a higher level of education. Women who felt that the construction work-force offered them limited prospects began to join this migration. It is a sad but telling commentary on women's perceptions of their trade, but understandable none the less when the number of skilled male masons and carpenters who make up the brawn drain to the Middle East are considered.

In the building groups in Kirillapone the women were also instrumental in organizing a savings and loan association, administered by the SAVE Field Office. Among their own teams the activities of women have ranged from organizing the traditional *Seettu* (an informal savings group with rotating access to each month's collection), to holding convivial gatherings at the *Thosai* (pancake) kiosk on pay day.

However, in wider, formal gatherings the women, despite their training, remain inhibited and are still the silent majority. Although political patronage has been eroded by the alternative patronage unwittingly developed by SAVE, the twin problems of education and income continue to deter most women from aspiring to their share of power and formal decision-making. This is perhaps most clearly demonstrated by the failure to contest the election of the women's representative in the community committee. One effort by SAVE to persuade a woman in the work-force to challenge her failed by three votes, but the workers did not renew the challenge the following year, although this could equally be a reflection on the tokenism associated with the office of women's representative.

Conclusion

In retrospect the housing project, the largest income-generating activity in the Kirillapone programme, appears to have been the most obvious vehicle for meeting both the long-term and short-term needs of the women. First, as the major users of housing, involvement of women in planning and design proved invaluable. Second, the close relationship between the improvement of housing and the physical environment had significant implications for family health. Third, construction skills not only improved the ability of women to maintain their housing stock but also provided them with access to a market where construction skills were scarce. Lastly, participation in the housing loan scheme provided women, and particularly women who headed households, with access to formal credit facilities.

The Kirillapone project began as a conventional community development project, attempting to ascertain 'felt needs' of the community through a survey and discussions and to devise solutions for community problems through the existing leadership and organizations. However, the practical application of this theory of bottom-up development revealed some glaring shortcomings in the earliest phase of the project. As the responsibilities of women in the community became more apparent, SAVE found itself compelled to re-examine vital aspects of community development such as participation, articulation, and prioritizing of needs and decision-making. In attempting to redress the imbalance between responsibility and power, SAVE began to design and implement strategies that would empower women through training, employment, income, and organization. Some of the strategies adopted brought women into non-traditional avenues of work. Others enabled women to earn an income, supplement existing resources, reduce the burden of household duties, or simply associate with other women in trying to improve their lives. As women began to avail themselves of these opportunities they began to be aware of a new independence and a new sense of power and influence.

The new opportunities for independence provided by the capacity to earn an income added another new dimension to the existing domestic instability. Common law marriages had always been easily contracted and as easily broken, with the desertion rate high as males sought work outside the locality, and then often failed to return. Participation of women in the work-force appeared to have the effect of turning the tables on the men. Working in close proximity and living within the same environment, a number of married men and women in the construction teams developed new, extramarital relationships which threatened not only domestic stability but also, for a while, peace in the neighbourhood. One woman went so far as to throw her husband out, then, having had her marriage legalized through SAVE a few months previously, she hired a lawyer and filed suit for maintenance of their children. Nevertheless over time the shanty made adjustments to the new situation. A considerable number of men and women were reconciled after this brief 'honeymoon' with freedom. Some women moved out of one house and into another in the shanty while in other situations, a few women took up employment in the Middle East.

However, this has not opened up new frontiers of freedom, but simply provided an escape route from domestic slavery into wage slavery. At the same time there is no doubt that the financial independence of women better equips them to perform their household and childcare responsibilities. The reduction of disease, improvement in the nutritional status of children, higher school attendance, and a number of other benefits to children provided by their families were all results documented by SAVE. One of the strategies adopted by SAVE to involve the women more actively in the programme was *shramadana*. SAVE used the traditional areas of women's work, in health care, cooking, and the maintenance of the physical environment to provide women with training and opportunities for earning a living. The training of health auxiliaries and nurse-aides had long-term benefits for the entire community while it gave the women beneficiaries new, marketable skills. The construction of a community kitchen, and the organization of women's groups who used it, gave the women valuable training in nutrition and enabled them to earn an income through the sale of meals to the building site work-force.

The training of women in construction skills, considered a non-traditional area of work at the time, was, in retrospect, the most significant link with women's traditional work. Despite the vicissitudes of both the training and construction phases, the involvement of women in the final phase, that of mainten-ance, came easily and naturally. This was largely because women traditionally have been considered responsible for cleaning and maintaining the home and environment. In Kirillapone maintenance of housing stock and the physical environment is a neighbourhood or communal exercise, carried out on a regularly organized basis through *shramadana*. Invariably the volunteers are women and, more recently, children, both boys and girls. In addition the project offered the women new opportunities for exploiting the urban labour market. The baseline survey showed that most employed women were domestic or unskilled casual labourers. By investigating the demand for skills in the urban market SAVE began to train women for specific jobs. Training in industrial sewing, for instance, guaranteed employment. SAVE took a bigger risk in training women in construction skills which were regarded as 'men's work'. Their experience revealed that in training women in non-traditional areas of work, wider intervention at the national policy-making level is required to ensure that such efforts have replicable results.

Nevertheless the Kirillapone experience does underscore the question of women's dependency and vulnerability in an economic system that is not designed to accommodate their responsibilities and needs. The intervention of SAVE provided much-needed training and guidance which gave them the confidence to compete in the labour market. Yet what will be the situation of the next generation of women in Kirillapone? SAVE's predefined role was a limited one. How long can and should an intermediary maintain its support if it is to ensure enduring results? What policy decisions are required to sustain such action and what role can an intermediary such as SAVE play in supporting such policies? These are questions that concern all NGOs and all governments, for better linkages between the two groups are required if the innovative approaches of pilot projects are to bear fruit. The experience of working together has enabled the women of Kirillapone to better articulate their communal needs and achieve greater control over the conditions that govern their lives. This has evolved through informal training and experience. Where there had been a passive acceptance of the hardships of urban squatter life, women are now aware of what can and cannot be achieved by joint action. The autonomy of women is more difficult to measure for it is dependent on a range of variables, from sexual freedom to the capacity to argue over the price of bread in the open market. But the choices and decisions that a woman may make when she is skilled, confident, and financially independent, combined with an awareness of her own contribution to, and role in, the community to which she belongs, must surely add in no small measure to her own sense of worth.

Notes

An earlier draft version of this chapter was published as Fernando (1985) 'Women's participation in the housing process: the case of Kirillapone, Sri Lanka', *DPU Gender and Planning Working Paper* no 3, University College, London.

1 A 'garden' may take its name from the original owner of the land or a particular geographical feature such as a canal or copse of trees, or from the original squatter who might have made a profitable business of erecting and subletting makeshift housing.
2 The categories of permanent, temporary, and self-employment used in the baseline survey had the following definitions: *permanent* workers are wage-earners registered as employees in a formal organization; *temporary* workers are engaged in casual work paid on a daily basis where work is limited to a single assignment over a few days; *self-employed* workers are engaged in independent retailing of goods or artisans working on their own.
3 In 1979 the rate of exchange was 30 rupees to £1 sterling.
4 Researchers from the Marga Institute used a number of techniques

to help the community identify needs. Questionnaires were administered to 120 people, that is 15 per cent of the population (60 men and 60 women in 51 households) and to 21 school-going children. In addition case studies were undertaken with women, informal conversations were held with residents, and participant observation was utilized as far as possible. Particular emphasis was laid on information which might facilitate the realization of SAVE's objectives of encouraging greater self-reliance in the community. The author was working for the Marga Institute and undertook the survey and other field work for SAVE. She later became Director of the US Save the Children Kirillapone Project.

5 The Marga Institute, acting on behalf of SAVE, was able to implement a few short-term projects, such as repairs to houses and the enrolment of children in school.

CHAPTER 6

Government housing policy and its implications for women in Guyana

LINDA PEAKE

Introduction

Guyana, a former British colony situated on the northern coast of South America, is the only avowedly socialist and the only English-speaking country on the mainland (see Peake 1987). Once refered to as the 'breadbasket' of the Caribbean, since the mid-1970s the country has been in a state of crisis and now ranks amongst the world's poorest countries. Its decline, although partly attributable to the world recession and its dependence on three primary exports (bauxite, rice, and sugar) is largely explained by the corruptive practices of its government. Claiming to follow a path of co-operative socialism Thomas (1983) reveals that, in fact, government policies have led to the emergence of a state capitalist society. The aim of the government, to secure an élite position for its members, is legitimized by its constant assertions to be acting in the interests of low-income groups. It is within this context of economic decline, social decay, and political corruption that the effects of the government's housing policy on low-income women will be assessed. Particular consideration is given to women belonging to social groups from whom the government receives its support, that is Afro-Guyanese women living in urban areas. The analysis focuses on two of the most prevalent forms of housing available in the 1970s and 1980s, aided self-help projects and government-rented apartments.

The chapter is divided into three sections. A brief introduction outlines the government's official position both in relation to women in general and in relation to their entitlement to housing. The historical context and the current crisis of housing policy since Guyana's independence is then outlined. Against this background the participation of Afro-Guyanese women in both an aided self-help on the coastal strip, the Virginia Women's Homestead, and in government-rented apartments in Georgetown is appraised. The chapter concludes with an assessment of the extent to which the housing needs of low-income Afro-Guyanese women are being met.[1]

Women and government policy

As a result of the United Nations Decade for Women (1976–85) increased attention has been paid to recognizing the roles and needs of women. All Caribbean territories subscribe to the prescription of the UN Decade for Women, and in Guyana since 1980 a Women's Advisory Board with a staff of three women has been established in the Office of the Prime Minister. This has the aim of working towards the 'integration of women into development'. The People's New Constitution was promulgated in the same year, Article 29 of which reiterated the government's commitment to the full participation of women in all phases of national life:

> Women and men have equal rights – and the same legal status in all spheres of political, economic and social life. All forms of discrimination against women on the basis of their sex are illegal. The exercise of women's rights is ensured by according women equal access with men to academic, vocational and professional training, equal opportunities in employment, remuneration and promotion, and in political, economic and social activity, by special labour and health protection measures for women, by providing conditions enabling mothers to work and by legal protection and material and moral support for mothers and children, including paid leave and other benefits for mothers and expectant mothers.
>
> (Government of Guyana 1980: 10)

Seven years later changes are still being made in matters relating to affiliation and maintenance, pension benefits, and rights relating to the acquisition and division of property. Despite these promising legal developments, the socio-economic position of low-income Afro-Guyanese women remains highly unfavourable. This is likely to continue until the misconceptions held about these women are analysed and broken down. In particular there is

114

much confusion arising from the non-recognition of both women's triple roles in productive, reproductive, and community managing work, and changing household structure (Moser 1985a).

In Guyana, despite stereotype assumptions about the structure of the household and the division of labour within it, women have always spanned public and private spheres (although their recorded participation in paid work is relatively low). In 1970 women comprised 19 per cent of the labour force, and were employed in traditional female activities such as nursing, teaching, and office and shop work.[2] An unspecified number also work in the Guyana Defence Force. These official figures should be treated with caution. What they fail to reveal is that increasing numbers of Afro-Guyanese women are employed in the informal sector in the urban areas, particularly as traders selling both cooked and uncooked food and items illegally brought into the country from overseas.[3] No attempt has been made to assess the income-generating potential of the traders and because they flout the law the PNC government is determined to clamp down on their activities. Thus an important source of livelihood, particularly for Afro-Guyanese women might disappear, adding to the already high unemployment rate.

Women in Guyana have a long history of involvement in waged work and income-generating activities, yet 'much more . . . has been written about Caribbean women in the context of the family than is written about their work and other roles' (Powell 1984: 101). This is because women are defined by the state primarily in their reproductive role as childbearers and child-rearers, with their roles in waged work and in contributing to the maintenance of the environment going unrecognized, as the following quotation reveals:

> The portion of the life-span of the average women which is taken up with child-bearing has markedly contracted. This, together with the lengthening of her life expectancy due to better medical facilities, has left her with more *free time* which continues to increase as more labour-saving devices tend to become available to her. . . . Further, the physical effort involved in many areas of endeavour has over the years been substantially reduced and brought within her grasp.
>
> (Government of Guyana 1976: 1, my emphasis)

Furthermore it is often assumed that this free time will be spent on community participation. As a briefing paper on self-help from the Ministry of Health, Public Welfare and Housing (nd: 1) shows this view is widespread: 'It is hoped that the non-working wives may be mobilised to develop some community programme'. It is considered that outside their reproductive role women are non-productive, yet in Guyana over one-third of households are headed by women who must be involved in productive work to ensure the survival of their households.[4]

WOMEN AND GOVERNMENT HOUSING POLICY

It would appear that housing is one area of public life in which certain advances have been made for women. The *State Paper on Equality for Women* (Government of Guyana 1976) made no mention of inequalities between men and women in relation to housing. Part of the reason for this is that to a certain extent a number of the legal inequalities have been removed. The 1969 Rent Control Ordinance for government-rented housing broadened the meaning of the term 'tenant' to include the 'reputed' spouse of the tenant residing with that tenant six months prior to the death of the tenant. Prior to 1969, only the *de jure* wife or husband of the tenant was entitled to continue as the legal tenant. The amendment finally gave legal recognition to the conjugal patterns commonly found in Guyana, that is common law unions and visiting unions. In self-help schemes priority is given to applicants with families, regardless of the sex of the household head and the Self-Help Agreement seeks to protect the rights of women who are not heads of households but who have contributed to self-help work. This gives recognition to the greater involvement of women in the construction activities of self-help schemes.

Turning to owner-occupation, the legal position is that the services of a woman in the home should be taken into account when determining the rights of each party to property acquired during the union. This is now ensured by making it a legal necessity for both parties to sign the mortgage contract. Instrumental in making this legal change was the parliamentary secretary at the Ministry of Health, Public Welfare and Housing.[5] Apart from being the parliamentary secretary for housing she is also the chairman [sic] of the Conference on the Affairs and Status of Women in Guyana (CASWIG).[6] This is a non-governmental umbrella organization formed to eliminate discrimination against Guyanese women. Despite its female leadership, however, CASWIG has made no attempt to improve the position of women in relation to housing. It does not see housing as a priority area, although it claims one of its major objectives is to encourage the sharing of responsibility between women and men in the home and in the community. Although women's needs, it may be thought, would have been recognized by the woman parliamentary secretary for housing who also has a strong interest in women's affairs, the appointment of women to policy-making bodies in Guyana is an activity best seen as an end in itself as opposed to a means to an end: it has not led to a greater sensitivity to women's needs.

These legal changes have most benefited middle-class women with sufficient finances and knowledge to secure access to courts of law to ensure their entitlement to equal rights. For many low-income women, their last recourse in their attempts to secure housing is to appeal to their legal rights, of which many are ignorant. Rather, their efforts to obtain a dwelling for themselves and their dependants arise from a desire to improve the inadequate, often squalid, environments in which they live. Two such efforts will be examined in detail after the following section which outlines the government's philosophy and approach to housing provision.

The history and current crisis of housing in Guyana

Unlike most countries in the region, Guyana's problems are not associated with high rates of population growth and urbanization, but with underpopulation and the extremely skewed spatial population distribution. Of a population totalling 768,607 (in a country of 215,000 square kilometres, approximately the same size as Britain), nearly 90 per cent are concentrated on the narrow coastal belt, which is now relatively highly urbanized.[7] Current distributions have historical roots and the principal factors underlying the spatial configuration of settlements and population in Guyana can be traced back to the combined effects of physical features and to the policies of the colonial rulers. The interior of dense forests and mountainous terrain is difficult to penetrate and remains virtually unsettled. However, the rich alluvial soils of the coastlands provided fertile ground for sugar and rice plantations which, together with the presence of bauxite and other minerals near the coast, led to the development of settlements along the coastal belt. The pattern of settlement outside the capital, Georgetown, and the sugar estates, however, is relatively sparse.

Of equal importance is the racial composition of the

population, also a legacy of the country's colonial inheritance. African slaves were first taken to the area as early as 1621 by the Dutch West India Company to work on the sugar plantations. With the abolition of slavery in 1834 and the subsequent import (until 1917) of East Indians as indentured labour, the social structure underwent a dramatic change. The last published population census of 1970 revealed that 51 per cent of the population comprised people of East Indian origin (Indo-Guyanese), 31 per cent of African origin (Afro-Guyanese), 10 per cent mixed, 5 per cent Amerindians, and 3 per cent divided amongst Portuguese, Chinese, and White.[8] The population growth rate between 1946 and 1970 was 122 per cent for Indo-Guyanese and only 41 per cent for Afro-Guyanese: given the traditional ethnic basis of support for the two major political parties in Guyana this rapid relative increase of the Indo-Guyanese sector of the population has had serious social and political implications.

The Indo-Guyanese largely support the opposition party, the Marxist People's Progressive Party (PPP) led by Cheddi Jagan, while the Afro-Guyanese support the ruling party, the People's National Congress (PNC) led by Desmond Hoyte (and until his recent death, by Forbes Burnham). The PPP held power from 1953 when the transition from British colonial rule began, until 1964 when the PNC took power. In 1966 Independence was granted. Since this time the PNC has retained power by pursuing an implicit racial strategy of divide and rule, and more recently as the racial basis of its support has diminished, it has employed an ever more blatant approach to the rigging of elections (Latin America Bureau 1984).

As a consequence of the racial tension engendered by the PNC government there have been periodic eruptions of violence, with major implications for the spatial distribution of the population and the government's approach to housing. Racial conflicts in the early 1960s on the coastal belt and in the inland mining town of Linden resulted in the forced movement of 15,000 people to settle in racially segregated communities. Many had no option but to settle on government-owned land with some 3 per cent of the population (3,000 families) now living in squatter settlements. Thus the establishment of squatter settlements in Guyana is not the same phenomenon as in Asian and Latin American cities. In the latter it is associated with heavy rural-urban migration, rapid population growth, and high rates of urbanization. In Guyana it was undertaken as a solution to racial conflict. It is not viewed by low-income groups as a solution to the housing crisis. Nor are squatter settlements confined to urban areas, they also occur in rural areas and on the rural/urban periphery, particularly in the sugar belt where vacant land is available.

It was not until 1970, with the PNC announcement that the country was following a path to socialism and had become a Co-operative Socialist Republic that housing was accorded any national priority in policy terms. The 1970 census revealed that at this time 66 per cent of households owned or were paying for their dwelling while a further 31 per cent leased or rented. These percentages varied between the urban and rural areas. In the latter, where the Indo-Guyanese dominate, home ownership was three times as common as in urban areas where renting, mainly through private landlords, was the norm.

In common with other Third World governments in the early 1970s, Guyana moved from an emphasis on 'top-down' public housing projects to 'bottom-up' self-help projects. Given the government's ideology of co-operative socialism, co-operatives were to be the instruments through which the social and economic reorganization of Guyanese society was to be achieved.[9] This was especially the case for housing. Housing was viewed not only as a 'roof over one's head' but also in terms of community membership. The slogan of the 1972–6 Second Development Plan, 'Feed, house and clothe the nation', reiterated this philosophy. The government's aim was to increase the level of self-reliance and self-sufficiency among the population, and it assumed that co-operative maintenance of property would provide the basis for collective participation in other activities.

It is claimed by the PNC government that self-help housing has been an important dimension of Guyanese housing policy for the last thirty years.[10] In 1968 Aided Self-Help projects were brought within the remit of the then Ministry of Housing and Reconstruction; however, by 1982 only 4,000 families were housed in them (Hanson 1982). There are two varieties of self-help projects in Guyana: aided self-help (ASH) housing societies and co-operative self-help housing groups. In ASH housing societies members pay for house lots at the cost of development and repay the Ministry of Housing for loans covering the cost of the materials used in construction.[11] With spiralling costs of building materials and land development many ASH housing society members were unable to repay their mortgage loans and were encouraged to join co-operative self-help groups. In these members pay a fixed percentage of their income towards the cost of their homes. No one member pays more than another for the house they occupy but payments can be spread over varying periods. The same system applies to payments of municipal rates, maintenance, and land development costs. Housing co-operatives can be subdivided into two categories; first, those that are concerned only with acquiring land and houses, and second, community co-operative villages, which are concerned with utilizing the principles of co-operativism in order to develop a sense of sharing and self-reliance within the community.

The most important period for self-help housing was the 1970s, when government subsidies included salary costs and reduced interest rates on loans. From 1974 to 1976 and in 1978, public sector employees were released from their work-places on full pay (although the level of production at the self-helpers' work-place had to be maintained at the same level). Self-help groups were also granted mortgages by the Guyana Co-operative Mortgage Finance Bank at 6 per cent interest per annum. (Market rates in 1981 were 12–14 per cent.) In addition the Central Housing and Planning Authority (CHPA) gave subsidies to self-help groups which included bulk-purchase of materials, infrastructural works, technical supervision and instruction from skilled construction workers and transportation of materials and equipment to sites, which amounted to 40 per cent of the cost. In the 1980s, however, the removal of government support has resulted in self-help groups working in their free time without the benefit of professional instruction from skilled construction workers, and with applicants no longer being screened to ascertain whether they can afford their mortgage payments.

The PNC government appears to have been unwilling to modify the necessary mechanisms through which the goal of co-operative socialist housing could be realized, that is by allocating housing according to need and not by ability to pay. It has done little to encourage co-operatives, however, and consequently they have an abysmal record. Although housing co-operatives in the 1970s did receive some support they are co-operatives in name only. The majority have made no substantial contribution to economic activity nor to increasing the power of low-income groups to control the distribution of resources in society (Standing 1979). Moreover, when building activity finishes, the co-operative society ceases to function. This has been the pattern of self-help housing in Guyana, indeed the majority of self-help groups are not registered as co-operative societies.

Unfortunately, for the decade 1970–80 official estimates of the number of new dwellings built by the government differ widely. Hinkson (1980) put the number at 3,088 (out of a total estimate of 30,180) (Ministry of Health, Public Welfare and Housing 1981), while Griffith (1981) put the figure even lower at 2,206.[12] Although a few co-operative self-help schemes are still operating, it is now more common for people to build their own homes individually. Private households, it is estimated, build about 70 per cent of the new housing stock per annum (Hanson 1982). As no trade unions are engaged in house-building the remaining 30 per cent of houses are built by private developers, at an average sale price of G$ 75,000 (Dick 1984).[13]

Throughout its twenty-one-year period of office, the record of the PNC government of providing housing (and all other services) for low-income groups has steadily deteriorated. In the 1980s, with its socialist credentials in tatters, its commitment has disappeared altogether.[14] Although hard hit by the lack of foreign exchange in 1981 the government allocated a mere G$ 5.5 million for housing development (1981: G$ 2.65 = US$ 1.00). The low level of political commitment to housing is further illustrated by a reversal in policy, in which housing has been downgraded from an integral element of development to a mere item of welfare. This was evidenced in 1983 when the portfolio for housing was removed from the Ministry of Works and Housing to the low-status and overburdened Ministry of Health and Public Welfare (Griffith 1982). By early 1985 the government allocation for housing was further reduced to only G$ 2.5 million leading to both the cessation of government-sponsored house-building by co-operatives and the decision to sell off government-rented apartments. As a result of these actions the government has reneged on its commitment to 'house the nation'. Since 1986 those unable to afford to build or buy their own homes have been restricted to finding their own solutions to their housing needs. The following section describes the options open to low-income groups in the early 1980s using two case studies to illustrate the attempts of Afro-Guyanese women to secure housing.

Case studies of Afro-Guyanese women and housing

In the 1970s and early 1980s, when the PNC government still had housing to allocate, despite its stated aim of housing people according to their need, it formulated a housing programme based on family income.[15] The government had two types of housing to offer: rented apartments and ASH housing. The broad guidelines adopted were that families with incomes of up to G$ 250 per month qualified for government-rented apartments. On incomes as low as this families were not considered capable of repaying the mortgage loans for home-ownership. Above this income, people were either encouraged to join co-operative housing groups and build by aided self-help, or to purchase plots on which to build their own house individually. Hanson (1981) estimated that if a household were to receive a mortgage loan of G$ 30,000–35,000 (the official 'low-income' housing range) it would need an annual income of over G$ 7,000, yet the 1977 Labour Force Survey revealed that 50 per cent of households had annual incomes of less than G$ 2,800. Hanson (1982) further estimated that over 77 per cent of the urban population and 96 per cent of the rural population could not afford to buy houses in the price range of G$ 30,000–35,000.[16] With the bulk of the population not being able to afford to buy did the government fulfil its objective of housing low-income groups?

In practice, the PNC government has provided housing only for the Afro-Guyanese population. The racial basis of political party support has resulted in the need for Indo-Guyanese to be more self-reliant and independent of the PNC government whose basis of support lies primarily with the Afro-Guyanese community. As the vast majority have access to land in the rural areas (either their own or rented from family) Indo-Guyanese build their own houses and depend on assistance from friends and family rather than call on government resources. Those without access to land, in the urban areas, resort to private renting from Indo-Guyanese landlords. Despite being the focus of government support the attempts of Afro-Guyanese to secure access to state housing – either rented apartments or ASH housing – are fraught with difficulties as the following case studies reveal.

CASE STUDY 1: THE VIRGINIA WOMEN'S HOMESTEAD SELF-HELP SCHEME

This case study describes the problems encountered by the women who built the Virginia Women's Homestead and shows that even though this project took place in the 1970s, during the most active period of self-help housing, the women still incurred difficulties in their attempts to grapple with the cumbersome, obsolete, and time-consuming statutory procedures associated with self-help housing in Guyana. An analysis of the records available in the Ministry of Health, Public Welfare and Housing, and interviews with the women themselves (in April 1985) revealed that while the slow pace of plot acquisition and development was partly due to the rate at which members could save money with which to build their houses, the major delays were associated with administrative inefficiency and a lack of proper guidance on co-operative ventures by both the local council and the then Ministry of Works (Transport) and Housing. Despite the discouragingly slow pace of development that the interruptions and active opposition led to, however, the women never lost sight of their goal and succeeded in building their own homes.

The decision to build the Virginia Women's Homestead at Cane Grove, 26 kilometres east of Georgetown, was initiated in 1968 by three women living in the local area who were all renting their homes. Seeing a plot of vacant land with good access to the medical, educational, and shopping facilities in the village, they decided to try and use it to build homes for themselves. Myrtle, who first thought of the idea, sought permission to use the 2 hectare plot for building houses and setting up a co-operative poultry farm. She and two of her friends, Hyacinth and Eugenie, then asked other local women renting houses to join the group. The process of finding sufficient members took two years. This length of time can be explained by the fact that group members had to fulfil both formal and informal eligibility criteria, which together severely limited the number eligible to join. The formal eligibility criteria drawn up by the Ministry of Health, Housing and Labour were that the applicant should not own another house at the time of application; they should be prepared to do self-help work; they should be able to make an initial deposit of G$ 300; and they should be earning sufficient to enable him/her to qualify for a mortgage. The informal criteria were that only Afro-Guyanese PNC supporters were welcome to join the group.

The intention was not only for women to become members; initially in the late 1960s, a few men joined the scheme but were amongst the first to leave once delays were experienced. Myrtle stressed that it was only the women members, to whom the issues of acquiring tenure and improved living conditions were important, who were prepared to push matters with ministry officials. This proved essential to the implementation and completion of the projects. During the decade it took to build the Virginia Women's Homestead the individuals in the group changed a number of times. By mid-1975 the group of twelve included only four founder members, but thereafter its all-female composition remained fairly stable.

Of the twelve women members seven were heads of their households. Their characteristics did not differ significantly from the women in the five households headed by men. The women were aged between early 20s and mid-60s, with the number of their dependants ranging from one to eleven. Household salaries also had similar ranges of G$ 200–605 per month for woman-headed households and G$ 220–500 per month for man-headed households. The households differed, however, in terms of the number of adults available for self-help building. In the five households headed by men all the men were involved in income-earning activities (as a policeman and as minor officials in the Ministries of Agriculture and National Development) and the women were housewives, whereas in six of the woman-headed households the women were engaged in waged work (as a teacher, a rice farmer, a poultry farmer, a domestic, and a district co-ordinator for the Ministry of National Development) with the remaining woman living on money from her children (she was building the self-help house for one of her sons who was studying in the USA). Given the delays in the project, however, it was not until house construction began in 1977 that this inequity in the amount of time each woman could devote to construction work revealed itself, but because of delays experienced in the construction phase, women heads of household were able to keep to the building schedule.

Early in 1970 the women approached the Ministry of Works (Transport) and Housing who arranged to have their surveyors draw up a plan of the Homestead. The women were allocated the land in 1970. However, it was not until April 1972 that it was surveyed and the lots laid out. The plot consisted of a rectangular block of twelve house lots (1.3 hectares), two reserved lots for community farming (0.26 hectares), and a road dividing the plot in two. The surveying was the first step in what was to be an extremely long-winded process before house-building could commence. First, a plan of the plot was sub-mitted to the Commissioner of Lands and Surveys. The women were legally required to ensure this occurred within thirty days of the plan's completion. The plan was then sent by the commissioner to the Central Board of Health (CBH) with an application for the issue of the First Certificate for transport and infrastructure building purposes (a transport is a legal document conferring ownership of the land to the occupants). Legally, building of infrastructure and house foundations cannot commence until this is issued. This requires the CBH to refer these proposals to the Local Sanitary Authority for a field inspection and report. On receipt of this report the CBH can approve the issue of the First Certificate. However, this is subject to the approval of the CHPA. It was not uncommon for the CHPA to reject plans approved by the CBH because their requirements and specifications differed. In this case a process which could be completed in six months took four years. This process then had to be repeated for the issue of the Second Certificate for house-building purposes.

The slow pace of development caused a number of members to leave the group, taking with them the money they had pooled for down payments. Finding new members who could contribute the requisite amount was not an easy task. It was to take until 1974 before the group was complete again and the pace quickened. Early in 1975, even though the First Certificate had not been granted, the women approached their Community Development Council for assistance with the building of the plot road and the provision of pipelines for the water mains, and themselves started to level the land and dig drainage ditches. After seeing the results of their physical labour the women were encouraged to contact the district co-operative officer to register as a co-operative. Again, another long waiting period ensued. Numerous representations made to the self-help officer from the Ministry of Works (Transport) and Housing and the regional minister, between June and December 1975, yielded no response. Eventually, however, in January 1976 the self-help officer sent application forms that enabled them to be registered as an Aided Self-Help Co-operative Housing Group.

Encouraged by this development the women recommenced building drains and constructing the internal access road and bridge to the plot. Co-operative status requires sending monthly progress reports to the ministry, which if not undertaken for three consecutive months is interpreted by the ministry as the co-operative's ceasing to function. The women, initially unaware of this system, did not send in any reports until May

125

1976, only to be informed by the ministry officials that their lack of compliance with this procedure would cause further delays. However, in July the CBH finally approved the plans for the First Certificate, and by October the women completed the building of the bridge, the drains, and the road. The women could now advance to the second stage of the administrative procedures of applying for a Second Certificate. Fortunately for the women this time the process was to take less than six months. Once the Second Certificate was acquired, the plans were deposited with the registrar of deeds for the conveyancing of freehold title. The relevant local authority could then issue a building permit and house construction could commence.

During 1976 the women had met once every fortnight to discuss such matters as preparation of the road, weeding of the main drains, and encouraging members to complete their down-payments. By February 1977 they had saved G$ 5,400. Despite the fact that the women had achieved their down-payment targets and had completed heavy building work, certain people, such as the parliamentary secretary to a nearby co-operative village, considered that local officers in the Housing Ministry were deliberately trying to frustrate the women's efforts. Repeated attempts by the ministry to obtain details of the project from the local community organizer were unsuccessful. As the ministry could not gain any idea of the costs involved, they had difficulties programming the project into their budget. The community organizer and the building supervisor (both men) had, however, told one of the ministry officials that they had been 'instructed' by its senior officers to have nothing to do with the Virginia Women's Homestead Project. Thus, as late as February 1977 the community organizer had still not registered the group as a housing co-operative.

In March 1977, with the Second Certificate issued, work finally began on building the self-help homes. At this time help from the CHPA in the form of technical supervision from a building supervisor and carpenters and the bulk purchase and transportation of materials to their plot was still available. Despite this help the implementation phase of the project was also beset with problems, with construction of the houses taking two and a half years. Heavy rains, shortage of supplies, and problems with the building supervisor who, the women claimed, stole large quantities of the wood and paint allocated to them to sell elsewhere, all contributed to the problems the women faced. The water supply was delayed due to further technical hitches and with no mains water available, plumbing could not be completed. The electricity supply was also delayed. Although poles were set up, cables could not be attached because of the rains and the women's need to insure their houses and sign letters of occupancy before the Guyana Electricity Company would connect the cables. This was another procedure of which the women had not been informed by the community organizer. Early in 1979 with the bulk of the work completed the women started to dig the inter-lot drains and to plant their kitchen gardens and fruit trees. By August building was complete and in September 1979 the Viriginia Women's Homestead was officially opened. Despite the major ideological and material constraints the women had faced over the ten-year period, they had succeeded in building their own homes. Unfortunately for the women their difficulties did not end there.

Following the pattern of self-help housing groups in Guyana, once construction was completed the women ceased to function as a group. Only Myrtle, the secretary, attempted to keep the women together and she found this difficult: 'Now all they manage to do is to say hallo to each other'. There is no communal cleaning of the drains, for example, and no one is responsible for collecting mortgage payments (G$ 60.00 per month) or rates. In 1984 the Water Board cut off the supply of potable water because a number of women had defaulted on their water rates payment. The women failed to make a collective effort to resolve this problem, and now they each have to collect their water from the canal behind the homestead. Furthermore, after building their houses the women had intended to construct a chicken farm and a children's playground. These projects never materialized and by 1985 the women had handed over the chicken farm site to the PNC to build an office.

The women had succeeded though in their objective of building homes and in the process they had demonstrated their ability to organize collectively, to save money, to secure loans, and to engage in both skilled and unskilled construction work. Acquiring construction skills was not the only positive aspect of the co-operative self-help housing experience of the Virginia Women's Homestead women. Being able to choose their own site and location ensured that they remained close to their workplaces: ten of the twelve women worked in the local area of Cane Grove and the remaining two had jobs in Georgetown. Also important to the success of the venture was the fact that all the women, although not necessarily friends, had many features in common, coming from the same area and ethnic group and all supporting the ruling party. A number of potential areas of conflict were therefore removed.

The problems faced by the women since their homes have been completed have not stemmed from a lack of money to pay bills or a lack of building skills, but from the breakdown of the co-operative spirit that kept the women together over the period it took to build their homes. Throughout the decade it had taken to complete the project the women had little interest in the formal aspects of forming a co-operative and had, in fact, legally been an ASH group only for the final two years of the project. They had achieved the purpose for which the co-operative was needed, that is saving of money, without any legal framework. It is not surprising, therefore, that the 'co-operative' ceased to function once building work was complete and the women had achieved their original objective of building new homes for themselves. In the 1980s, however, with no new housing co-operatives being established women are forced to build on their own, which considerably heightens the problems they face. The alternative is government-rented housing, which the next case study focuses on.

CASE STUDY 2: GOVERNMENT-RENTED HOUSING IN GEORGETOWN

The view that most low-income groups in the Third World live in self-help housing is inaccurate: many of them occupy rented housing (Gilbert 1983). Low-income groups in Guyana are no exception. Officials in the Ministry of Housing in 1985 estimated that it maintained 2,000–7,000 dwellings. Government-rented housing was originally viewed by ministry officials as a transitional stage for families before owning their own home; the houses were intended as decanting centres for slum clearance projects, but the lack of owner-occupied housing has resulted in many having to stay in the rental sector. This notion of impermanence accords with the classic view of Turner (1976) who argued that renters would move on at a later stage in their life cycle to become owner-occupiers. Gilbert (1983) has put forward an alternative hypothesis that renters are not necessarily potential owner-occupiers, rather they comprise the most disadvantaged groups in urban areas who are unable to own their own homes because of exorbitant house prices and non-availability of land. This latter hypothesis is consistent with the situation in Guyana, which also serves to illuminate a particular aspect of women's reproductive role, the maintenance of client relations with public sector agencies. This is well illustrated by the number of applications for government-rented housing, over 90 per cent of which were from women, of whom 95 per cent were Afro-Guyanese. It did not appear, therefore, that women were discriminated against in the public sector in terms of eligibility for a dwelling. Furthermore, there was an explicit recognition within the Ministry of Health, Public Welfare and Housing of the needs of woman-headed households: no demands were made to interview male kin and neither was any pressure exerted on women to prove they were living alone or to register a male partner as the legal tenant.

As government rent charges were minimal (and have not been increased for over twenty years) women heads of households were not seen as a less reliable credit risk than men heads. There were fifteen categories of rents in the range G$ 5–60 per month depending on the age and size of the dwelling. Applicants were supposed to be allocated them on the basis of household income. The apartments with the lowest rents of G$ 5.00 per month comprised two bedrooms and a living-room with access to a shared lavatory. These units were available only to the largest low-income households. There is a strong correlation between household size and per capita income in Guyana. In the early 1970s 72 per cent of the larger households, in which category households headed by women are concentrated, had the lowest income levels (World Health Organisation 1976). The next lowest rent of G$ 8.40 per month was for a single-room apartment with an outside lavatory and bathroom. These were available only to woman-headed households. Thus there is a concentration of women in the two lowest quality rented dwellings. Furthermore, it was not until the eighth category, with a rent of G$ 18.40 per month, that a separate kitchen was included in the apartment, a facility obviously not obtained by those women who by virtue of their low incomes could not afford rents at this level. To determine the factors controlling the eligibility of women for government-rented housing the characteristics of seven women who applied for these dwellings between March and May in 1985 will be examined. (All the sixty-odd applicants in this period were women, with only a few accompanied by their male partners, and all bar one couple were Afro-Guyanese. The seven women referred to were chosen at random.)

The seven women ranged in age from 24 to 59. Only one was

unmarried and one divorced, with the remaining five claiming to be married. Of these five, however, only one, Winifred, lived with her husband and four of her six children. Berbinna, with five children, lived separately from her husband with whom her relationship had broken down. She thought that her husband would return if she had adequate accommodation since it was a lack of such that had caused the initial strain in their relationship. Since 1977 she had been living with a relative, with fourteen children, who had a three-bedroomed house. Berbinna, her five children, and her mother lived in the hallway and not surprisingly she complained that relations with her relative were constantly strained. Beryl, with six children, also lived separately from her husband who had left her. Myrtle had a visiting union with her husband. As a corporal in the army, posted outside Georgetown, he could see her only at weekends. They had one daughter, 6 years old, living with a relative in Berbice, to whom they paid money in return for caring for their daughter. The remaining married woman was Yvonne, with nine children. Her husband worked on a ranch in the interior and she saw him only a few times each year. The non-married women included Stella, who was divorced and had five children, four of whom had left home, but had left three grandchildren for her to take care of, and Odessa, who was single with one child.

Winifred then was the only woman living with a man on a daily basis; the others were *de facto* woman-headed households, and therefore should have been eligible for even the cheapest category of government-rented apartments. In reality, however, the women were not eligible for a number of reasons. Given that the top category of rent for government apartments was G\$ 60.00, it could be surmised that those women affording to pay rents above this value would have little or no chance of being eligible for a government apartment. All of the women, except Berbinna, were paying rents which ranged from G\$ 7.00 to G\$ 90.00 per month, and two, Odessa and Winifred, were paying above the top category of G\$ 60.00 for government apartments. Since 1984 Odessa had been renting a room in a friend's home, but wanted to move to one with more space since she was sharing her room with her daughter and her friend's three children. Winifred, who had been living with her family in a privately rented three-bedroomed flat since 1977, wanted to move as the floor was rotting and the ceiling was also in a poor condition as the children in the flat above urinated through it.

Despite paying a high rent of G$ 90.00 per month Odessa found her monthly salary of G$ 360.00 as a typist insufficient for a mortgage. Although looking at apartments in the private rental sector for over a year she had not yet found one suitable. Despite the fact that her annual income was above the level at which people were encouraged to join co-operatives the housing officer seemed prepared to try and find her a government-rented apartment on the grounds of her being a single parent. Winifred, as a National Guard Senior Supervisor with a monthly income of G$ 570.00, earned double the salary limit for a government-rented apartment. In addition her wages combined with those of her husband and eldest daughter would, the housing officer assured her, be sufficient for her to obtain a mortgage of up to G$ 50,000. Winifred was therefore ineligible and as she was unwilling to build a house, given a lack of time, the only option open to her was to buy privately. The experiences of these two women would suggest that the criterion of income was not interpreted by housing officials strictly according to the ministry rules. When income was at a level (approximately G$ 7,000) which allowed a mortgage to be obtained it would override all other criteria. However, below this level, other factors came into play, such as being a woman head of a household. It would appear, therefore, that the ministry officials had responded to the high number of woman-headed households applying for rented housing; however, when the situation of Berbinna is taken into account, the criteria appear less straightforward.

Berbinna, like Odessa and Winifred, also earned above the maximum of G$ 250.00 per month, making her ineligible for a government apartment. As a National Security Guard her monthly salary was G$ 428.00, but from this she had to support five children and her mother. As a woman heading a large household with no accommodation except a relative's hallway her case for government-rented accommodation appeared stronger than Odessa's. The only difference between the women's cases was that Berbinna was willing to pay up to G$ 100.00 of her monthly salary on rent while Odessa was not. Once aware of this the housing officer was not prepared to put Berbinna on the waiting list for a government-rented apartment. This criterion, of the amount each woman was prepared to pay, overrode all other circumstances of woman-headed households and determined whether they could be rehoused or whether they would have to continue to live in unhygienic, overcrowded, and squalid conditions.

The situations of the remaining four women, who were all in private rented accommodation, appeared to confirm these findings. Myrtle had lived on her own since 1984 in a private two-roomed flat for which she paid G$ 30.00 per month and shared with four families (six adults and three children). Yvonne, paying G$ 7.00 per month, had lived in her small privately rented room with her nine children since 1972. The room was in a house with seven others, all similarly occupied, with everyone sharing one malfunctioning lavatory. Since 1983 Beryl had a room for herself and her six children in the house of a friend, for which she paid G$ 45.00 per month. Stella was the only woman to have had a two-roomed privately rented flat, for which she paid G$ 25.00 per month. This, however, had a leaking roof and no bathroom, with the only source of water coming from a broken-down communal water standpipe.

Of these four women only Yvonne was offered government-rented housing. As a housewife looking after her nine children, Yvonne's only source of income was the G$ 200.00 per month her husband sent her. She could afford to spend only up to G$ 35.00 per month on rent, although this would represent a noticeable increase on the G$ 7.00 she presently paid. The housing officer confirmed that at this level she would not be able to afford rents on the open market and would be eligible for a government-rented apartment.

Myrtle, Stella, and Beryl were offered land on which they could build. Because they were willing to pay a monthly rent of over G$ 100.00, they were not allocated government-rented apartments. Although both Myrtle and Stella were not in waged work and therefore had time to organize house-building, the housing officer asked no further questions as to their capability and the suitability of their personal situations for this undertaking. Myrtle had the money to build a house (but not enough to buy) with her husband earning G$ 560.00 per month, and occasionally making money herself from selling food. Her child was also looked after, giving her time for house-building, but it was unlikely she could achieve this on her own with her husband able to help only at weekends. As a divorced housewife, Stella lived on G$ 350 per month, which she received from her children. Although this amount was insufficient to secure her a mortgage it was enough for private renting. The lack of private rented accommodation, however, left her, at the age of 59, with the only option of building her own home. Beryl, earning G$ 372.00 per month as an office cleaner, was in a similar position. Although younger than Stella, she was in full-time employment with six children to raise on her own, circumstances that the housing officer did not appear to see as affecting her ability to find the time to build her own home.

In theory it would appear that low-income women are in a favourable position in terms of their access to government-rented housing. However, the case study has shown that the reality is often one of long delays (of up to five years) living in cramped, unhygienic, overcrowded conditions with only a small chance of being allocated a dwelling. The desperate living conditions of private rented housing, which led to four of the women declaring that they were willing to spend a quarter of their monthly income on rent, forced them into a situation of having to build their own homes individually. On the basis of the criterion of the willingness of the women to spend up to G$ 100.00 per month on rent (regardless of their total income level) the decision was made as to their eligibility for government-rented housing. Only in Winifred's case was the total household income (of approximately G$ 9,000) an inhibiting factor. Indeed the other six women, except for Yvonne, with yearly incomes in the range of G$ 4,000–6,000, earned over the total amount above which they were not officially eligible for government-rented housing. Of these five only Odessa was granted access to government housing, yet her financial circumstances were very similar to those of Berbinna, Beryl, and Stella and her living conditions slightly easier. While willingness to pay this G$ 100.00 per month appears to benefit the most financially disadvantaged women it penalized those on the margins of this group, especially *de facto* woman-headed households whose personal circumstances were not seen as a sufficient reason for being allocated government housing and yet at the same time these very circumstances mitigated against their being able to build their own homes.

Conclusion

Since the mid-1960s the PNC government has claimed to be committed to improving the standards of low-income groups and, since the mid-1970s, to securing equality for women. The PNC government has attempted to achieve these objectives by transforming from a capitalist to a socialist economy in order to increase public ownership, eradicate poverty, and at the same time promote self-reliance through the philosophy of co-operativism. The gap between policy and practice, however, is large.

Women's rights to housing have been acknowledged both by housing ministry officials and by legal changes, which have conferred property ownership rights on women. These rights, however, have been conceded solely in relation to women's reproductive roles as domestic workers, while legal changes have not benefited low-income women. Ministry officials recognize that the servicing, managing, and maintaining of the built dwelling is largely carried out by women. Indeed, the preservation of the house in terms of initiating maintenance and repairs, was seen as the greatest area of involvement of women in the housing process. This is not surprising given that women's role in construction work is overlooked or viewed largely in relation to women's domestic tasks. However, the concern of women to satisfy their needs in terms of acquiring access to housing led, in the 1970s, to their becoming increasingly involved as producers in the self-help movement.

The negative aspects faced by the Virginia Women's Homestead women (delays in registration, lack of knowledge of complicated procedures, and a lack of help from male officials) which contributed to the time it took to complete their houses, were overcome by the solidarity they achieved in their determination to satisfy their need for housing. This is arguably the most positive feature of co-operative self-help housing for low-income women. In a country where delays in provision of materials are common, and corruption is rife, women working on their own to build their houses could easily find these problems insurmountable. And while the co-operative spirit did not lead to co-operativism in other areas of life it did serve the purpose for which it was required – providing new houses for women. However, economic problems that have beset the country since the mid-1970s have led to the cessation of government-sponsored building programmes. Thus those women not eligible for public-sector housing are forced into individualized self-build housing. This is particularly disadvantageous to woman-headed households with less time available to participate in construction and a low, and often irregular, income that does not enable them to contract skilled labour. Given the alarming shortage of experienced builders in Guyana (UNDP 1982) government support for the co-operative sector could have resulted not only in increased access to housing but also in training women in construction skills, which would have provided low-income women with potential for earning an income.

Those low-income women already in self-help have acquired tenure rights. With the pending sale of government-rented apartments, the right to own will also be recognized for present tenants.[17] However, with tenants then being responsible for maintenance and repairs women will have to rely on their own meagre resources with no back-up from the state. Furthermore, the situation of those women temporarily living with friends or relatives, or in the private rental sector will worsen dramatically. With no new house-building by the government and no rented apartments within their control, the responsibility for housing low-income groups will be removed from the public sector. As a result no subsidized housing for low-income women will be available. Apartments for rent will be provided solely by private landlords and the increased demand for them will allow rents to escalate, causing further problems. (Although legislation – the 1969 Rent Control Ordinance – exists requiring private landlords to have the rental value of their premises assessed, its effect is minimal.) Thus low-income women will have no control over the type of housing produced for them. The effects of this are most likely to be felt by the low-income Afro-Guyanese households, and in particular woman-headed households who rely most heavily on government support. The only alternatives open to these women will be to remain in their present unsatisfactory conditions or to build homes in the squatter settlements. The historical origins and peripheral locations of these make them highly undesirable, but given the PNC government's total inability to satisfy the needs of low-income Afro-Guyanese women in relation to housing this would appear to be the only solution open to them.

Notes

This chapter is based on an earlier draft, Peake (1986a) 'Low-income women's participation in the housing process: a case study from Guyana', *DPU Gender and Planning Working Paper* no 10, University College, London.

1 One of the major problems in assessing the extent to which the housing needs of low-income women in Guyana are being met is the paucity of data. Statistics and basic data fundamental to developing a housing policy for the Guyanese people are not available for analysis. Many records have been lost in the course of the five or six changes of premises of the Housing Department in the last five years. The available information is incomplete, out of date, and unreliable, and has often not been compiled in a form that facilitates analysis. Data on the overall level of housing stock were still being compiled. It is not possible, therefore, to determine the proportions of different household types, such as woman-headed households, vital for the planning of suitable-sized dwelling units. The distributional data, needed to assess whether public housing finance is helping low-income women, such as tenure across racial and income groups and socio-economic class, are also non-existent. Particularly important is the decennial population census. However, the last published census in Guyana was conducted in 1970. Although a further census was conducted in 1980 the results have not been published. Consequently calculations of housing needs have to be based on extrapolations and statistical projections from the 1970 census. Changes in the rate of natural increase and of increasing urbanization and migration which have taken place in the intervening period (1970–87) cannot be taken into account. Hence estimates do not accurately reflect the housing need of particular household types or localities (especially important in urban areas). As Standing (1979: 53) has asserted: 'There is no doubt that housing needs are poorly met in Guyana, though it is hard to assess either the standard or trends because of data limitations'.

2 Standing (1979) has given the female unemployment rate for 1970 as 19.6 per cent (compared to 15 per cent for males).

3 In the 1970s the government banned the import of over 100 different foodstuffs in an attempt to promote self-sufficiency. The women traders blatantly ignore this ban as they can find a ready market for the many items no longer available in the country. By December 1986 the ban on wheat flour, a major staple, was lifted.

4 Buvinic, Youssef, with von Elm (1978) calculated from a sample of 115,863 that the marital status of these woman-headed households in Guyana in 1970 was as follows: 28 per cent never married, 33 per cent married, 33 per cent widowed, 3 per cent divorced, and 3 per cent separated.

5 Cde. Bend-Kirten-Holder herself had lost four separate properties in previous marriages as the mortgages had been signed over to her husbands. It was this personal experience that made her determined to change the legal position in relation to women.

6 Formed in 1970 CASWIG has twenty-eight organizations affiliated to it, including church, social, professional, and political groups. Significantly the two radical women's organizations in Guyana are

not affiliated to CASWIG. These are the Women's Progressive Organization (WPO), the women's arm of the PPP, and the women's arm of the Working People's Alliance, the 'third' party in the Guyanese political system. The credibility of CASWIG has suffered since its inauguration: its recommendations have not been taken seriously by any ministry, it has been moved between ministries repeatedly, and its impartiality as a non-government organization is seriously under question because of Cde. Bend-Kirten-Holder's position as a leading member of the PNC and its affiliated Women's Revolutionary Socialist Movement (WRSM). Consequently by 1975 it was a spent force.

7 The population estimate of 768,607 is for the end of 1975 (see Standing 1979). Other estimates, for 1977, put the population total at 902,000. Given the high level of out-migration during the late 1970s and 1980s, the conservative estimate appears more realistic. Thomas (1983) claims that the population is actually decreasing.

8 Portuguese and White have always constituted separate ethnic groups in the population censuses as an indication of the inferior social position attributed to the former compared with the White, that is British, who owned and managed the productive process.

9 Co-operatives have a long history in Guyana and were officially encouraged as early as 1948 by the British colonial authorities. By the end of 1974 over 120,000 people were members of co-operatives, covering such areas as housing, education, transport, savings societies, consumer items, workers' societies, and building construction.

10 Self-help housing was formally introduced in 1953–4 when the government in conjunction with the Caribbean Development Commission sponsored ten projects, each providing fifteen houses, along the coastal strip.

11 The Housing Development Act, 1970, provided for the operation of a Revolving Fund in the then Ministry of Health, Housing and Labour, which enabled the ministry to purchase, develop, and sell land and to finance the construction of houses for sale and rent. The Housing Fund provided 'front-end finance': after houses were allocated the Guyana Co-operative Mortgage Finance Bank (GCMFB) would reimburse to the fund its expenditure and would then formally register individual occupants as mortgagees. Together with the Housing Fund, the GCMFB was able to restructure the pattern of the mortgage market by channelling funds towards those officially designated as lower income groups.

12 Within these totals estimates also vary for the different types of dwellings built. Estimates range from 1,531 to 2,527 for self-help housing; 94 to 368 for rentals; 159 to 581 for rental purchase; and 667 for hire purchase.

13 In 1980 Strachan (1981) estimated private house prices in Georgetown ranged from G\$ 30,000 to G\$ 170,000.

14 As Hanson (1982: 3) has shown:

> In most countries, especially the middle income ones, . . . housing is often 16–25% of total fixed investment and 30–40% of the investment in construction. However, in Guyana it appears that in recent years housing has dropped to only 11–12% of fixed investment and 23–25% of construction investment. These are some of the lowest figures I have seen in the World, even in the lowest income countries.

15 The 1977 Labour Force Survey indicated that the distribution of income in Guyana is highly skewed: while the top 10 per cent of households earn 36.3 per cent of total income the bottom 80 per cent earn only 45.6 per cent. A characteristic of the lowest-income households is that less of their income is available for housing, because they spend a higher proportion on food. The 1976 National Food and Nutrition Survey of Guyana revealed that in households with incomes below G$ 300 per month, approximately 87 per cent of income was spend on food while only 44 per cent of income was spent on food in households with a monthly income above G$ 300.

16 Lending institutions are often unwilling to invest in clients who want housing below G$ 30,000 because of the financial risks they see attached to such ventures. Not surprisingly, a significant proportion of the finances for house-building comes from informal lending between friends and relatives. Although the Guyanese Co-operative Mortgage Finance Bank provides mortgage loans of 90 per cent, people often have difficulty in securing the other 10 per cent. The ancillary costs of house acquisition are also above what many potential owner-occupiers expect. The high cost of legal fees for conveyancing, mortgages, insurance, and rates often result in new owner-occupiers defaulting on their loans.

17 In an attempt to raise revenue, a decision was made in 1982 to sell government apartments to tenants or to increase rents. A Rent Revision Committee was set up to make recommendations and ministry officials carried out a survey of rented dwellings. Before receiving this survey the Minister of Finance announced in January 1985 that the dwellings would be sold. The dwellings are to be managed and maintained on the same basis as self-help housing co-operatives, allowing the tenants to make contributions to their maintenance by self-help labour. Housing ministry officials anticipate numerous problems with this decision because the legal and technical issues involved are unlikely to be resolved before the sale commences.

© *1987 Linda Peake*

CHAPTER 7

More than bricks and mortar: women's participation in self-help housing in Managua, Nicaragua

IRENE VANCE

Introduction

In the current literature on low-income housing there are a growing number of studies which focus on the difficulties surrounding the implementation of community participation in housing improvement programmes. While a substantial number of these studies point to the limitations of trying to promote a 'top-down' participation programme on the basis that this will be met with resistance by the target group, very few studies examine factors operating at the project level which limit participation, or offer an analysis of the constraints which exist between the group of self-builders. Explanations to date refer to the laziness of the participants, and to lack of will and time to participate in voluntary labour, to corruption, and to co-optation of local leaders. In all these studies little reference at all is made to women and to their work in construction, nor to the division of labour, and gender roles generally.

This case study of community participation in a self-help building scheme examines the changes that took place in gender relations and roles when the opportunity for genuine bottom-up participation occurred and its consequences both between women, and between women and men.[1] The project was carried out by the residents of San Judas, a low-income *barrio* in Managua, Nicaragua, during a period when the country was undergoing radical political, economic, and social changes.[2] The Sandinista government was brought to power in 1979 after two years of popular insurrection which overthrew Anastasio

Somoza, ending forty years of dictatorship by his family. The insurrection was marked by the mass mobilization of people from all sectors of society, and in particular it provided women with the opportunity to participate. In the period immediately after the war, the popular bases of power, which had emerged in the struggle, were legitimized by the government, and popular participation through the mass organizations was regarded as fundamental in all national and local-level decision-making.[3] The largest of these organizations is the *Sandinista Defence Committees* (CDSs). They are neighbourhood committees organized at street level which extend nation-wide. The political weight of the CDSs and the mass organizations was demonstrated by their participation in the national legislative body, the Council of State. As originally conceived it consisted of thirty-three seats. Months prior to its inauguration the mass organizations had pressurized for changes in the planned composition of the Council to reflect better popular interests. The result was that representation was broadened and seventeen seats went to the mass organizations from a total of forty-seven seats making up the Council of State.

The San Judas project was the first self-help scheme to be implemented under the new revolutionary government. Mobilization around the issue of housing improvements began within the community and prompted the decision to form a housing collective. Unlike many self-help schemes in which participation is top-down, this was a bottom-up initiative, generated largely by women. This scheme provides an opportunity to examine what happened to women in terms of their relationship with men, and what happened at the community level concerning women and their different roles as producers, reproducers, and community managers. Addressing these questions at the various stages of project implementation shows that the active participation of women in all phases of the planning process not only helps to meet the practical needs of women (as the principal users of housing) but also can be an end in itself, that is it meets a more strategic need, by providing the basis for a redefinition of the different roles of women in society.

The project was successful; forty-eight houses were built collectively, but conflicts did occur. The chapter deals with the extent to which the conflicts were the result of the triple role of women not being recognized at the planning stages and the degree to which stereotypes surrounding the sexual division of labour excluded women in various stages of the project. The case study contributes to the debate about the roles of women and men in society in general and in political participation in particular. It reveals that strategies by government at national and local levels, to provide low-income housing solutions which seek to incorporate community participation by both men and women, must recognize the differences between men's work and women's work on the basis of gender. Since the project was carried out shortly after the Sandinista victory in July 1979, the next section will briefly describe the political and economic context in which the project took place.

The national context

Prior to the revolution most Nicaraguan people lived in extreme poverty. Levels of poverty are reflected by a number of socio-economic indicators which include a high degree of malnutrition, high infant mortality, inadequate housing, and sanitation, and the general lack of access to medical care and education.

From a population of 2.7 million according to the 1971 census, 60 per cent of the people lived in unacceptable housing. The housing problems were exacerbated by an earthquake in 1972 which devastated much of the capital: 50,000 homes were lost, most of which were never replaced. Over 50 per cent of the population was illiterate and in rural areas this figure was nearly 70 per cent. Lack of health care and services meant that six out of every ten deaths were caused by curable diseases. Life expectancy was the lowest in Central America (NACLA 1976, 1978; Wheelock 1979). Within this pattern of poverty, women and children were particularly affected. The infant mortality rate was between 120 and 146 per 1,000 live births and over 70 per cent of children suffered some degree of malnutrition during their lives (PAHO 1979).[4] Maternal mortality was among the five leading causes of death for women in the 15–45 age group which indicates the absence of prenatal and postnatal care of mothers. Preventable diseases were the principal causes of death; diarrhoea and infectious diseases accounted for 31.4 per cent of all deaths (Bossert 1982).

By 1975 women not only comprised 51 per cent of the total population, but also headed 48 per cent of Nicaraguan households. This instability of the Nicaraguan household is not merely a question of the irresponsibility of men or attributable to cultural attitudes; it is linked to the economic model of development of Nicaragua under Somoza. Since the 1950s and 1960s the extension of plantation agriculture for the production of agro-export crops has resulted in the proletarization of the countryside.[5] The dispossessed peasant farmers increased the agricultural labour force dramatically. Low wages, and the seasonal demand for labour, meant that men were not able to support their families, giving rise to increased migration to the city. Employment in the cities was equally precarious, since the industrialization that did take place was highly mechanized and did little to absorb available labour.[6]

This economic reality contradicts the dominant ideology of women being materially and emotionally dependent on men, restricted after marriage to childbirth, childcare, and domestic labour. Low-income Nicaraguan women have had no choice but to seek waged labour, outside the home, to support their children. The proportion of women wage-earners rose from 14 per cent in 1950 to 21.9 per cent in 1970 and 28.7 per cent in 1977 (Randall 1981). Despite the high percentage of women in waged labour, few are engaged directly in industrial production. Most women are self-employed and work in services or in selling, where earning capacity is precarious. In 1981 of those self-employed people earning less than US$ 80 per month in Managua, 77 per cent were women.[7]

It was these conditions of deprivation and oppression that drove people into popular insurrection and to seek the overthrow of the Somoza regime. The armed struggle and mass mobilization of low-income sectors were the first experiences of popular participation and provided a learning experience in popular organization at different levels. Women played a major role in the war and were heavily involved in the fighting. In the final stages 30 per cent of the fighters were women. The CDSs, in addition to carrying out the bulk of the fighting, ran hospitals and health services and guaranteed distribution of food. In the chaotic months at the end of the war the mass organizations played a crucial role in running the country.

When the Sandinista government came to power, in addition to the legacy of poverty, they inherited a bankrupt economy without foreign reserves and a debt of US$ 1.6 billion. In the face of this economic crisis and in recognition of the high level of popular participation that had been achieved the people were regarded by the revolutionary government as the country's most important resource. For example the mass organizations had direct representation in ministries providing services, and professionals therefore were accountable to and worked directly with, communities and community leaders.

Despite the economic problems the country faced the government set the improvement of the conditions of the low-income sectors as one of its major priorities. The Programme of Economic Reactivation in Benefit of the People 1980 announced measures to reactivate the economy, to reorganize the structural basis of production, and to attend to the needs of those most marginalized by the previous regime. In this respect the Sandinista government recognized the specific oppression of women as waged workers, and as a result one of the goals of the Sandinistas became the emancipation of women. A series of legal reforms have been enacted to alter the position of women in the area of personal status, family relations, and to prohibit the exploitation of women in advertising and the media (Molyneux 1985b). These include efforts to improve working conditions. Women in agriculture now have the right to receive their own wage packet. In the cities efforts have been made to set up production collectives for women. To date, however, these have been restricted to traditional female activities, such as clothing collectives and food preparation. Female domestic workers through the formation of the Union of Domestics have won a ten-hour day, double pay for holiday work, and a minimum wage of US$ 40 a month. Maternity leave and measures to improve safety standards at work have been introduced. Some effort has also been made to socialize childcare in order to release women into the work-force and allow them to participate in social and political life. Although the facilities still reach only a minority of women, by mid-1984 over forty childcare centres had been set up countrywide (Molyneux 1985a).

Women have been encouraged to consolidate their organizational experiences gained during the insurrection and to extend their participation in all aspects of social and political affairs. Within months of coming to power, the government and mass organizations began nation-wide literacy and health campaigns. From a total of 100,000 volunteers, trained to teach basic literacy, 60 per cent were women. Likewise in the Popular Health Campaigns held in 1981–2, of 78,000 health workers involved, 75 per cent were women. Largely as a result of women's involvement these early achievements in literacy and health have been very impressive (Melrose 1985).

As part of the reactivation programme the Ministry of

Housing and Human Settlements (MINVAH) was created to tackle the massive housing deficit, estimated at 240,000 units. Immediate priority was given to low-income urban residents. Within the first few months the government announced the Law of *Repartos Intervenidos* which placed 420 *barrios* under state control administered by MINVAH. In these *barrios* private landlords had failed in their legal duty to install basic services. Moreover, many residents had paid for their plots of land but had not received titles. The new law specified that purchase payments were paid directly to MINVAH and funds used to complete the installation of infrastructure. The CDSs were critical in the implementation of this policy. Their role was to ensure that poplar organization, which had played a vital role in the war, continued, this time within community work around housing. The CDSs were responsible for prioritizing the particular needs of low-income groups in the *barrios* and in some instances organizing work brigades. To stimulate community solutions MINVAH set up a Materials Bank to provide construction materials at controlled prices. Area improvements and upgrading of existing neighbourhoods in preference to large-scale new building schemes was the principal strategy of the government. Site and services were rejected on the basis that they reinforced individualistic as opposed to collective responses to area improvements. The residents of San Judas were among the first of the community groups to request the collaboration and assistance of MINVAH to improve housing conditions in their neighbourhood.

The project setting

The settlement of San Judas began in the late 1950s and today it is one of the oldest and most densely populated *barrios* in Managua, with a population of 37,000. The earliest occupants were migrants from rural areas seeking seasonal farm work. Plots were sold by subdividers on a system of 'rental with promise of sale'. Here the buyer would assume the title with the final rental payment. The early development and growth of the *barrio* was sporadic, and lacked any element of urban planning. Subdivisions were sold without the installation of basic services. As a result the area largely remained as farmland until the 1972 earthquake when the population of the *barrio* almost doubled. Vacant plots were quickly parcelled off by the subdividers creating extensive overcrowding.

A variety of housing types are to be found in San Judas. These include independent houses consolidated over the years and built of solid materials, and a large proportion of less solid structures, of wooden boards, cardboard, and pieces of tin. The most precarious housing type, however, is rented rooms with multi-occupancy: these represent 'infill' development established since the earthquake. The rooms, built around a communal space with water, washing, and cooking facilities, lack sewerage and pluvial drainage. Street access is by a network of small passageways, which reduces light. These rooms represent the most unhygienic and cramped living conditions. It is not uncommon for two or three families to share one room and up to seven families to share services.

San Judas is a low-income community, made up of unskilled factory workers, and self-employed men working in a range of services as mechanics, chauffeurs, taxi drivers, and some construction workers. Work for both men and women is irregular and men often experience several months without employment. There is a continual cycle of migration both within the city and to rural areas in search of seasonal work. Unemployment and underemployment is highest among the least skilled women who are restricted to jobs in the lowest paid sectors, such as washerwomen, domestics, and sellers.

Women and community mobilization

Early community mobilization by women was introduced through the church. This was because the greater proportion of church attenders were women, and activities associated with the church were traditionally the only significant area of public participation for women outside the home. Under cover of church activities women were able to become involved with the *Sandinista National Liberation Front* (FSLN) and in political work. As Maria Silva remembered:

> We in San Judas were Sandinista right from the start. We had everything organized for the final struggle against the National Guard. When they tried to take the *barrio* in June 1979 we were ready. In the early days, though, when we were organizing – in 1977 and 1978 – I had a small shop, selling cold drinks. It was a good place to organize from, you see people would come to my place, stop for a drink and pick up information or messages. I remember, those early

days, when the first comrade came from the Sandinista Front, to give us political orientation, a very young comrade from the Ministry of Health. My daughter Estrella carried messages and my son went off to the mountains.

The residents of San Judas were well known for their participation in the popular insurrection. No heavy fighting took place in the *barrio*, but many young men and women left to join the FSLN fighting forces. Women with family responsibilities were also able to participate in the struggle, organized at street and block level by the Civil Defence Committees (CDCs). Through neighbourhood networks, food supplies and distribution were controlled, clandestine hospitals and first-aid were organized, 'safe' houses were set up, and information on the movements of the National Guard were transmitted to the Sandinista fighters. For the majority of Nicaraguan women the insurrection period provided the first opportunity for their roles as political activists and community organizers to be recognized. Many women had been organized at the community level from the early 1970s. As Maria Silva remembered:

> I lived on the lakeside, by the slaughter house, conditions were terrible, we were 'the poorest of the poor.' Only the church cared for us. There was about 300 families, we got together with the priest and got enough materials to put up some houses, we even put a pharmacy in my house, but the National Guard moved me on from the lakeside, they thought I was a communist. It was after this that the church started with us to organize against Somoza. I had two more children, my husband left me but I never gave up my community work.

FROM MOBILIZATION TO COMMUNITY DECISION-MAKING: ORIGINS OF THE HOUSING COLLECTIVE

After the war, the same level of community organization generated in the CDCs (renamed after the war to Sandinista Defence Committees) continued. In San Judas the *barrio* committee organized salvage operations from the war. Work brigades were set up to repair damaged property, food was distributed, and clean-up campaigns and health days were organized to avoid epidemics. Importantly women continued to mobilize for improvements in the *barrio*. The *barrio* committee comprised four male representatives, one from each of the four zones of San Judas, and four women representatives who had special duties, including health, community development, propaganda and information, and culture. This equal representation in San Judas is a typical feature of community level politics in post-revolutionary Nicaragua. It reflects an increase in the numbers of women assuming decision-making roles. For example, women represent 50 per cent of the total CDS membership. The *barrio* committee in San Judas chose to take immediate steps to tackle two major problems of the *barrio*, namely housing and unemployment. Within months of the end of the war several production collectives were set up and Maria Silva, representative of zone four on the *barrio* committee, was elected to take special responsibility for housing and community development.

Maria organized a census of the *barrio*, via the CDS street committees, to establish the number of families who were refugees and to record the conditions of housing and tenure patterns. It was clear that if they were to tackle the housing difficulties they would have to look beyond the newly formed Ministry of Housing. Maria searched for funding and through her church contacts a donation of US$ 100,000 was acquired for housing from a national religious organization, CONFER.[8]

An unusual characteristic of the terms of the donation was that the donor agency played no formal part in the formulation of the scheme. Nevertheless, absolute control by the participants was restricted since the only condition made by the donor agency was that the funds should be channelled through the Ministry of Housing. Therefore the San Judas self-help scheme became the first project to be co-ordinated by the Department of Home Improvements, within MINVAH.

Self-help schemes and community programmes had not formed part of the activities of Somoza's Housing Bank.[9] Within the new ministry there were no personnel with experience of working directly with communities. This called for a period of adjustment and for re-education of officials, whose class perceptions and professional interests had to be removed. The San Judas project was therefore seen very much as a training programme for the ministry personnel, as well as for the community. Various ministerial staff were involved at different stages of the planning and programming with the residents of San Judas. Three were assigned to work directly with the collective, a female architect, a male civil engineer, and a male social worker. As part of the retraining of ministry personnel, the officials on community schemes were encouraged to work at the site with the participants, sharing in the physical work where possible and offering encouragement and guidance rather than directing operations from their office positions.

According to MINVAH's plans the formation of the housing collective was not only to be an exercise in housing construction to satisfy the shelter needs of the participants. It was also seen as part of a much broader programme of skills training in which the participants were to be encouraged to participate at all levels in the planning and execution of the housing scheme, with responsibilities for management and decision-making to be shared by the membership, and not reserved for the leadership.

The housing project contained a number of stages. These are considered below.

Stages of preparation for the housing project

THE PARTICIPANTS
The selection criteria were formulated by the *barrio* committee, MINVAH officials, and Maria, who, as she put it, 'knew the people far better than any ministerial official'. In San Judas the criteria were based on *need* rather than on any proof of fixed economic status or family type. This differs from the majority of housing projects where income is the most important eligibility criterion. The criteria included those living in overcrowded or shared accommodation, refugees, or households whose present accommodation was located precariously close to the storm drains. The census showed that there were at least 200 urgent cases. Since the donation could not cover all these needs, the final selection of participants was made by the *barrio* committee with an initial selection of forty-eight households.

The majority of the participants were low-income households, with an average of six or seven persons and total earnings that periodically fluctuated between US$ 50 and 200 a month. (In Nicaragua, earnings of less than US$ 80 are considered as low-income.) At the time of their selection most of the households had been dependent for several months on food aid, distributed by the *barrio* committee. Only two men in the project had retained their jobs throughout the war, while five were unemployed for long periods during the project.

Of the sixty households who were finally selected, almost half were households headed by women, twenty-two of whom were women supporting their children, separated from their husbands, or widowed. This high percentage of woman-headed households in the project is in keeping with national statistics for the country as a whole. The age range of woman heads of household in the project was 24–53, with the mean age being 35 years. Of the women household heads, 36 per cent had not attended school, and only 10 per cent had completed their primary education. Their jobs included unskilled factory work, domestic service, and taking in washing. The menial nature of these jobs was reflected in the income range of the woman-headed households which was much lower than average, at US$ 50–150.

COMMUNITY INVOLVEMENT IN DESIGN
The original plan presented to the participants was a basic core-unit with tiled floors and all services installed. Discussions on design issues were taken in a series of meetings in which MINVAH presented several design models. These meetings were mostly attended by women, and only a few men. Most men said that 'at these meetings all you get is a lot of chat, a lot of women talking. We can attend when the real work begins'. The interest shown by women at the design stage can be understood since women in their role as wives and mothers spend more time in the home. They were therefore more interested in and most affected by design decisions, and this was reflected in the changes made in design. For example the original plans showed semi-detached units, but the participants voted for detached units so that they 'could have a large plot for planting'. Tending the household garden had traditionally been a woman's task in the rural areas and provided subsistence for the household. In the final plan the plot size was 203 square metres with a constructed area of 44 square metres representing a built area of only 21 per cent, which left the rest of the land free for small-scale cultivation. Women had another important role in design; for example, in the use of internal space, the unit had no partition walls so that each family could adapt the space to their own needs.

The final alterations to house design came from a community effort to include more women who had participated on a voluntary basis throughout the planning stages. Several women attended the collective meetings, and went to the *barrio* committee office in the hope of getting a place. For example Vilma Silva recalled:

> I filled in the forms in the census, but I didn't get selected in the first round. Neither did my neighbour Manuelita, but we both really needed a house. The owner of the land where we live now lost everything he had in the war, so we needed to move quickly for his sake. So I wrote again to Maria, I went to see her every day at the

149

office to see if there was any news, any chance we might be accepted. That's how I became a beneficiary by being involved in the meetings, by taking part, and hoping I could get a place through hard work.

Maria, the *barrio* committee, and the membership requested the ministry to cut costs per unit thereby allowing for the construction of twelve more units, giving a revised total of 60 units. The modifications in design meant that the participants would have to purchase the sanitary units, pay for the installation of electricity, plastering, tiling the floors, and laying footpaths. The women were keen to retain the tiled floor so although the modifications meant that each household would be responsible for laying the tiles, the ministry provided the materials. The participants voted to accept these changes and with them the extra financial burden. To meet these extra costs the participants set up their own collective savings, held regular fund-raising events and in this way, bore the responsibility of consolidating the project.

The choice of site was limited by the small amount of vacant land in the *barrio*. However, the selected location met the needs of both men and women. The site was alongside the main road, and next to a new community complex, which included a large market, health clinic, post office, bank, library, school, and child day-care centre. For those who worked outside the *barrio*, transport facilities were available and the close proximity of services allowed women to combine their childcare responsibilities with productive work. It also fulfilled MINVAH's objective of consolidation of the existing urban area.

There were differences of opinion between the ministry and the community over the concept of what comprised a 'permanent unit'. Both women and men would have preferred to build a wooden-framed house set on a few layers of blocks, because it was quicker to build, easy to modify according to family needs, required minimal building skills, and was more appropriate to the climate. Equally important, in rural areas women traditionally had responsibilities for building and repairing the house. Working in wood was therefore a familiar construction technique for most of the participants.

The ministry objected on the grounds of cost and maintenance problems associated with wooden structures. They proposed to use reinforced block, zinc sheet roofing, and wooden doors and windows to provide a permanent unit and to give the participants their first experience in modern construction techniques. In the architect's schedule three of these units could be built each month. After prolonged discussion the ministry's view prevailed. The choice of building materials indicated that the ministry officials were adhering to western models of a minimum standard unit and failed to recognize the constraints that this type of design would impose on the participants, particularly women. First, the change from traditional to modern house design would extend the timing of the project, and second, it would require knowledge of special building skills. The establishment of these requirements failed to recognize the nature of women's work and ignored the sexual division of labour.

SKILLS TRAINING AND ORGANIZATION

Before the building work commenced the weekly meetings concentrated on a training programme run by the social worker to establish a more formal administration structure to assist in the running of the collective during the building phase. Until this time, an informal structure had operated in which Maria chaired the meetings and Gloria acted as treasurer. They held their positions by popular consent. Elections were held to appoint office-holders to four separate committees: these were administration, finance, maintenance, and discipline, and each had three or four members. In the elections Maria and Gloria retained their key positions, although the tendency on the committees was for the co-ordinators of each to be men and the secretaries to be women. The only exception was the maintenance committee where the co-ordinator was a woman.

In the training programme office-holders received practical instruction in administrating documents and record-keeping. Study sessions for all members included 'How to run a meeting', 'How to make decisions', and 'What is a housing collective?'. Several sessions were devoted to discussing broader issues of co-operation and organization of work teams. Using cartoons they acted out in a social drama some of the potential scenarios they thought were likely to arouse conflict on a building site. However, the issue of men and women working together was never discussed as an area of potential conflict. Attendance at these meetings was not compulsory, but the majority of those who did attend were women. Many of the men stayed away, considering that 'this wasn't real work, just more chat'. The absence of men from these meetings, however, did affect events when the building work began, and this is considered below.

Building work was to be undertaken by work-teams. According to the ministry, these were to be balanced between skilled and unskilled workers, with an equal mix of men and women, taking into account factors such as level of political awareness, sex, economic activity, and previous experience of construction work. In doing this the ministry were proposing a radical departure from the culturally accepted work relationships between the sexes. Not only were they promoting the idea that men and women should work side by side on the building site, but also they were advocating a policy of gender equality, with no distinction between men's work and women's work.

Alberto, a team leader, who had twenty years' experience in construction, put forward proposals that were in marked contrast to those of MINVAH. He suggested four brigades with twelve male officials and twelve male unskilled helpers with women merely assisting men in supporting tasks. Not only did Alberto's suggestions explicitly exclude women from the skilled construction work, but also his plans were equally unrealistic since most of the men had no knowledge of building construction. Selection of work-teams was discussed at meetings, but no decisions were taken because the women and unskilled men resisted allocation until work had commenced and they had gained some experience of the different building tasks. Four team leaders, all of them men, were chosen on the basis that they had had experience in the building trade and could act as instructors on site. They took part in several sessions with the architect to discuss the technical aspects of building; the rest of the labour force had to learn on the job.

Implementation of the housing project

This section examines some of the problems that arose during the implementation of the housing project.

THE FIRST CONFLICTS

One of the first problems to affect the membership was the length of time taken to start the building work. The participants were selected in January 1980. Negotiations on design and site location, the training programme, and the clearing of the land took a year to complete. During this time considerable changes had taken place in the membership, for example, a few had found employment and moved to other *barrios*, some dropped out when they realized that they would have to build the houses by collective labour, and others felt that bureaucratic delays within MINVAH would halt the project and thus resigned.

The first building activity that involved the group's working together was clearing the site; this began in October 1980. The task was a slow and arduous one since the site was spread over 2.02 hectares, was heavily overgrown, and had to be cleared by hand using machetes. Division into work-teams for this activity was not seen as necessary. Many women were accompanied by their children who worked all day alongside their mothers. There were no written rules on representation per household at this stage, only an understanding that as many people as possible should attend since the work was so tiring. Records showed that the attendance of women was consistently higher than that of the men. Since the site was located near a geological fault another task at the preparation stage was to take seismic tests. This entailed an equally arduous task of digging a deep trench which had to be filled in again with everyone taking part in this activity.

Within a month, however, of the building work starting the team leaders recorded several problems. The work brigades were not functioning since there were too few skilled men to train the larger number of unskilled workers. Attendance was varied, and work performance, particularly of women, was poor. Therefore the team leaders could not rely on having a regular team on any workday. On the basis of these problems the team leaders recommended that women should send men to represent them on the building site. The proposal provoked angry reactions from women, particularly those who had a good work record. First, the report had been compiled by the team leaders and reflected their interpretation, which the women regarded as biased. Second, the report explicitly linked the slow progress at work to the presence of women on site. The major grievance of the women was that when they were clearing the land there had been no objections about the quality of their participation or work performance. They had carried out most of this work, while the men 'took it easy'. Sylvia opened the discussion with these comments:

> Look when we were clearing the land, you men were happy enough to let us women sweat and toil with the machetes, and our children too. Some of us women have other responsibilities and cannot be

here all the time. You all know in my case that I have work on Saturday mornings, but my 13-year-old never missed a Saturday morning, and you all know that I joined him as quickly as I could each afternoon. That arrangement was good enough for you leaders when we cleared the land, so why isn't it good enough now?

Equally as important, women objected to the report because the ministry's plans indicated that men and women would participate in *all* activities. They felt that the team leaders were at fault for not taking their responsibilities as trainers seriously, instead they 'shouted orders all the time'. Thus if the men were unimpressed by women's work performance, the women were equally critical of men's behaviour towards them on the site. Cristina expressed her views in this way:

> The problem with the leaders is that they like to shout orders at the women, they don't show us what jobs to do, it's all shouting, do this, bring me that, fetch the water, we just have to run after the men and when they don't need us we just have to stand around until they shout at us again.

This particular meeting ended in complete disorder with feelings running very high. Some women feared they would be expelled. The ministry officials were privately worried at the level of discontent and felt that some leaders might threaten to abandon the project altogether if the disputes were not settled. The officials' only suggestion was to reform the work-teams at the beginning of the second stage and draft a formal contract of work.

It is important to understand why there was so much conflict on the building site. During the clearing of the land no conflict arose. This was because traditionally working with a machete was considered to be both men's and women's work. In contrast to traditional house-building practices, housing constructed using modern materials and requiring technical skills is men's work and the construction industry is exclusively the domain of men. It was therefore considered 'unnatural' for the men to have women involved in 'men's work' on a construction site. On the other hand, women who had a good attendance were taking the opportunity provided by the ministry regulations to learn how to work as equals with men. To achieve this equality in work relations with men the women had to overcome many obstacles, for instance their lack of skills, their exclusion from the work-place, and the requirement to demonstrate their reliability. This was difficult since women also had to bear the main responsibility for reproduction, childcare, and housework. Such responsibilities made conflicting demands on their time and energy. For example, during the course of the project, some women became pregnant but the ministry officials and the participants failed to recognize, at the planning stage, that women had domestic and reproductive responsibilities, yet these determined to a large extent the ways in which women organized themselves in collective work. The men, who did not have such conflicts, did not recognize women's responsibilities and continued to claim that the qualities of a good work-force were regular attendance and reliability. This automatically excluded women with heavy demands on their time. The women had legitimate reasons for criticizing the men for being poor trainers. By being excluded from the skilled tasks they were relegated to the role of passive onlookers with their contribution limited to carrying water and blocks. A complicating factor was that some women were uneasy about engaging in the tasks on the building site. They tended to stay on the sidelines and did not push the men to explain the various skilled jobs. It was only in meetings that they felt confident enough to criticize the attitude of the men towards them. On the building site, however, most were intimidated by the atmosphere created by men at work, the older women in particular complaining that the men's crude jokes were insulting. Some women preferred to remain at home, took little part in the work, and when they did turn up on site treated the occasion as a picnic. This did little to ameliorate the tension between women and men. These women and the team leaders were reinforcing the old patterns of sexual division of labour, in which men do productive work and women reproductive work.

REFORMULATION

The ministry attempted to reform the work arrangements through a set of conditions drawn up in a formal work contract. The contents of the contract demonstrated that the ministry officials were influenced by the opinions of the team leaders. For instance Clause Twelve stated that:

> For married women it is obligatory that their husbands participate in construction work; single women must make the effort to find a male relative or any other person to work on their behalf.

The team leaders also requested that an additional clause should be added, which stated that 'no children could be accepted as

155

adequate representation of a household on the building site'. Clause Twelve of the contract together with the team leaders' report appeared to confirm some of the women's fears that they would be expelled from the scheme if they failed to find a male partner to work on their behalf. To understand the basis of this fear requires a more detailed examination of women's personal circumstances.

Gloria's 26-year-old sister, Carmen, was one of the youngest women to be included in the collective. When she was selected she was living with her husband at her mother-in-law's house. From the date of her selection to the start of building work a year had elapsed during which her husband had deserted her. She had moved out of her mother-in-law's house and was living with Gloria. She shared one room with her two small children, aged 4 years and 18 months. Her husband refused to support her or the children, so she was financially dependent on Gloria but contributed to Gloria's household by selling clothes. Gloria's son came to work with Carmen on the building site. However, if children were to be excluded, Carmen had no adult male relative who could represent her.

The Espinoza family had been selected because they were a large extended family living in very overcrowded and unhygienic conditions. The mother, Dora, was the original participant, but she could not get her brothers to work for her so she gave the allocation to her daughter, Carmen. Carmen was several months pregnant but her relationship with her husband was very strained and he refused to work for her. Although Carmen desperately wanted the house and was prepared to work for it, if Clause Twelve was adopted by the collective she knew she would have to forfeit the house unless she could convince her husband to work for her. In effect these women, and many others in similar circumstances, had no option but to work for themselves. They could not afford to pay for men to represent them, so they resisted signing the work contract.

General discussion about various clauses of the contract dragged on for weeks and stalemate meant that women continued to turn up for work without a male relative. The team leaders continued to specify poor attendance as the most limiting factor to the progress of the scheme, but none of the sanctions in the work contract were implemented. Within a month, Adolfo and three other men and the social worker from the ministry were absent from the project for three months, engaged in military training with the militia force. During this time they were not obliged to find replacements to work on their behalf. Three other men also left and arranged that in their absence they would pay US$ 40 which could be used to hire labour. These incidents show that the reformulation plans as set out in the work contract were not adhered to and were seen by men and women alike as unrealistic.

Gradually women did gain recognition from the team leaders for their work. Several factors were responsible for this. At the inauguration of the first nine houses, the ministry presented certificates of merit for consistent good work. Several women received certificates. In addition, those women who had male relatives who could work on their behalf and who had good work records were influential in improving the status of women on site. In particular Cristina, who became pregnant during the project, worked alongside her brother, a mason, and from him she learned the basic skills of his trade. Likewise Gladys, who worked with her 16-year-old son, also gained a basic knowledge of various tasks. These women gradually acquired confidence and were respected by team leaders, and this respect in turn improved the general relationship between the men and the women on site.

ALLOCATIONS

The allocations of finished houses on which no final decision had been made by the ministry sparked off a further series of disputes between men and women. At the completion of the first stage, Maria, as director, drew up a list of families most in need of rehousing. The ministry objected on the grounds that the selection should be based on various criteria such as work record. Maria insisted that the houses should be allocated by the collective and not the ministry; she claimed that:

> Only the assembly of collective members has the right to allocate the houses. We know who has the greatest needs among us, we know which of the women live in the most miserable conditions, and only we know who has worked and struggled in this community. The people have won the right to decide these sort of issues, it is not up to those in the offices to decide any more.

The membership were united in their opposition to the ministry taking decisions, but they were divided as to how the allocations should be made. Maria, and a few of the women who had an irregular work record, stressed that the houses should be allocated on the basis of need. The regular attenders, both men and women, felt that they should draw up a set of criteria on house allocation that included attendance at work, contribution to the collective fund, and the need for rehousing. There was a third body of opinion held mainly by the skilled workers and the team leaders, which held that each family should be able to select their own plots. Each group had different reasons for holding opposing views. The men were dubious about the fairness with which a selection could be made by Maria or the collective members. The single women were keen to see Maria's suggestions adopted. With the contract of work unsigned details of sanctions for irregular attendance had not been settled but single women did not rule out the possibility of expulsion. At the time that allocations became an issue, the final cost of the houses was still unknown. The men wanted to have details of repayments because they feared that the houses built in the final stages of the programme would be more expensive. In these uncertain circumstances the single women were concerned that they would not be able to make the repayments if they did not receive allocations in the first phases, and would therefore be forced to renounce their houses.

Eventually the allocations in the first phase were decided by a raffle from twenty families. Maria put forward those households that she considered eligible. Of the nine who were housed, three were single women (one a widow), and six were households headed by men. However, at the announcement of the successful participants there was a controversy about the selection of Chico, who was a team leader. There were mutterings among the group that 'he had a good job with the Ministry of Education, he had no great need, and he could afford to wait since he lived with his sister'. Rumour had it that he had spoken privately to the architect, and secured his selection by promising to remain as foreman on site for the duration of the project. Examination of the final selection, however, suggests that within the community, despite initial differing views, both men and women put more weight behind the importance of need as opposed to performance at work. This was demonstrated by the action of Antonio, a team leader, and Gladys, a single mother, who had both been selected but chose to hand over their allocations to Jose Manuel, whose wife was in hospital, and Bertha, one of the widowed women in the collective. These actions reinforced the allocation terms that Maria had publicly argued for.

Stage two was not problematic in terms of allocations, since it was clear from the outset that four houses were to be built (two for storehouses and two for the storekeepers). In stage three further problems occurred. For instance a violent dispute developed between Julio and Gloria's sister, Carmen, because they both wanted the same plot. Both felt their personal needs warranted their receiving it. Gloria, who usually never participated in disputes, entered the argument on her sister's behalf.

> It seems to me that those who shout the most, and use vulgar language, are the ones who think they can get ahead. Julio might have worked better than Carmen, that I will not deny. But are we going to give Julio this house just because he pushes for it? There is no order here, that's exactly how things were in the old days, those who threw their weight around got ahead, the rest of us had to get by. If Carmen hasn't worked as well as she should then I will come and work on her behalf, but we cannot have types like Julio getting their way.

Feelings ran so high that by the end of the meeting Gloria had resigned as treasurer.

The degree of discontent indicated that deep divisions existed with allocations policy. Men and women had different sets of rules; most women wanted allocation on the basis of need, and most men wanted allocation on the basis of time and work invested on the building site. A skilled man like Julio was prepared to use status to negotiate an allocation for himself in stage three. Julio had achieved his goal in securing the plot, but the rest of the men disapproved strongly of his behaviour. It is significant that throughout the arguments some members identified Julio's selfish and intransigent attitude to be *somocista*.[10] After the revolution *somocismo* and *machismo* were used synonymously and attempts were being made to reassess the roles of the sexes. Julio's aggressive behaviour towards Carmen was seen as a display of *machismo* and was challenged publicly by Gloria and Carmen. Many references were made about the incident between Carmen and Julio long after the event. It was remembered by both men and women in this way: 'Carmen may have forfeited her house, but Julio had forfeited his dignity'.

After the quarrel between Julio and Carmen, allocations were made without rancour. There was a shift in selection procedure towards allocating on the basis of skills as well as need, but this did not exclude women, since they continued to receive houses.

Despite the misunderstandings between the men and the women in the collective, progress on the houses continued with an average attendance at weekends of about 75 per cent. Some women had learned building skills and took on tasks that normally would have been done by the men. At stage four, reached after two years, houses were allocated to all the remaining regular attenders. The final six houses to be built were allocated to those who had been penalized for poor attendance.

THE ISSUE OF WOMEN'S WORK AND THE DIVISION OF LABOUR

At the outset of the project there had been difficulties between men and women over the question of the division of labour. The contribution of women had been seen to be limited to carrying water and blocks to the masons, and preparing the communal meal. This general conflict arose because of the differing perceptions of men's work and women's work. Also at issue was a distinction between the commitment of both men and women. Men tended to put more value on the physical and skilled work on the building site, than on the general administration and management of the project. This issue is illustrated by the lack of recognition of Maria's work.

At one point during the project, Maria was criticized by the men for not participating on the building site, 'to show a good example' to the rest of the women. Maria, as director, never participated in the building work, and was rarely present on site during work hours; however, her commitment to the project matched that of any of the skilled men when measured by the number of hours she spent handling collective business. Maria had campaigned to acquire the funds for the scheme. She had petitioned the city council to supply a tractor for clearing and preparation of the site. Throughout the period of the building work, she maintained a bargaining position with the ministry officials. It was her awareness of the precarious economic situation of individual collective members that led her to approach the Ministry of Social Welfare and successfully negotiate a food allowance for workdays. Maria also handled all the negotiations for the installation of electricity and water with the service institutions. Maria's contribution to the collective work, however, remained 'invisible' and lacked full recognition up until the point where she informed the collective that she might be forced to resign her position and to find paid work, in order to survive economically. This triggered a quick response from the collective members. Some men volunteered to help Maria financially and to 'represent' her family on the building site in recognition of her work for the collective. By contrast, when some men experienced periods of unemployment they offered to work extra hours on the building site during the week, but only after negotiating a weekly wage with the collective assembly, which indicated that while men would work for remuneration, women were expected to give their time and energy voluntarily.

As well as the subordination of women to men in work relations, there was the more traditional form of gender subordination of wives to husbands and male kin. This is illustrated by one of the disputes that occurred towards the end of the project. The architect introduced a new responsibility for members that was very unpopular. She proposed that the community should make out a nightly rota to guard the building materials, which were located in an open space and liable to be stolen. The ministry officials were not in a position to replace materials and security was therefore a collective responsibility. In discussion that followed this announcement the men objected to the involvement of women in this duty. Manuel opened the discussion by shouting that he would not do guard duty for the collective because he already had commitments at his place of work several times a week. He was, however, furious at the suggestion that women should be included in the rota: 'This is a job that requires a weapon, it's dangerous work, we can't have the women doing it'. Nubia, a young single mother who was much involved in the women's organization AMNLAE, replied that women were already involved in guard duty organized at a *barrio* level by the CBS. 'Women have already taken up arms, in militia practice. There is no difference in protecting our own materials from protecting our own community against *contra* attacks, and women are doing that in this *barrio*.'[11] Narvaez, a team leader and member of the administration committee, said that a rota including women would not work because

> just as the single women haven't the time to work on the building site, they won't have time to do guard duty. They have to be in-doors with the children and just as they can't find males to represent them at work they are hardly likely to find males to represent them now, unless their 'husbands' appear at night.

Narvaez's insinuations about their sexual conduct enraged the single women. They shouted back at him:

> Some of us have chosen to have children, but not husbands, because some husbands are too much trouble, and a bad influence on children. Besides we can put the children to bed, and do an early shift, from nine to midnight. Don't blame the women if this rota doesn't work.

Aside from the comments of Narvaez about single women, the majority of men viewed guard duty as a job that excluded women. In particular, the husbands who had wives present at the meeting insisted that it was a family responsibility, and that husbands or male relatives should bear the responsibility for the task. Further, Antonio expressed his fear for the safety of women, asserting that any robber was liable to assault and abuse the women and on these grounds he would refuse to let his wife take part. Antonio's wife, Vilma, spoke at that point, saying that she would do the guard duty, despite her husband's objections. What is noteworthy here is that Vilma was using the public arena of the assembly meeting to challenge the power and authority of her husband. In the private domain of their home, expression of her opinion would have been ignored. By contrast, the meeting provided a forum for women to tackle the lack of freedom in the home, and to question the old prejudices of their husbands. Vilma was supported by other women at the meeting, and as a result women succeeded in being included in guard duty rotas. Not all women would find it easy to have the time to take part but they felt they had won a significant victory in establishing their right to participate.

Conclusions

The participation of women in the implementation phase of 'top-down' low-income housing projects has usually been limited because they are thought to lack the relevant skills. Furthermore, even when women have participated in construction efforts in 'bottom-up' housing programmes, their contribution has rarely been acknowledged. This case study has identified the problems experienced by women who have been participating in self-help housing construction, and has demonstrated that in certain circumstances they have proved to be successful self-builders.

This analysis of women's participation in the San Judas

project has shown, first, that women successfully acquired construction skills. Second, it has demonstrated that despite major physical and ideological constraints experienced by low-income women, they made a major contribution to the construction of forty-eight houses; third, that they gradually succeeded in gaining acceptance by men of their presence and importance on the building site; and lastly, the study indicates that women persuaded the various ministry officials responsible for overseeing the project that they were capable of skilled manual labour.

These achievements were undoubtedly facilitated by the political context in which the project took place. On one level, the practical and political experience women gained during the revolutionary struggle equipped them with a variety of skills and gave them a measure of public visibility. On another level, and equally important, was the ministry's commitment to community participation and equality which provided an opening for women to participate in the project. As the case study shows this occurred neither automatically nor easily. While positive discrimination guaranteed that many low-income women were included in the project, inadequate provision was made for their full involvement in the implementation phase. As far as the latter aspect is concerned, the responsibilities of women in production and reproduction were not fully taken into account, as for example over the inevitable periods of absence of women during pregnancy. Moreover, planning for the implementation phase failed to recognize the various needs of different women. For example, women who headed households were restricted by lack of resources whereas women with men partners were restricted not only by lack of resources but also from ideological constraints emanating from their subordination to male authority within the household.

Many of the disputes between men and women, which emerged particularly at the allocation stage, are perhaps part of a more general conflict between altruism and reciprocity under a regime that called for a fundamental change in traditional attitudes. The costs of different contributions were not fully taken into account. Therefore, although many men resented the presence of women on the building site and complained that they were not contributing an equal amount of skills and labour, this conflict was probably in part resolved because altruism rather than more rigid notions of 'reciprocity' became a cornerstone of a project in which both low-income men and women were beneficiaries of a donation.

Even though much of the initial reluctance towards women's participation by the men was reinforced via the ministry (as evidenced in the discriminatory terms of the work contract), because officials were 'willing to learn' from the experiences of grassroots involvement in community participation, problems associated with traditional attitudes at both community and ministry level were eventually reconciled.

In many self-help projects in other parts of the world, allocation of housing units is made on the basis of each according to their financial and labour inputs. For women who cannot compete on an equal basis with men, this means that they often fail to complete their houses within the strict time schedules of the programme, and/or are eliminated from the project. The Nicaraguan project was targeted to meet the needs of the lowest income sectors and therefore repayments to generate similar projects were calculated on the basis of household income, not on the costs of the house.

No doubt the concluding remarks of this paper must relate to the replicability of this type of scheme elsewhere. First, at a local level, participatory self-help takes *time* to develop. Flexibility and commitment, therefore, on the part of the project staff is critical and above all, control of the project must be left to the participants, and this requires the political will of government to transfer power and channel resources to community groups. Second, if governments and aid agencies are concerned to meet the needs of the lowest income sectors of society, then the target group will include large numbers of women.[12] If the needs of women continue to be unrecognized and steps are not taken to encourage their active participation at all phases of project execution it is unlikely that women will be able to have any influence or control over the type of housing that is produced for them.

Notes

An earlier draft version of this chapter was published as Vance (1985) 'Women's participation in self-help housing: the San Judas *barrio* project, Managua, Nicaragua', *DPU Gender and Planning Working Paper* no 4, University College, London.

1 Fieldwork for this case study was carried out between September 1980 and January 1982, based on participant observation through

living in the neighbourhood and working on the building site throughout the duration of the project.

2 *Barrio* is a Spanish term for an urban district or neighbourhood.

3 Other mass organizations include the Association of Agricultural Workers (ATC); the Sandinista Trade Union Confederation (CST); the Association of Nicaragua Women (AMNLAE); the Sandinista Youth Movement (JS).

4 Studies carried out between 1969 and 1975 revealed that 57 per cent of children under 5 years suffered some degree of malnutrition and between 1965 and 1975 the proportion of children suffering second and third degrees of malnutrition increased 105.2 per cent from 50 to 102 per 1,000 (USAID 1976: 105, 185).

5 Over 38 per cent of the rural population had become landless by 1978 (Deighton *et al.* 1983).

6 It is estimated that two-thirds of the urban labour force remain outside permanent wage employment and women comprise 70.1 per cent of this category (Molyneux 1985a).

7 At the time of fieldwork the official exchange rate was 10 *cordobas* to US$ 1.

8 CONFER is the National Confederation of Nicaraguan Religious Organizations.

9 The Housing Bank was the Ministry of Housing during the Somoza regime. Although it was a public ministry with responsibilities to provide popular housing for low-income groups, it operated more as a private bank particularly after the 1972 earthquake when Somoza personally took control of the building industry. The Housing Bank was a convenient way to secure loans from abroad to continue Somoza's own private business interests in land and property speculation (Wheelock 1979).

10 *Somocista* and *somocismo* are terms synonymous with the corruption associated with the Somoza regime, and are used in a derogatory manner.

11 *Contras* are the counter-revolutionary forces under the leadership of some of Somoza's ex-National Guard who periodically carry out raids on isolated peasant villages, sabotage key installations, destroy crops, and kidnap and murder civilians.

12 A statement in the International Seminar in Lund, Sweden (October 1985) estimated that women and children make up 70–80 per cent of the population in most low-income settlements worldwide.

CHAPTER 8

Mobilization is women's work: struggles for infrastructure in Guayaquil, Ecuador

CAROLINE O.N. MOSER

Introduction

In Latin American cities low-income women work, not only in their homes and in waged-work activities but also in their neighbourhood communities. Along with men and children they are involved in residential-level mobilization and struggle over issues of collective consumption. The inadequate provision by the state of housing and local services in Latin America has resulted in open confrontation as people organize themselves to acquire land through 'invasion', or put direct pressure on the state to allocate resources for the basic infrastructure required for survival. This case study describes and analyses the critical role that low-income women play in the formation, organization, and success or failure of local protest groups, and considers the implications of their participation, both for the women themselves, and for the nature of struggle and consciousness at the point of residence.

Although it is now widely recognized that 'work' does not only mean paid work, and that consciousness can develop in forms of struggle well beyond the factory floor, nevertheless it is the struggles of waged workers that still receive the majority of attention.[1] For those concerned with women's work and its implications for women's consciousness the inappropriateness of such a narrow focus has long been apparent. This is the case not only because the majority of women's paid work takes place outside the factory in a variety of types of subcontracting or home-based piece-work, but also because women, unlike men, are primarily involved in other forms of work relating to their reproductive roles. Acceptance of the sexual division of labour, and the home as their sphere of dominance, has meant that women take primary responsibility for the provision of consumption needs within the family. This includes not only individual consumption needs within the household, but also needs of a more collective nature at the community level, with the point of residence thus extending spatially to include the surrounding neighbourhood.

Residential-level protest and struggle, in which communities organize themselves to confront the state about consumption-related issues, is not a recent phenomenon. However, in the past two decades in Latin American cities the so-called 'crisis of collective consumption' has resulted in the proliferation of popular residential struggles as local communities have challenged the state to take responsibility for the wide diversity of consumption needs which have been progressively socialized. A major focus of concern has been whether these popular struggles provide the basis for the development of urban social movements, in which broad class alliances are linked together in political struggle, not at the point of production as was traditionally the case, but at the point of residence. The fact that residential-level struggles are seen as inherently weaker than those around production issues is said to relate to the fact that issues of collective consumption do not necessarily coincide with class interests or antagonisms.[2] In much of the recent work on residential-level struggle the role played by women has been mentioned only descriptively in passing (Castells 1977a, 1982; Downs 1980; Singer 1982). If analysed conceptually it has been in terms of feminist consciousness, on the implicit assumption that through consumption-based struggles low-income women should develop an awareness of the nature of their gender subordination and their strategic gender needs (Gamarnikow 1978; Rose 1978; Kaplan 1982; Castells 1983).

A case study of the participation of low-income women in a self-help *barrio*-level committee, Indio Guayas, in the mangrove swamp periphery of the city of Guayaquil, Ecuador, provides the opportunity to examine a number of these critical issues concerning the importance of women in residential-level protest.[3] To what extent does the form of struggle amongst low-income families reflect the division of labour within the family and consequently the gender divisions within society – that is are men primarily concerned with the formal world of work carrying on their struggles at the point of production, while women are primarily concerned with reproduction (in the sense of raising and maintaining the family) carrying on their struggles around issues of consumption at the point of residence?

The extent to which it is seen as 'natural' for women to assume such importance in residential-level struggles should be reflected both in the nature of their mobilization and the manner in which it is interpreted. If women's mobilization is perceived of as an extension of their realm of interest and power in the domestic arena, family consumption needs are assumed to be women's practical gender needs, and it is most likely that it is in their gendered roles as wives and mothers, rather than as persons, that mobilization is legitimized both by the women and by their men kin. The fact that women themselves are responsible for preserving and reinforcing the sexual division of labour would then limit their capacity to identify more strategic gender needs, in other words to understand that their oppression is rooted not only in class conflict, but also in gender conflict, and in the nature of their relationship with men.

What are the implications of the fact that women play such an important role in local-level mobilization, both for women themselves, and for residential-level struggle? What are the consequences for the women if they do move beyond the perimeters of the 'domestic realm' into political action, thereby breaking the 'tacit agreement' between the sexes? What is the significance for those involved in residential-level struggle if it is identified primarily as women's struggle? Does this mean that in the same way that women's domestic labour is unvalued, so is residential-level struggle, because women's struggle is simply ignored or viewed as an inherently weaker basis for wider urban class struggle than men's struggle at the point of production? Examination of these issues in the case study is intended to contribute to the debate concerning the extent to which the analytical separation of the two forms of struggle, identified as an economic division between production and consumption, is in fact a gender division between men and women, reflecting the division of labour within the family. Ultimately this raises the question as to whether class is the only determinant of struggle, or whether another largely ignored determinant is gender– subordinated in production-based struggles but more openly manifest in consumption-based struggles. This would suggest that residential-level struggle may also be inherently weaker than production-based conflicts because the conflict between gender and class is more openly manifest.

The chapter is divided into four sections. The first, by way of background, describes the developing crisis of collective consumption in Guayaquil and the self-help response by low-income families. The second section examines the origins of popular participation in more detail. The third is concerned with the roles women play in the different committees; in addition the achievements of women's protest in one particular *barrio* are outlined. The final section focuses on the implications of the experience of residential-level struggle for the development of women's consciousness. In this complex and somewhat speculative area issues are explored at two levels: first, the consequences of the participatory experience for *barrio* women in terms of the extent to which this creates opportunities for transforming relationships within the family; second, the implications for women leaders, both personally and politically, of co-option by national political parties in return for *barrio* services.[4]

The development of Guayaquil and the crisis of collective consumption

Clearly the experiences of women in one of the many hundreds of self-help committees in the low-income areas of Guayaquil cannot be viewed in isolation, but must be understood in terms of the diversity of external economic and political factors which influenced its development. Therefore it is important to provide a brief reference to the wider contextual background.[5]

Guayaquil, founded by the Spanish in 1537, is Ecuador's largest city, chief port, and major centre of trade and industry. It is situated on low land 160 kilometres from the Pacific Ocean. Historically its growth has been closely linked with Ecuador's primary export-oriented economy, which is critically dependent on shifts in the world commodity and oil markets (D. MacIntosh 1972). It experienced expansion during the 1920 cacao slump and the 1960s banana slump, as well as during the post-1950 import-substitution industrialization policy. The very unequal distribution of income in Ecuador and the low level of per capita income has limited the possibilities for industrial development (JUNAPLA 1973). However Guayaquil remains an industrial enclave whose growth reflects the agricultural sector's declining capacity to retain its population as much as the city's potential to create industrial employment (Hurtado 1969; Cueva 1972; Moore 1978). Guayaquil has a population of over 1 million, with 30 per cent of its annual growth rate resulting from migration, mainly people of mixed Indian and Creole stock from the surrounding departments.

In Guayaquil commercial activity is focused around the 40 gridiron blocks of the original Spanish colonial city, which are encircled by the inner-city rental tenements. To the north, separated on higher ground, are the predominantly middle- and upper-income areas, while to the west and south are the tidal swamplands which provide the predominant area for low-income expansion. Settlement in this peripheral zone, known as the *suburbios* (literally suburbs), involves both the creation of solid land and the building of bamboo and timber houses linked by a complex system of catwalks. With most of the low-income population excluded from the conventional housing market (public and private), 'invasion' of the land in municipal owner-ship was, between 1940 and 1980, the predominant means by which housing was obtained.[6]

Indio Guayas is the name given by the local residents to an area of swampland, about ten blocks in size, located on the far edge of Cisne Dos, one of the administrative districts of the city. The settlement has no clear physical limits but has some 3,000 residents, the majority of whom belong to the Indio Guayas *barrio* committee. Data from a household survey undertaken in 1978 show a mean age for both men and women of 30 years.[7] Free unions are the predominant form of relationship, with most households headed by men and having an average household size of 5.8. The community is representative of the lower-paid end of unskilled non-unionized labour surviving in highly competitive small-scale enterprises, which are character-ized by underpaid and irregular 'casual' work in a variety of marginal service sector activities. The men are employed as mechanics, construction workers, tailoring outworkers, unskilled factory workers, or labourers, while the women are employed as domestic servants, washerwomen, cooks, sellers, and dressmakers (Moser 1982).

The motivation to 'invade' this municipal floodland and acquire a 10 by 30 metre plot is primarily to own a home, and thereby avoid prohibitive rents. Thus there are few absentee landlords and most plots are occupied by the owner.[8] The decision to acquire a plot is predominantly a family one.

Potential inhabitants hear about vacant plots almost entirely through their families (37 per cent) or friends (40 per cent). More than half had relatives living in the *barrio*. Distinct patterns of settlement can be identified in which extended families settle in the area over time. An elder son establishes a house for himself and nuclear family. After a few months or even a year or two, he will acquire a second plot nearby and bring his mother and siblings to the first plot which he transfers to their name although he pays for the two plots himself. In a second pattern, more common with women, a resident keeps constant surveillance on plots falling vacant to ensure that her family has first access to them. Both men and women visit the area looking for vacant plots. The inhabitants of Indio Guayas identify eight different ways of acquiring a plot making a clear distinction between paid and unpaid acquisition (Moser 1982). Both individuals and groups are involved in the process of cutting back the mangrove swamp and marking out the area, the majority either 'professional squatters' acting for personal profit, or plot owners working for themselves. In all cases this work is usually carried out by men since it is considered physically arduous and at times dangerous. It is only when the family occupies their plot that women become involved in the process of consolidating their home.

The majority of inhabitants (84 per cent) bought plots on which no house had been built. Consequently this is a community heavily involved in house construction. A wide knowledge exists not only among professional construction workers but also among most family members. Women make daily repairs to their houses while living in them and children cover holes in the roof and paper the walls with newspaper to keep out the wind. The constant movement of building materials, brought in on donkey carts, pick-up trucks, or on bicycles gives a strong visual impression of a community permanently involved in construction and repair. The conception that self-help housing is an extended process does not apply in Indio Guaya, where two-thirds of inhabitants built their houses in a three-month period. This suggests that sufficient capital was saved prior to the acquisition of the plot. This is not typical of all squatter settlements in Latin America and may be a consequence of the tropical climate of Guayaquil or the relatively inexpensive cost of a basic living structure. The most important building materials are standardized with corrugated iron roofs, split-cane walls, and wooden floors. Further upgrading is costly and therefore undertaken by few. It involves filling in of the swamp under the house, replacing the wood floor with cement, and substituting bricks or breeze blocks for bamboo walls. Families work on their own homes, with paid labour usually employed in the first, skilled stage of sinking and joining together the mangrove foundations on which the house rests. Although about a quarter of houses in the survey were built by paid labour over 50 per cent were built mainly by the household, since the skills required are fairly rudimentary. Most of the carpentry is undertaken by men, with women often buying the building materials as well as providing unskilled assistance. For most households construction of such a house is accomplished without major difficulties, other than sufficient cash for buying building materials. Far more problematical is the lack of basic infrastructure and it is this that causes communities to protest to the local municipality.

The origins of popular participation

Community level mobilization in the *surburbios* is neither automatic nor immediate. The development of self-help organization which occurs is influenced by factors internal and external to the communities, and these are examined in turn below.

In the *barrio* plots are not always occupied immediately when acquired, but are held as a future investment to be occupied when infrastructure has reached the area. The distance from the city centre, lack of electricity, running water, sewerage, and, above all, roads, all deter families from living on their plots. Women are most reluctant to move there because of the dangers to children of the perilous system of catwalks, the considerable additional burden of domestic labour under such primitive conditions, and the very real fear of loneliness. It is the men, generally less concerned with issues such as these, who persuade the family to move. But it is the women who bear the brunt, and the distress experienced by many in the early months and years should not be underestimated. Initially walking on catwalks is so frightening that many crawl on hands and feet, venturing out as infrequently as possible. The logistics of acquiring water from the tankers, or food from shops up to 2 kilometres away, are time-consuming and physically gruelling, with women recounting hazardous stories of wading through mud to acquire necessary provisions. As Maria, one of the earliest women to the area, described:

> The life on the catwalks was terrible. To live on the catwalks without light, without water, without anything, was excessively terrible. To live in the hope that friends from outside would help to get water was terribly difficult. Often there would not even be a drop of water to drink. Because if one wanted to eat one would have to bring the tank of water from over there, and they charged so much for bringing it here in canoe. When my husband had time he sometimes carried it. I did not carry any because I was afraid, because those catwalks were very high and they would often collapse. Women would fall off and they would injure themselves, they would get sticks stuck in themselves and get, what do you call it, gangrene. Two women died of that. They got one of those mangrove sticks stuck into themselves and they died.

For many women it is the first time they have left their parents' home and because the move frequently forces them to give up work, such as laundering or domestic service, it also involves greater economic dependence on their men. The lack of a reliable water supply is a particular problem for the numerous women who earned a living from laundry work. Families acknowledge the positive aspects of home ownership in that it enables money previously spent on rent to be used for house-building, education, and consumer goods. However, there are also negative consequences particularly experienced by women. In accepting the additional domestic burden many of them become aware of their need for new and different forms of solidarity and support. Prior to moving to the *barrio* hardships were most often shared by close family or kin.

As there are no roads in the *barrio* women are forced very suddenly to rely on previously unknown neighbours. However, they quickly develop complex social networks for mutual aid. These may be formalized through godparenthood. The unreliable nature of the labour market, which causes financial insecurity, and the high desertion rate experienced in free union relationships, are both factors which constantly reinforce support networks between women. Above all, however, it is the struggle for survival in a situation where even water is a scarce and valuable commodity, which forces women to develop and retain friendships with their neighbours, and gradually results in an increasing awareness among women of the need to try and improve the situation. Women living in the same street are constantly thrown together; when the water tanker fails to arrive they stand in groups discussing how to share what they have; when a child is killed falling off the catwalks women gather to console a grieving neighbour. In situations such as these women complain and commiserate together, and through interaction of this kind they become aware that the problem is not simply an individual one but common to all women. As Susana, later to become president of the *barrio* committee, remarked:

> In this area where we are now two little children died. A man also died by being electrocuted. He was making the light connection when the tide was in, there was lots of water, he got caught and died. There were some terrible cases that happened here. And seeing that it was extremely difficult to be able to live under these conditions, that's when we decided to get organized in a committee.

In the early stages of settlement growth, socio-economic differences between neighbours are not visibly marked. All live in rudimentary bamboo houses and have young children; differences in previous experience, or their men's occupations, are largely irrelevant when surviving in the same hazardous conditions. Although women become aware of their common suffering, this experience itself does not always provide sufficient motivation for common action. The Latin society places great emphasis on the submissive, dependent, and mothering role of women (*hembrismo*) as against the dominant, aggressive, and fearless role of men (*machismo*). Women do not question the fact of their responsibility for the domestic arena, which they see as natural, and that makes them the primary sufferers. Much of their conversation comprises woeful stories of endless misery with consolation gained from the recognition that this is the fate of all women. The suffering role of women is universally reinforced by the highly popular television soap operas and photo novels (imported mainly from Mexico, Brazil, and Spain). Even when attempts are made to reassess roles within the family it is difficult to change long-standing attitudes. Thus Maria, discussing her attempt to 'better' herself, recalled:

> I listen to the radio because they give advice about the home, about how to behave with the husband, how the husband should behave with the wife, that he mustn't be bad, mustn't keep her alone at home. It's nice to hear that. When he's here on Saturdays he listens in and he laughs.

External factors are also important for an understanding of mobilization. The existence of a widely known procedure of petitioning for services in return for votes by self-help committees proves a catalyst for initiating popular participation among newly settled communities. The long history of *barrio* committees in Guayaquil (beginning in the 1940s) has been associated with a political system in which populist parties bought votes by providing infrastructure. Until the late 1960s committees were short-lived, formed prior to elections and disbanded soon afterwards. It was only in the late 1960s with the post-Guevara tremors which shook liberal Latin America that they took on a more 'institutionalized' form. Along with the church, student, and middle-class women's organizations, which flooded the *suburbios* with dispensaries and clinics, came President Kennedy's 'Alliance for Progress' programme. As a condition of a large US AID grant for squatter upgrading, the Guayaquil Municipality was forced to create a Department of Community Development whose purpose was to assist communities to 'fight for infrastructure'. The 1972 Plan 240 to infill the mangrove swamps was organized around local *barrio* committees, although by 1976, when the project was terminated for lack of funds, most committees had disbanded or existed in name only. Nevertheless the experience of local organization gained during this period was an important one for the *suburbio* inhabitants.

The formation of *barrio* committees

Barrio-level committees in the *suburbios* of Guayaquil contain both women and men members.[9] It is the differences in motivation and commitment between men and women that requires identification. Since individual *barrio* committees have limited power to petition for infrastructure, it is necessary to examine leadership roles in terms of the history of a group of spatially overlapping committees. This reflects a complex process of fusion, especially pre-election, and fission, usually post-election following the unequal allocation of resources. The *barrio* committee of Indio Guayas was formed in 1975 as a splinter group of another committee owing to discontent with the incumbent leadership. As Susana, who invented the name Indio Guayas, explained:

> The first committee here was terrible. All the president did was to steal the money. He was simply engaged in swindling the people. Many presidents of committees live off their members. They don't care if anyone dies or drowns. But to be a leader I think one must be

truly human. And also to live here. Because otherwise how does one know what the needs are? I was experiencing that reality in the flesh living here. I made the people understand that we would not achieve anything if we stayed in that committee and that we should organize ourselves, whoever might be the President. But provided he really fought for the interests of this area. So one evening we met in my house, some thirty of us from this area, and we organized the committee that I am directing. At that time I was not president, my brother-in-law Julio was. But as he is lax, he does not like to fight if he meets any problem, he gives up saying, 'I don't want to know anything about it'. I would say to him, 'Julio, you will not have anything'. I was vice-president, so I became acting president and I went out into the streets to go after things. I would go with women to see what we could get. So I became president.

Although it is the women who urge their neighbours to form a committee they do not automatically see themselves as leaders, as the above quotation reveals. Rosa, woman president of a nearby committee, had a similar experience to Susana's when, 'out of curiosity', she first participated in a petition to the mayor.

In those days I cooked and washed. I had no idea about the business of struggle. I was so fed up with the bad organization of that committee that I persuaded my two neighbours to come to my house. They elected me president and we formed a committee. I had no idea what to do. But it is the obligation of women to struggle. It is our duty to ensure that things improve. Women are more dedicated than men. Women are stronger, they make decisions while men vacillate. So that's how we started.

Examples such as these indicate that women participate in protest initially out of desperation at their living conditions and then, out of a sense of duty, move into leadership positions over frustration at the corrupt management of the incumbent men presidents. It is important to note, nevertheless, that the majority of committees still have men as presidents, although those headed by women have increased. In the area of Cisne Dos four out of twenty committees were headed by women in 1976 but by 1982 the number had increased to eight.[10] Women, however, have always formed the majority of members. Over time distinctions emerge between those few prepared to take on the difficult responsibility of presidents and the majority who, for a variety of reasons, remain ordinary members.

Men and women become presidents for different reasons. Although the majority would emphatically stress their commitment to 'help the community', which at one level is certainly the case, this response also reflects the official line of the Community Development Department that for community work not to be corrupt it must be unpaid and voluntary. This conflicts with the reality which clearly shows community 'work' to be both arduous and costly in terms of time, an unaffordable luxury in a low-income community. Obviously there are economic interests involved in the work. Men, however, are able to be far more blunt and open about their personal motivations than can women. 'Professional' men squatters for instance use their position as *barrio* presidents to legitimize their operations 'advising' overnight invasions of unoccupied land for remunerative tips. Local men shopkeepers and artisans use committee work to establish their reputation and thereby increase clientele in the neighbourhood. In the community itself a somewhat ambiguous attitude exists concerning unofficial payments. When the president is a man it is a recognized, if criticized, part of 'work'. Certainly women presidents see men's involvement in financial terms. As one woman president explained:

> The great majority of the men leaders sell themselves, sell their conscience. Most of these leaders are not disinterested. They do it for an ulterior motive. Even if they see Ecuador is sinking they do it for the money.

Women, unlike men, have to be seen as selfless and 'pure', with their participation justified in terms of working to improve living conditions for their families. For this reason women's motives for becoming president are far more complex, often not recognized by the women themselves, and also can change over time. While many men leaders had previously belonged to trade unions and had prior experience of local organization this is not the case with women.[11] Equally the evidence does not suggest prior experience of politics by parent or spouse was a determining influence in a decision to accept the responsibility of leadership.[12]

The life histories of women show that those who experienced traumatic suffering in childhood or early adulthood are more likely to involve themselves in residential struggle, out of a determination that their own children, particularly their daughters, should not suffer in a similar manner. For example, Susana, president of Indio Guayas, is the eldest daughter of a woman who had six children by five different men, most of them casual lovers. One was murdered in a fight, others simply walked out, and the children were brought up in abject poverty. Susana, as the eldest, took the responsibility for her brothers and sisters while her mother worked. She began working at 12 and at 15 married a much older man, who had sufficient resources to allow her to train as a dressmaker. She still retains responsibility for her siblings while limiting her own family to two through birth control. Histories such as this are very common. Obviously for all women experiences do not have similar repercussions. Nevertheless the evidence indicates that the experience of *internal* personal pain and suffering are as important as *external* struggle (such as the experience of political organization in the trade unions) in developing an awareness and recognition of the nature of oppression and a determination to confront it. As important as 'class consciousness', then, is the gradual development of a consciousness of gender oppression and the subordinated position of women. As Susana, addressing an audience of both men and women in the weekly local meeting, said:

> We must fight. Above all I want the women, the housewives, to help us, to come with us wherever we go to get the services we need. Why? Because you are at the heart of your homes. You are the ones who suffer the actions of your husbands. The woman is a slave in the home. The woman has to make the ends meet.

The functions of *barrio* committees

Local committees are made up of fifteen elected officials, including the president, four named officials, and up to nine representatives. Although officials are regularly elected, in reality a core group of three or four make important decisions, both because of the time constraints of different members and the frequent necessity in committee work for rapid action. In a society with a strict norm concerning the extent to which women can work alongside men to whom they are not related without causing malicious gossip or marital friction, women prefer to work with other women. Consequently the composition of the committee tends to be influenced by the sex of the president. Thus when Indio Guayas was formed with Julio as president it comprised eight men and four women. A year later when Susana took over there were eight men and seven women, but by 1982 there were nine women and five men.

Despite this favourable balance of numbers the women remain in a subordinate position because the work involves contact with men officials and political party representatives. In order to minimize conflict they always try to ensure that either their spouse or another woman accompanies them, especially when they are required to journey outside the *barrio*. The close friend-ships that develop between women leaders are an acceptable way of showing that each woman is minding the other women's behaviour. Over time committees headed by women function alongside ones headed by men. However, because of the recognition of the important role that women play in *barrio* committees, they never become single-sexed.

The *barrio* committee performs a number of functions, particularly in the early stages of settlement consolidation, and regardless of the composition of elected officials, it is the women members who take responsibility for much of the day-to-day work. The lack of police stations in peripheral areas such as Indio Guayas means that the most important function of the committee within the community is to try and maintain social order. A second important internal function of the committee is to provide support to its members at times of personal crises such as an unexpected death, or imprisonment. Support in the form of money comes from voluntary collections, responsibility for which is undertaken by women committee members.[13]

The most important 'external' function of the *barrio* committee is to petition for infrastructure. This is a complex operation which is mentioned only briefly here in terms of the particular role played by women. In common with low-income commun-ities in cities throughout Latin America, the *barrio* committee attempts to influence the manner in which resources are allocated (Cornelius 1975; Collier 1976; Eckstein 1977; Nelson 1979). This requires local committees to allow themselves to be co-opted by political parties which exchange services in return for votes and political support (Sepulveda 1977). It also means, however, that the extent to which *barrio*-level mobilization is successful is largely determined by national political factors beyond the control of *barrio* residents. The different stages of mobilization involve considerable time-consuming 'voluntary' work. During the co-option process there are a succession of lengthy meetings (in addition to the regular Saturday neigh-bourhood meetings) within the *barrio*, as well as with party representatives and local government officials. The preparation and presentation of petition documentation is undertaken as well as the organization of 'spontaneous' demonstrations to protest at the Mayor's office in the City Hall. Since the provision of infrastructure is in direct exchange for votes, the *barrio* committee has particular political commitments. These include attendance at party headquarter briefings, organization of busloads of supporters for political gatherings, and extensive *barrio*-level canvassing. Finally, when the infrastructure is provided, the committee must ensure that the community's plan of work is implemented and that neighbouring committees do not divert the infrastructure through bribes to implementing agency officials. In the committees the women are responsible for this work.

The experience of the Indio Guayas committee was typical of most *barrio* committees. As previously mentioned, it was founded in 1975 during the period of military rule in Ecuador (1972–7) when few resources were allocated to low-income communities such as those in the *suburbios*. Until 1977 and the return to democratic government, Indio Guayas's committee was primarily concerned with its internal functions in the *barrio*. As Indio Guayas and the surrounding area had not been settled before the previous elections, the *barrio* committees were unco-opted. Thus intense political activity took place during the run-up to the 1978 national elections. Eventually Indio Guayas together with twenty other local committees were formed into a Front (*Frente*) and co-opted by a newly formed centre-left political party, *Izquierda Democratica* (the Democratic Left). In the *barrio* the decision concerning the choice of which party to support was based less on its political line than on the perception of its capacity to deliver the promised infrastructure in return for election votes. In the 1978–82 period Indio Guayas, with the other members of the Front, retained its long-term commitment to the same political party as it finally acquired, after many problems, infill, electricity, and water.

The implications for women of participation in *barrio* committees

THE ORDINARY MEMBERS

Since infrastructure is exchanged for votes the number and commitment of ordinary members is critical to the success and long-term survival of the *barrio* committee. Although in most families both the man and woman join as members of the committee, it is the women who regularly participate. Where men do attend their participation is neither regular nor reliable and is often undertaken after considerable pressure has been applied both by the committee and their women.

Political party leaders, administrative officials, and *barrio* men all see it as natural that most of the participatory work should be undertaken by women: 'because women have free time, while men are out at work'. Although this may be true for some, particularly during the daytime, it is also a convenient myth. Most women, throughout their adult lives, are involved not only in domestic and child-rearing work but also in a diversity of income-earning activities, even though these are more likely to be undertaken from home (Moser 1981). Time spent in mobilization is therefore detrimental both to domestic and to productive work, and women make considerable sacrifices, often risking their jobs as well as neglecting children, in order to participate. Obviously age and household commitments limit women's ability to participate but in fact women of all ages do, although those with very young children have greatest difficulty. The attitude that committee work should be left to women is reinforced by the women themselves. Just as it is natural for them to take full responsibility for domestic work in the home, women see it as their responsibility to improve the living conditions of their family through participation in *barrio*-level mobilization. As Maria mentioned, 'It is the duty of a good mother and wife to improve the neighbourhood for her children'. In this way women justify their responsibilities in terms of their gender-ascriptive roles. Equally they perceive themselves as benefiting most from, for instance, piped water, since the work of water collection and haulage is undertaken primarily by them. Thus the lack of reliable participation of men is lightly and often jokingly dismissed, as laziness, selfishness, and irresponsibility, the predominant characteristics of male behaviour in the domestic arena. For their part, most men are willing to allow their women to participate, provided they can see the benefits to the family and ensure their own domestic comforts are not disturbed. Although mobilizations involve women travelling outside the *barrio*, and at night, the fact that it is a group activity means that it is considered 'safe'.

In Indio Guayas the women have been involved in community petitioning for more than ten years. Over this period the experiences and achievements have had important effects on the women's personal lives. Participation in protest meetings provides women with an opportunity to get out of their homes and meet their neighbours. In the tedium and monotony of daily domestic work it provides excitement, if at times exposing them to hostility and violence, as the following account indicates:

> Susana said we must make a big demonstration, we must get all the people out. And Euclides [a man president] said 'If they make any trouble for you, knock Pendola's [the Mayor's] door down with your feet and you will see that they will give you something'. And so it was. We came along the catwalks, Jose [a man president from the next door committee] along one side and Susana on the other side, going all around calling all the people to come to the City Hall. We went in seven buses packed with women and children; people full of mud, without shoes, because they had to go around like that, just like that the women went. We went around 10 in the morning. And we made a real big problem for Pendola. The Mayor was real mad, he said that the police must evict us from there. And we didn't budge. 'We want infill', everyone was shouting. We were happy because like that we could achieve something.

Popular mobilization involves endless waiting, in queues with petitions, in buses to reach destinations, and at political meetings for the relevant politician to appear. This provides women with frequent small-group situations and the opportunity to discuss common problems and share intimate experiences: typical conflicts in their relationships with men, problems concerning their own sexuality, and marital disputes over the use of birth control. As a group, women make consensual judgements about women who allow themselves to be sexually abused, and increase each other's confidence to return home and confront their men over issues such as sex or money. Group struggle provides catalytic situations for shared confidences which gives the women the opportunity to examine and question their own lives. In their personal lives most women moved very rapidly from the parental control of childhood, to the control of their children's father and, therefore, have had limited previous experience of independence or recognition of their own power, even if in a limited arena. Group experience of shared problems and common successes produces an awareness of personal consciousness.

The extent to which such participation gives women the confidence to question the subordinate nature of their personal relationships cannot be measured. Nevertheless, individual examples provide evidence of the manner in which the experience of group protest over time has assisted *barrio* women in their decision to take greater responsibility for their lives. Both Anna and Josefina were living in free union relationships with local artisans, a carpenter and a tailor. In their early years of living in Indio Guayas both brought up young children and provided unremunerated assistance to their men's work (Moser 1981). Neither had any economic independence and both endured the physical abuse of husbands who were heavy drinkers. Anna's situation was made worse because her husband openly, and with his mother's support, lived between two households. Four years later both women had taken steps to make themselves economically independent. Josefina returned to night school to complete her primary education, while intermittently selling cloth to rural family contacts. Anna was attending dressmaking classes and working as a laundry-woman. With her own income she had gained sufficient confidence to retaliate when attacked by her husband, and to prevent his access to the house for three months until he stopped drinking excessively and beating her up. Both women clearly identified popular participation as critical in assisting them to recognize the possibility of obtaining some degree of economic independence.

The experience of protest exposes low-income women to the nature of the Ecuadorian political system. They see corruption in the way decisions are made, and exploitation in the manner in which the poor are constantly manipulated for political ends, resulting in increased cynicism about the political system. Although literate women have had the vote in Ecuador since 1928, politics is still considered essentially a male world with women traditionally accustomed to vote in accordance with their father's or husband's view. In Guayaquil the low-income vote has usually supported populist leaders such as Velasco in the 1950s and then Bucaram in the 1960s. Popular participation often provides women with their first direct contact with a range of political views, which in the case of Indio Guayas from 1978 onwards included *Izquierda Democratica*. Obviously not all women are equally affected by this experience but those that begin to make their own decisions about political support are no longer prepared to conform to family conventions about voting. The effect of popular participation on women, however, should not be exaggerated, since each protest by its very nature is a relatively short-term activity. Even during the protest period there are often strong pressures that prevent women from participating. Women clearly identify the principal problem not as their domestic commitments but as the hostility of their men. As Margarita described it:

> Many of the women got tired of going on because there was always trouble with the husbands, they are jealous, they don't want to let them, and one needs time for the business of politics, get up at dawn, leave the house early, and come back at night. You only survive if you can overcome that problem. But for a lot of them it's too much. You know how men can bully and then they get frightened. What will the children live on?

However, the history of mobilization in Indio Guayas throughout the 1978–82 period indicates that once women have participated, the experience is not forgotten. Not only is it a bond that unites women, a frequent topic of discussion, recalled in retrospect as 'a good time', but also the same women can be called on, again and again, when their support is required.

WOMEN LEADERS[14]

For a few women the experience of popular participation has fundamental consequences not only personally but also politically. Women leaders emerge, presidents as well as prominent committee members, who during the process of co-option look towards political leadership roles. However, those women who try to move beyond the women's domestic arena into the men's world of politics do so at enormous personal cost and little reward. It is in the criticisms encountered and the conflicts confronted by women leaders that the powerful societal mechanisms which control women and confine them to their domestic roles are most blatantly manifested.

In the community, women leaders are viewed ambiguously, alternately admired and criticized, subject to both verbal and physical abuse. Susana's description of an early conflict over the selective provision of infill is indicative:

> Because we got the works the people on H Street were furious. There were blows, sticks, stones. The people knocked down a catwalk because they thought the infill was coming. And a woman fell down and broke her skull, and so they put the blame on me. 'That whore's daughter, she ordered the catwalk to be knocked down.' So they blamed me for the woman cracking her skull. They were going to beat me up but I didn't let them. I came out with a milk bottle, I was going to buy milk for the coffee. It was 7.30. It was nothing but mud. All the people shouted at me. I was absolutely livid. I said to her, 'So you say I ordered the bridge to be knocked down!' 'Yes, you said it.'

So I threw the bottle and threw it at her head; but as it was wrapped in a paper bag it didn't break and didn't do her any harm, and I grabbed at her and tore at her clothes; as she wasn't wearing a bra, all her tits were sticking out. Somebody rushed up with a blanket to cover her. Then she went and filed a complaint with the police. So I also filed a complaint against her. It was an awful problem.

As women leaders become more powerful they are increasingly distanced from their women neighbours and friends. That political leaders and officials rush in and out of the area visiting their homes is viewed with hostility and jealousy by other women who feel 'trapped' at home. Gossip that criticizes their roles as wives and mothers is the most powerful weapon used to besmirch their reputation. The following accusation, made about a woman leader by her close neighbour, is typical:

She neglects her children. The girls know how to cook but they just don't want to. The trouble is that there is no one to make them do it. The children are badly brought up, they just run around the street.

The importance of conforming to the expected role of a woman as wife and mother fulfilling domestic obligations is also used by women to justify non-participation. One of Susana's close neighbours, who suffers from chronic exhaustion and severe depression, complained:

I can't just let everything go. Nobody will do it for me, you see, like Señora Susana. She goes off and doesn't cook, because her sister does the cooking for her. Whereas when I come back I have to cook and wash and everything so often I don't go for that reason, and then she sometimes gets annoyed when I don't go. But she has fewer kids than I do, and her husband stays at home, whereas mine gets home tired, wants his meal and to get to bed. If I were in her shoes I would go.

This gossip is an interesting distortion of reality. Although Susana's husband works at home as a sub-contracted tailor, he never expects to cook, while the assistance provided by Susana's sister, although important, does not solve the fundamental problem of her domestic commitments.

The most difficult personal problem faced by all women leaders is that of marital conflict. While their men are content, even proud, at the outset, a number of factors often contribute to a rapid deterioration in the marital relationship; first, the time-consuming nature of the work, particularly at a time of national political activity; second, the rampant gossip which assumes that because women are working with men they must be prostituting themselves; and third, that as women become public figures they achieve greater importance than their spouse, both inside and outside the *barrio*. Susana describes some of her feelings on the problem, and how she has tried to cope:

> I have had problems for years, since I first went on the committee. Ever since then there has been lots of trouble. But I don't go around telling everyone about it, I just keep quiet. They come for me, I say fine and I get dressed and go. He says it's all right if I am fighting for our street only, but not for all those others. I tell him that's selfish. If I am a leader and people have trust in me, I cannot let them down, I must go on until I get the works for them.
>
> It may be that he doesn't like it because I have to see a lot of men, because most of my work is with men. But if I don't want to do anything, nothing will happen to me, because that depends on oneself. I have been with him for twelve years and in all those years I have never failed him. It gets worse and worse. One week we are all right and the following week nothing but fights. But I don't care. I don't pay much attention to him. I don't suffer. I eat. If I stopped to think I would be miserable. I am not going to let him dominate me too much. He would like me to do nothing and let him do whatever he likes. Once he sees that I don't obey him, he'll have to decide whether he wants to go on or go to the devil. What does marriage do for us? I have always worked since I was a young girl. So I'll just have to work a little harder if he goes, to support myself and the children. Is that such a problem?

Susana, discussing the problem in 1978, when she stoically resigned herself to being locked into her home when her man decided she had done sufficient 'running around with men', still saw the problem as a private affair. By 1982, however, the conflict had become public, and degenerated to such an extent that in a Front meeting Susana's husband, Juan, publicly forbade her to accept the presidency of the Front, moments after she had been elected in an open ballot. In the ensuing confrontation the women verbally attacked Juan as '*macho*', but added:

> The system is the critical problem. Even if we all vote for her, even if twenty of us democratically vote for her, in the end you, Juan, have the only vote that matters. It is you who has the final vote. It's the husband who decides everything.

The problem was finally resolved by a compromise solution, in which Juan agreed that his wife would remain president, but only until the imminent elections were over.

Women leaders try in a number of ways to cope with marital criticism and local abuse. The most common response is for them to observe traditional female images and roles to an exaggerated extent to compensate for the contradictions created by political work. As women working in a 'man's world' they are scrupulously 'respectable' in their behaviour, always ensuring that they are accompanied by kin or a woman friend when travelling outside the *suburbios* and attending political meetings, dressing unprovocatively, and consciously avoiding compromising situations. Publicly they constantly justify their participation in terms of a common concern for the needs of their children rather than their personal ambition: 'I work for my children. In the future they will be able to say, "Her mother was loyal to us, let us help her"' (Margarita).

Despite their efforts, women leaders are faced with conflict on all sides and become painfully isolated. They are used but not accepted as equal by male leaders, and forced to rely on friendships with other women leaders, with whom they are often in conflict due to the competitive allocation of resources. A middle-class woman active in politics summarized the problem in the following way:

> Women have a very difficult time. The patriarchal culture means that they are not helped at all, just used. If I was married I wouldn't be running all over the place. I would have to stay at home. Because of the problem of *machismo*, women are not allowed out. But the competition between women is enormous. Women have to struggle against other women as well as against men.

Of all the low-income women it is those who emerge as leaders who try to challenge conventional attitudes to women. Thus Susana, while blatantly justifying her work to her husband in terms of her role as a mother caring for her children's needs, quite explicitly recognizes her own personal needs:

> I wasn't born to slave away at the sewing machine. I do believe that a woman has to do the cooking and cleaning, but not to be stuck at home all the time and nothing else. We must see something better, get some profession, do something for the community and also work. They probably think that I order my husband around, that I am very overbearing. But I am not overbearing, it's merely that the woman has the same rights as the man. Because if he wants to go out, so do I, although of course not to get drunk, but to have a good time.

The attempts by women leaders to change the nature of their marital relationships invariably culminates in the breakdown of the union. Although the woman frequently forms a second union, this is generally with a younger, often less aggressive man, on whom the woman is not financially dependent, indeed she may well support him. It is important to emphasize that although economic independence solves the immediate problem for the individual woman concerned, it does not necessarily result in any fundamental restructuring of the relationships between women and men generally.

THE CO-OPTION OF WOMEN LEADERS BY POLITICAL PARTIES

Not only do women leaders join *barrio* committees for different reasons from men, but also the way in which they are co-opted by political parties differs in a number of respects. Ecuadorian political parties have become increasingly aware that women leaders, while fewer in number than male leaders, have a particular importance. Since the majority of ordinary members of *barrio* committees are women, women leaders often have far greater ability to organize them. Moreover, women are by reputation more reliable, committed, loyal, and less fickle than men in changing allegiance from one party to another. Evaluating the participation of women leaders in the Front of *Izquierda Democratica*, a local political party representative commented:

> The women from the *suburbios* are fabulous. They are critical to the Party. The women are the real leaders. They commit themselves with real passion to the work, while the men play around. In the Front Susana is the epicentre. They all work round her. If she changes they all follow. But she has to learn to think with her head as well as with her heart.

Opinions such as this reflect attitudes in a political party which co-opts women leaders, because of their local power, while failing to take them seriously as people. A national-level leader expressed his ambivalence to the role that women leaders play in national politics, when he said:

> The openings are there. Women simply don't take advantage of them, and don't want to go into politics. From birth they are taught to respect men, to respect their brothers and not to be independent. So they are not prepared to fight. That is why there are no women in the National Congress, and only a few at other levels. But when a woman is in politics, when you get one, *'esta muy fuerte'* [she is very strong], more than men. When a woman has power the men say that she is very dangerous and they don't like her.

In campaign speeches and political party slogans the virtues of low-income women were extolled with particular emphasis on their roles as mothers and wives, while their activities within the party are limited to women's affairs and they are prevented from gaining any real power. In *Izquierda Democratica* this policy reached a crisis in 1982 when the party tried to organize *suburbio* women leaders into a Women's Front under the leadership of the upper-class wives of national political leaders. The blanket refusal of leaders such as Susana, Margarita, and Rosa to join the Women's Front highlighted the impossible position of working-class women leaders caught in a conflict not only of gender but also of class. The assumption that as women they a priori have interests in common with other women, including the patronizing wives of upper-class politicians, fails to take account of the fact that both as political leaders and as members of the working class they feel they have more in common with other working-class leaders, male or female.

Although *barrio* women leaders are co-opted to obtain votes for political parties it is more difficult for them to achieve elected positions in Ecuadorian politics. Four different stages of political involvement can be identified: *barrio* leader, activist in political party, elected municipal councillor, and elected national congress representative. Men quite frequently reach the third stage, but lack of financial resources makes them unable to survive in the system of political pay-offs and they rarely last more than one term in office. Women, by contrast, rarely reach the third stage, yet are far more ambivalent about their political ambitions. Some, like Rosa, see the problem primarily in terms of personal inadequacy, as the following comment indicates:

> The Party thinks that at the base it doesn't matter if it's a woman or a man, but at the political level it must be a man. I will overcome this problem. Men use women, but then get jealous, because when women get educated they try and take over. All the men fear that Susana and I will become councillors. The Party will not give us an opportunity. I want to study, why should I just wash dishes? If I am given the opportunity to stand again I will. When I stood as councillor in 1977 I did not understand politics. I did not understand the Municipal Law. I had no confidence. Now I am prepared. I know how to read documents. The Party did not teach me. I kept on asking Ledesmo [National Congress Representative] to give us seminars on administration. If we don't prepare ourselves when will we achieve anything?

Most women leaders, however, show great reluctance about moving beyond the level of *barrio* leader. As Susana, speaking in 1982, said:

I don't know if I want to stand as a councillor. Politics just causes problems, problems in my home and problems with everyone here. Men like playing around, but I know what I can do well. I can get things done. Look how many people have got water around here. I got the water not only in Indio Guayas but all over. I am a leader not because I am that capable, but because the people have confidence in me, because they see I will fight for what I believe in. That's why I know this is where my power is, here in the *suburbios*.

As a woman leader Susana has far greater commitment to the community than is generally the case with men, who more frequently assume leadership responsibility in order to gain economic rewards or political advancement. However, the constant criticism she encounters in her work increases her personal guilt about neglecting her children and husband and reduces her self-confidence. This, combined with the fact that the political arena is effectively closed to women, ensures that leaders such as Susana limit their personal ambition, restricting it to short-term community gains rather than long-term political goals.

Conclusion

This case study from the *suburbios* of Guayaquil illustrates the way in which the work of women and men is separated, and the implications of this for popular participation. While men's work takes place outside the community in the factories and market-places and the power politics of City Hall and local government, the arena of domestic responsibility and welfare provision within the community is primarily organized by women. Thus popular participation and protest over issues of collective consumption is fundamentally seen as women's work, although men frequently retain leadership positions.

The fact that women, supported by their men, participate in activities considered to be a natural extension of the domestic arena imposes limitations on such action. Just as women's work as mothers and wives is not valued, so the political activities of women are not considered *real* work. Women recognize that the community is their most effective arena for action, and in so doing accept that their power stems from their gender-ascribed roles as wives and mothers. Consequently after their success in obtaining infrastructure for the community, most return to their homes. This leaves their subordinate position unchanged and unchallenged. Those few women in leadership positions who demand greater power, beyond the community level into the men's world of power politics, challenge existing gender divisions within society. Although they perceive their struggle in class terms, and not in terms of gender (which remains at the personalized level within the family), nevertheless their attempts to achieve political power challenge, albeit unintentionally, the subordination of women in Ecuadorian society. As a result they are caught between two struggles, of both class and gender, and alienated on all sides. They are viewed with hostility and jealousy by women of their own class and mistrusted by their spouses. At the same time they are used but not accepted by men political leaders of all classes while rejecting alliances with women of other classes. These women respond to their dilemma by ensuring that their personal behaviour conforms to the traditional female role, or by gaining economic independence. In neither case do the solutions openly confront the essential issue of gender struggle, thus demonstrating the lack of possibility under the prevailing conditions within Ecuadorian society for gender issues to move beyond the personal level and become formalized as a political issue.

In the introduction it was argued that the recent literature on urban social movements neglects the role of women. Further, where it is considered it is in terms of the emergence of the women's liberation movement which 'aims at overcoming the structural domination of one gender by the other' (Castells 1983: 309). The evidence from this case study indicates the inappropriateness of evaluating the struggles of low-income women in a Third World city entirely in terms of their feminist consciousness, and consequently the limitations of assuming the universal commonality, both trans-class and trans-culturally, of women's interests. At the same time it would suggest that any analysis concerned with establishing why residential-level mobilization fails to create the same level of class consciousness as it does at the point of production needs to take account of the issue of gender subordination.

Too little recognition has been given to the fact that this is one of the most divisive mechanisms of social control, reinforced not only by the state but also, if unconsciously, by men of all classes. For this reason it is critical to identify the extent to which gender struggle and overcoming gender subordination may in the last analysis be one of the most important preconditions for popular movements (in which women play such a significant role) to be effectively transformed into political movements. Only then will

191

low-income urban movements not only combine both production and consumption but also involve both women and men
equally.

Notes

An earlier draft version of this chapter was published as Moser (1985b)
'Residential-level struggle and consciousness: the experiences of poor
women in Guayaquil, Ecuador', *DPU Gender and Planning Working Paper*
no 1, University College, London.

1 Historically the dominant form of struggle, especially in First World
   countries, has been at the point of production, with the experience
   of exploitation between the capitalist and worker resulting in the
   development of worker's consciousness. Withdrawal of labour
   through strike action has been one of the most obvious outward
   manifestations of the particular level of solidarity, with the trade
   union movement playing a critical role in the operationalization of
   workers' consciousness (see Anderson 1967). Although women
   have been involved in production-based struggles the trade union
   movement, with its predominantly male leadership and male
   membership, through a number of different mechanisms, has
   positively reinforced and strengthened the ideology of the sexual
   division of labour. It has thereby helped to ensure that the point of
   production remains a men's world in which women may struggle
   over issues affecting the rights of workers in general, while they are
   simultaneously being marginalized as women workers. (See for
   instance Brown 1976; Hunt 1980; Moser 1985c; Wise nd.)
2 As Saunders has argued, 'Analytically there is a necessary non-
   correspondence between class struggles and sectoral struggles
   although empirically the two may overlap . . . urban politics have
   their own specificity with no necessary relation to class politics'
   (Saunders 1981: 274–5). Castells (1976, 1977b, 1982), Pickvance
   (1977), and Pahl (1978) also provide a detailed discussion of this
   debate.
3 The Spanish word *barrio* literally means district, area (of town), or
   quarter. However in the colloquial context it has a more important
   and non-spatial meaning of a community or neighbourhood. For
   this reason the Spanish word is used throughout the text.
4 Ecuadorian politics have been described as 'a pattern of constitutional rule in which power is passed often peacefully from one
   upper-class clique to another' (D. MacIntosh 1982). The consequence of an over-centralized hierarchical system of government
   means that local municipalities, without annual budgets, have to
   manipulate the system by petitioning central government for local

project funds. Consequently decision-making by politicians is personalistic, based on short-term political motives and a concern for buying votes rather than long-term effects of their actions.

5 See Moser (1981, 1982) for more detailed information relating to this case study.

6 See Moser (1982) for a detailed account of the history of *suburbio* land ownership. Three different types of 'invasion' can be identified: First, politically motivated organized 'invasions'; second, those manipulated by real estate interests; and third, the 'invasions' of 'professional squatters' who resettle every few years, selling off their previous homes. The first two types of invasions predominated prior to 1976 legislation which reaffirmed the ownership of *suburbio* land by Guayaquil's Municipality, while requiring it to sell to existing occupiers. While the 1976 legislation was seen as a vote-catching gesture on the part of the CFP Party of Assad Bucaram to give homes to the majority of the city's population, it was *de facto* a recognition of the state's responsibility to provide land on which the low-income population might build their own homes.

7 Fieldwork for this case study was undertaken from September 1977 to March 1978 and was based on participant observation through living in the *barrio*, and a survey of 244 households of three different block groups, selected to show changes in the settlement and consolidation process. Further fieldwork to provide longitudinal data was undertaken in January 1979 and August 1982.

8 The fact that there was virtually no renting was a direct consequence of the type of ownership pattern. Since there was no legal title to plots, ownership was by possession, which meant owners were very reluctant to let to others, since they might in turn claim ownership.

9 This contrasts with the majority of studies of residential-level mobilization which have described the history and functions of women-only committees. See for instance Chinchilla (1977), Kaplan (1982), and Schmink (1982).

10 By the 1980s the reputation of women presidents such as Rosa and Susana in the area around Indio Guayas resulted in younger women founding their own committees, many under the direct guidance of Susana.

11 For instance the president of the *barrio* committee next door to Indio Guayas was an important official in the local fire service union, while an important male member of the Indio Guayas committee, now a local shopkeeper, had previously been involved in union work in a banana-packing company in Guayaquil docks.

12 Comparative work indicates the importance of identifying both class and political orientation of party. Chaney (1979) in her work on Latin American middle-class women leaders shows the important influence that parents have on the political activities of their daughters in Peru and Chile. Randall (1981) in her *Sandino's*

Daughters: Testimonies of Nicaraguan Women in Struggle shows the important influence of radical rural *campesino* leaders on their daughters, and of radical urban middle-class sons and daughters on their mothers. In Guayaquil radical university student sons of working-class women were responsible for persuading their mothers to organize mass invasions prior to elections. However, the reverse is not necessarily true: often the daughters of women leaders from the *suburbios* are vehemently non-political in their attitudes.

13 By contrast, when a man abandoned his woman, or beat her up when drunk, these were considered domestic family concerns and not the responsibility of the *barrio* committee.

14 During the 1978–82 period, when Indio Guayas formed part of a political Front with twenty other local committees, much of the work, particularly prior to elections involved close collaboration. Consequently the fieldwork was broadened to include the experiences not only of Susana, president of Indio Guayas, but also of the other seven women presidents in office by 1982.

© *1987 Caroline O.N. Moser*

CHAPTER 9

Postscript: what hope for the future?

CAROLINE O.N. MOSER AND LINDA PEAKE

The case studies in this book illustrate the diversity of women's participation in housing and human settlements and draw attention to the regional differences and cultural variations that exist. They reveal the positive efforts of women to satisfy their needs for housing, whether in 'bottom-up' initiatives (Sylvia Chant, Caroline Moser) or in 'top-down' enterprises such as site and services projects (Leda Machado, Paula Nimpuno-Parente, Linda Peake), squatter upgrading (Marina Fernando, Irene Vance) and public-sector renting (Linda Peake). But it would be wrong to infer that these case studies are indicative of a global phenomenon. While there is a slowly increasing awareness amongst planners and policy-makers, activists and academics, that there is much to be learnt in terms of positive strategies from the experience of low-income women in human settlements, the evidence also suggests that the housing projects discussed in this book are not widely replicable. Given the gravity of the world's housing crisis they may well prove to be exceptions to the rule.

Low-income households throughout the world live in appalling housing conditions; dwellings are often cramped, unhygienic, unsafe, insanitary, makeshift, and lacking in basic facilities. Moreover, conditions are not improving. The housing crisis has been exacerbated by global economic recession and by the debt crises facing many Third World countries. Housing is invariably low on the list of government priorities, and is usually treated as a welfare issue rather than as an integral component of development. In the 1980s many Third World governments are making even less pretence than before to allocate financial resources to improve the living conditions of their low-income populations. Debt repayments are becoming increasingly difficult to meet. As a consequence of the oil crisis, and the austerity measures ordered as a condition of IMF loans, many governments are further reducing their expenditure on job creation, housing construction, and other social services. The costs of readjustment rest most heavily on the low-income groups, who are least able to bear them. Not only is there a decline in public expenditure, but also the amount they can afford to spend on housing is getting smaller because of their reduced purchasing power. In the 1980s and into the 1990s with space at more of a premium than ever, low-income groups will either do without housing altogether and live on the streets, or they will be channelled into increasingly subdivided slums and squatter settlements. As Hardoy and Satterthwaite (1987) have argued low-income communities will experience a decline in services, further concentration in informal sector employment, the use of more marginal and hazardous sites for housing, and a rise in the risk of diseases.

As Peake shows, the Guyanese government, in response to the problem of debt repayment, has abandoned its commitment to housing, both the consolidation of existing housing and the building of new houses. Consequently for more people, squatter settlements have become the only available solution. Machado, in the case of Brazil, further illustrates that even when a government has established a programme of low-income housing, women are effectively excluded. In many countries another social cost of readjustment appears to be a significant increase in domestic violence against women. This is associated with an increase in the number of households headed by women left on their own to raise their dependants, while men migrate in search of work or for other reasons simply abandon their commitments to the household.

Because of the escalating costs of housing programmes, site and service projects are not reaching low-income groups, and upgrading or other forms of self-help have become more important. These rely substantially on community participation and as the case studies have shown, on the participation of women. As discussed in Chapter 1 the objectives of community participation in housing projects vary from welfarist or anti-poverty concerns to economic objectives associated with project efficiency, effectiveness, and cost recovery, and to more feminist concerns associated with equality and the empowerment of women.

Evaluation of the case studies in terms of the objectives of women's participation is revealing, not only for the differences in objectives, but also for the contrasting consequences of the actual participatory process. Thus in the Kirillapone project in Colombo, Sri Lanka, at the initial project design stage the objective was a somewhat traditional welfarist concern to 'integrate women into development' as better mothers. Recognition that the problem was really one of employment led to a subsequent change to an anti-poverty approach in which all participants were provided with training in construction skills. Although both men and women initially had misgivings about working together as masons, traditionally regarded as 'men's work', this gradually became an accepted area of employment for women and enabled them to build their own homes. The change of emphasis in the Kirillapone project provides an example of a flexible approach to planning. This is more characteristic of small non-goveri.mental projects than of large government or bilateral-aid programmes. The original project objectives changed considerably, with the participatory experience leading to far greater autonomy on the part of women than had been anticipated.

Both the Women's Housing Co-operative in Guyana and the Dandora Site and Service project in Nairobi, Kenya, had similar anti-poverty objectives with their concern to provide women who headed households with access to adequate housing. In the case of Dandora, however, it could also be argued that in a context where women were more reliable and responsible than men in completing their houses and repaying their loans, they were included in order to achieve project efficiency. Only in the San Judas Project in Managua, Nicaragua, was the empowerment of women an explicit objective. The project recognized the subordinate role of women in society, and endeavoured to reduce the nature of inequality between men and women through joint building groups. As Vance explains this met with resistance from men not only in the design phase but also throughout implementation. Critical to changing attitudes within the community were both the proven ability of women to build their own homes, and the political support of a national government committed to equal participation by men and women in community projects.

While the objectives of women's participation differ in 'top-down' housing projects, in squatter settlements the case studies from both Guayaquil, Ecuador, and Querétaro, Mexico, show that women participate with clearly defined objectives relating to practical gender needs such as better housing or infrastructural services – needs which are required by all the family but which women in their reproductive, productive, and community-managing roles see as their responsibility to provide.

One of the most important themes in the case studies is the relationship between practical gender needs and the way in which low-income women in their triple role take responsibility for meeting such needs: from Querétaro to Georgetown to Nairobi, women in their reproductive role take responsibility for allocating resources to house improvement or negotiating with the state over the provision of housing: in their productive role women from Kirillapone to San Judas are involved in house construction; and in their role as community managers women organize locally both to obtain services and ensure their maintenance, as illustrated in squatter settlements in Colombo and Guayaquil.

All the case studies show the extent to which practical gender needs in human settlements and housing are met. It is also important, however, to assess the extent to which more strategic gender needs are met. These are often far less obvious or explicit, but essential to women in order to achieve the freedom to determine their own lives. Although in many cultures women spend more time in the home than men, they have little control or influence over their housing and the environment in which they live. For this to change, women's strategic needs must be met. Undoubtedly this is a sensitive issue: it is not appropriate for First World women to inform Third World women of the particular forms of their oppression or to suggest strategies for their alleviation. Increasing awareness of the similarities of concern of Third and First World women has led to mutually beneficial exchanges of experience revealing the varied strategies they have both adopted.

To this end the case studies reveal the importance of having sensitivity to, and an understanding of, the way in which gender relations are expressed in specific cultural contexts. They also serve as examples of the common housing and human settlement problems faced by women in the Third and First Worlds. For example the 'bottom-up' mobilization of women in Guayaquil, Ecuador, has parallels in the community kitchens set up by the wives of striking miners in Britain in 1984–5 and in the establishment of Gingerbread groups. Similarly aided self-help projects such as those in Guyana, Brazil, Kenya, and Nicaragua can be compared with women's experience in co-operatives and tenants associations in Britain while women's homelessness, a common feature of many Third World cities, is increasingly being recognized as a problem in the First World. As shown in the case studies, housing design and settlement layout affect the domestic labour of women in the Third World. Similar conclusions have been drawn in the First World (Matrix 1984; Women and Geography Study Group 1984). Parallels are also evident in transport provision, proximity to place of work, and access to services. Lastly domestic violence occurs throughout the world and organizations such as Women's Aid, which provide refuges for the victims of such violence, exist in both First and Third World countries.

Analysis of the case studies reveals that women have three main strategic gender needs: security, safety, and the abolition of the sexual division of labour. To gain security women need to acquire tenancies or ownership rights to land. Without these women suffer a number of disadvantages: they cannot protect themselves against unstable or violent domestic situations (Moser); the control men have over their households is reinforced (Chant); and as they lack collateral they are therefore deprived of the value of land and property as investment (Nimpuno-Parente).

To gain safety women need to live in an environment free from fear of male abuse towards themselves and their dependants. When women have the money to pay for skilled labourers to build their homes their trust may be abused (see Peake, Chant, Nimpuno-Parente). Lack of resources to improve housing conditions is also a problem for women in many communities, especially where men spend the money on their own individual wants (see Chant, Fernando, Peake).

Changing the sexual division of labour requires a recognition of the triple role of women and an increase in their opportunities for economic independence. As Chant and Fernando show, deprived of this right, the health of women and their dependants is likely to suffer. Machado and Nimpuno-Parente illustrate the difficulties that arise when employment opportunities are not considered in the selection and location of sites for housing projects. The problem is exacerbated when zoning regulations prevent the establishment of businesses in residential areas. As Vance and Fernando reveal access to formal credit facilities and training in relevant skills both increase women's economic independence and help erode traditional stereotypes of the position of women. But Chant and Nimpuno-Parente show that the contribution of women to house construction is often regarded mainly as an extension of domestic work.

In the case studies strategic gender needs have rarely been met. There are various reasons for this. First, government policy rarely results in the satisfaction of strategic gender needs. For example the Brazilian and Kenyan governments utilize criteria for housing programmes that discriminate against women. In Guyana, although women have not been denied tenure rights, the withdrawal by the state of financial support for housing means that the acquisition of tenure is of little value. In Nicaragua, despite awareness of the needs of women and the existence of political support, Vance shows that strategic gender needs were not wholly met.

It appears that only through women's participation and mobilization can challenges to the sexual division of labour be made. Evidence from the case studies suggests that conventional assumptions regarding the sexual division of labour are gradually changing. Further, through their own organization women are challenging cultural norms by attempting to transform conventional living and working arrangements. Vance, for example, shows how participation in housing provides a basis for redefining the position of women in Nicaraguan society. The women's experiences in the liberation war gave them the confidence to mobilize around issues in other sectors of the economy such as health care, education, and housing. Collective meetings during the construction phase of the San Judas project provided an opportunity for the women to challenge the authority of their male kin. Moser reveals that when women have the opportunity to meet informally they discuss their relationships with men, disputes over birth control, and so on. This shared experience can give women the confidence to increase their independence and take greater responsibility for their own lives. This may result in their leaving their partners or in taking up official positions on *barrio* committees.

Fernando shows how project leaders discovered that women were inhibited in official organizations and they therefore encouraged informal activities and alternative groups based on women's traditional roles (*shramadana*). Within these alternative structures women acquired skills that gave them improved access to economic opportunities and increased their self-reliance. Their financial independence increased not only their autonomy and control over their own lives, but also made the women more aware of the contribution they could make to their community, thereby adding to their sense of worth. Finally, Moser, Fernando, and Vance show that obstacles to the involvement of women include not only a lack of awareness among planners but also a lack of understanding or resistance within the community itself. Clearly educating men about the importance of women's participation is essential if a more equitable division of labour between the sexes is to be achieved and women are to satisfy their strategic gender needs.

Bibliography

Abreu, P. (1977) 'Mão-de-obra femininae mercado de trabalho no Brasil', *Boletim Técnico*, 3, 1, Rio de Janeiro: SENAC.

Adamson, P. (1983) 'The gardens', in J. Grant (ed.) *The State of the World's Children, 1981–1982, UNICEF*, Leicester: Blackfriars Press.

Afshar, H. (ed.) (1985) *Women, Work and Ideology in the Third World*, London: Tavistock.

Agarwal, A. and Anand, A. (1982) 'Ask the women who do the work', *New Scientist* (November) 4: 302–4.

Anderson, P. (1967) 'The limits and possibilities of trade union action', in R. Blackburn and A. Cockburn (eds) *The Incompatibles*, Harmondsworth: Penguin.

Angel, S., Archer, R., Tanphiphat, S., and Wegelin, E. (eds) (1983) *Land for Housing the Poor*, Singapore: Select Books.

Ardener, S. (ed.) (1981) *Women and Space*, London: Croom Helm.

Arredondo, G., Kusnir, L., and Largaespada, C. (1984) 'Analysis of women's participation in self-help building projects in low-income sectors of the metropolitan area of Mexico City', mimeo, Mexico City.

Austerberry, H. and Watson, S. (1983) *Women on the Margins: A Study of Single Women's Housing Problems*, London: City University.

Banco Central do Brasil (1983) *Boletim Mensal* 19, no. 4, Brazil.

Barnes, C. (1975) 'Women in Kenya's rural economy', in A.O. Pala, T. Awori, and A. Krystal (eds) *The Participation of Women in Kenyan Society*, Proceedings of a conference held in Nairobi,

Kenya, 11–15 August.

Barrett, M. (1980) *Women's Oppression Today*, London: Verso.

Barroso, C. (1982) *Mulher, Sociedade E Estado No Brasil*, São Paulo, Brazil: UNICEF/Brasilience.

Blayney, R. and Lycette, M. (1983) *Improving the Access of Women-Headed Households to Solanda Housing: A Feasible Down Payment Assistance Scheme*, Washington, DC: International Center for Research on Women.

Blumberg, R. (1978) 'The political economy of the mother-child family revisited', in A.F. Mark and R.A. Romer (eds) *Family and Kinship in Middle America and the Caribbean*, Leiden, Netherlands: University of the Netherlands Antilles and the Department of Caribbean Studies of the Royal Institute of Linguistics and Anthropology.

BNH (Brazilian Housing Bank) (nd) *National Housing Bank – A Brazilian Solution to Brazilian Problems*, Rio de Janeiro, Brazil: BNH.

——— (1966) *Nocoes Basicas*, Rio de Janeiro, Brazil: BNH.

——— (1978) *Projetas de Lotes Urbanizados*, Rio de Janeiro, Brazil: BNH.

——— (1980) Profilurb: *Programma de Financiamento de Lotes Urbanizados*, Rio de Janeiro, Brazil: BNH.

Bolaffi, G. (1979) 'Para uma Nova Politica Habitacional e Urbana: Possibilidades Econômicas, Alternativas Operacionais e Limites Politicos', in L. Valladares (ed.) *Habitacao Em Questao*, Rio de Janeiro, Brazil: Zahar.

Bossert, T.J. (1982) 'Health care in revolutionary Nicaragua', in T. Walker (ed.) *Nicaragua in Revolution*, New York: Praeger.

Bridges, J. (1980) 'The Mexican family', in M.A. Das and C.J. Jesser (eds) *The Family in Latin America*, New Delhi: Vikas.

Bromley, R. (1982) 'Working in the streets: survival strategy, necessity or unavoidable evil?', in A. Gilbert, in association with J.E. Hardoy and R. Ramirez (eds) *Urbanisation in Contemporary Latin America: Critical Approaches in the Analysis of Urban Issues*, Chichester: Wiley.

Brown, R. (1976) 'Women as employees: some comments on research in industrial sociology', in D. Leonard, D. Barker, and S. Allen (eds) *Dependence and Exploitation in Work and Marriage*, London: Longman.

Burgess, R. (1978) 'Petty commodity housing or dweller control? A critique of John Turner's views on housing policy', *World Development*, 9, 9/10: 1,147–60.

——— (1982) 'Self-help housing advocacy: a curious form of

radicalism. A critique of the work of John F.C. Turner', in P. Ward (ed.) *Self-Help Housing: A Critique*, London: Mansell.

Buvinic, M., Youssef, N., with von Elm, B. (1978) *Women-Headed Households: The Ignored Factor in Development Planning*, report submitted to the Office of Women in Development, AID, Washington, DC: International Center for Research on Women.

Caplan, P. (1981) 'Development policies in Tanzania: some implications for women', *Journal of Development Studies*, 17, no. 3: 98–108.

Castells, M. (1976) 'Is there an urban sociology?', in C. Pickvance (ed.) *Urban Sociology: Critical Essays*, London: Tavistock.

—— (1977a) *The Urban Question*, London: Edward Arnold.

—— (1977b) 'Theoretical propositions for an experimental study of urban social movements', in C. Pickvance (ed.) *Urban Sociology: Critical Essays*, London: Tavistock.

—— (1978) *City, Class and Power*, London: Edward Arnold.

—— (1982) 'Squatter politics in Latin America: a comparative analysis of urban social movements in Chile, Peru and Mexico', in H. Safa (ed.) *Towards a Political Economy of Urbanisation in Third World Countries*, Delhi: Oxford University Press.

—— (1983) *The City and the Grassroots*, London, Edward Arnold.

CBS/UNICEF (1984) *Situation Analysis of Children and Women in Kenya, Section 3*, Nairobi, Kenya: CBS/UNICEF.

Chana, T.S. (1979) 'Site and service strategy assessed', paper presented at International Regional Seminar on Sanitary Engineering, Cairo, November.

—— (1984) 'Nairobi: Dandora and other projects', in G.K. Payne (ed.) *Low-Income Housing in the Developing World*, Chichester: John Wiley.

Chaney, E.M. (1979) *Supermadre*, Austin, Texas: University of Texas Press.

Chant, S. (1984a) 'Las Olvidadas: a study of women, housing and family structure in Querétaro, Mexico', unpublished PhD dissertation, Department of Geography, University College, London.

—— (1984b) 'Household labour and self-help housing in Querétaro, Mexico', *Boletin de Estudios Latinoamericanos y del Caribe* 37: 45–68.

—— (1985) 'Family composition and household consolidation: the case of Querétaro, Mexico', *DPU Gender and Planning*

Working Paper no. 2, University College London.

Chinchilla, N.S. (1977) 'Mobilising women: revolution in the revolution', *Latin American Perspectives*, 15, 4, 4.

Clark, M.H. (1984) 'Woman-headed households and poverty: insights from Kenya', *Signs*, 10: 338–54.

Clarke, C. and Ward, P. (1980) 'Statis in makeshift housing: perspectives from Mexico and the Caribbean', *Comparative Urban Research* 8, 1: 117–27.

Collier, D. (1976) *Squatters and Oligarchs*, Baltimore, Md: Johns Hopkins University Press.

Connolly, P. (1982) 'Uncontrolled settlements and self-build. What kind of solution? The Mexico City case', in P. Ward (ed.) *Self-Help Housing: A Critique*, London: Mansell.

Cornelius, W.A. (1975) *Politics and the Migrant Poor in Mexico City*, Stanford, Calif: Stanford University Press.

CSE (1976) 'On the political economy of women', *Pamphlet No. 2*, London: Conference of Socialist Economists.

Cueva, A. (1972) *El Proceso de Dominacion Politica en el Ecuador*, Quito, Ecuador: Ediciones Criticas.

Davidoff, L. (1979) 'The separation of home and work', in S. Burman (ed.) *Fit Work for Women*, London: Croom Helm.

De Azevedo, S. and De Andrade, L. (1982) *Habitacaco e Poder – Da Fundacao Da Casa Popular Ao Banco Nacional Da Habitacao*, Rio De Janeiro, Brazil: Zahar.

Deighton, J., Horsley, R., Stewart, S., and Cain, C. (1983) *Sweet Ramparts, Women in Revolutionary Nicaragua*, London: War on Want and Nicaraguan Solidarity Campaign, Spider Web.

De Souza, L. (1981) 'O tabulho Feminino e a estru tura familiar', paper given at the Assosiacão Nacional de Pos-Gaduacao e Pesquisa nas Ciências Sociais, Belo Horizonte, Brazil.

Dick, C. (1984) *Housing the Nation over Two Decades: A Review of Official Policies and Achievements Regarding Housing in Guyana under the PNC Government*, Georgetown, Guyana: Ministry of Health, Public Welfare, and Housing.

DIEESE (Departamento Intersindical de Estatistica e Estudos Socio-Economicos) (1984) *Boletim DIEESE (May)*, São Paulo, Brazil: DIEESE.

Doebele, W. (1983) 'The provision of land for the urban poor: concepts, instruments and prospects', in S. Angel, R. Archer, S. Tanphiphat, and E. Wegelin (eds) *Land for Housing the Poor*, Singapore: Select Books.

Dos Santos, C. (1979) 'Velhas Novidades nos Modos de Urbanizacao Brasileiros', in L. Valladares (ed.) *Habitacao Em*

Questao, Rio de Janeiro, Brazil: Zahar.

Downs, C. (1980) 'Comissões de Moradores and urban struggles in revolutionary Portugal', *International Journal of Urban and Regional Research* 4, 2: 267–94.

Dwyer, D.J. (1975) *People and Housing in Third World Cities*, New York: Longman.

Eckstein, S. (1977) *The Poverty of Revolution*, Princeton, NJ: Princeton University Press.

Fernando, M. (1985) 'Women's participation in the housing process: the case of Kirillapone, Sri Lanka', *DPU Gender and Planning Working Paper* no. 3, University College, London.

Fundacão Joao Pinheiro (1980) *Avaliacao do Profilurb no Brasil*, Belo Horizonte, Brazil: BNH.

Furtado, C. (1971) *The Economic Growth of Brazil*, Berkeley, Calif: University of California Press.

Gamarnikow, E. (1978) 'Introduction, women and the city', *International Journal of Urban and Regional Research* 2, 3: 390–403.

Gardiner, J. (1977) 'Women in the labour process and class structure', in A. Hunt (ed.) *Class and Class Structure*, London: Lawrence & Wishart.

Gilbert, A. (1983) "The tenants of self-help housing. Choice and constraints in the housing market', a paper prepared for the 1983 Conference on the Spatial Dimension in Development and Planning, University of Guyana, Georgetown.

Girling, R., Lycette, M., and Youssef, N. (1983) *A Preliminary Evaluation of the Panama Self-help Women's Construction Project*, Washington, DC: International Center for Research on Women.

Government of Guyana (1970) *1970 Population Census*, Georgetown, Guyana: Government Printer.

—— (1972) *Guyana Development Plan 1972–76*, Georgetown, Guyana: Government Printer.

—— (1976) *State Paper on Equality for Women*, Georgetown, Guyana: Government Printer.

—— (1977) *Labour Force Survey*, Georgetown, Guyana: Government Printer.

—— (1980) *Constitution*, Georgetown, Guyana: Government Printer.

Griffith, M. (1981) 'The construction industry in relation to housing', *Discussion paper*, Georgetown, CHPA.

—— (1982) 'Directions for the housing department', *Discussion Paper*, Georgetown, Guyana: CHPA.

Hanson, D. (1981) *Policy, Finance and Organisation of Housing in*

Guyana, Georgetown, Guyana: United Nations Development Programme Report.

—— (1982) 'Analysis of housing in Guyana', *Discussion Paper*, Georgetown, Guyana: Ministry of Health, Public Welfare and Housing.

Hardoy, J. and Satterthwaite, D. (1987) 'The legal and the illegal city', in L. Rodwin (ed.) *Shelter, Settlements and Development*, London: Allen & Unwin.

Harms, H. (1982) 'Historical perspectives in the practice and purpose of self-help housing', in P. Ward (ed.) *Self-Help Housing: A Critique*, London: Mansell.

Hayden, D. (1981) *The Grand Domestic Revolution: A History of Feminist Designs for American Homes, Neighbourhoods and Cities*, Massachusetts and London: MIT Press.

Herner, J. and Ziss, R. (1980) *La Vivienda Popular en el Ecuador: Efectos Economicos*, Quito, Ecuador: Instituto Latinoamericano de Investigaciones Sociales.

Hinkson, J. (1980) *A Decade of Housing in Guyana*, Georgetown: Ministry of Health, Public Welfare and Housing.

Hunt, P. (1980) *Gender and Class Consciousness*, London: Macmillan.

Hurtado, O. (1969) *Dos Mundos Superpuestos: Ensayo de Dia no ti a de la Realidad Ecuatoriana*, Quito, Ecuador: INEDES.

IBGE (Fundacão Instituto Brasileiro de Geografia e Estastistoca) (1981) *Anuario Estatistico do Brasil*, Rio de Janeiro, Brazil: Diretoria Geral de Estatistica do Ministerio da Agricultura, Industria e Comercio.

IBGE/UNICEF (Fundacão Instituto Brasileiro de Geografia e Estastistica) (1982) *Perfil estatistico de crinacas e maes no Brasil – Caracteristicas socio-demograficas 1970–1977*, Rio de Janeiro, Brazil: IBGE.

IWTC (International Women's Tribune Centre) (1981) *Newsletter: Women, Money and Credit*, 15, New York: IWTC.

—— (1982) *Newsletter: Women and Water*, 20, New York.

JUNAPLA El (1973) *Estrato Urbano Popular: Informe de Investigacion sobre Guayaquil*, Quito, Ecuador.

Kaluzynska, E. (1980) 'Wiping the floor with theory: a survey of writings on homework', *Feminist Review* 6: 27–54.

Kaplan, T. (1982) 'Female consciousness and collective action: the case of Barcelona, 1910–1918', *Signs* 7, 3.

Keare, D., and Parris, S. (1982) 'Evaluation of shelter programs for the urban poor – principal findings', *World Bank Staff Working Paper*, no. 547, World Bank.

Latin America Bureau (1984) *Guyana, Fraudulent Revolution*, London: LAB.

Lycette, M. and Jaramillo, C. (1984) *Low-Income Housing: A Women's Perspective*, Washington, DC: International Center for Research on Women.

McDowell, L. (1983) 'City and home: urban housing and the sexual division of space', in M. Evens and C. Ungerson (eds) *Sexual Divisions: Patterns and Processes*, London: Tavistock.

Machado, L.M.V. (1985) 'Women and low income housing in Brazil: evaluation of the Profilurb Programme in terms of its capacity to define and reach female-headed households', *DPU Gender and Planning Working Paper* no. 5, University College, London.

MacIntosh, D. (1982) *The Politics of Primacy: Political Factors in the Development of Guayaquil*, unpublished MSc thesis, Columbia University, DC.

Mackintosh, M. (1981) 'The sexual division of labour and the subordination of women', in K. Young, C. Wolkowitz, and R. McCullagh, *Of Marriage and the Market*, London: CSE.

Madeira, F. and Singer, P. (1975) 'Estrutura do Emprego e Trabalho Feminino fno Brasil: 1920–1970', *Cadernos CEBRAP* 13, Rio de Janeiro, Brazil.

Mangin, W. (1967) 'Latin American squatter settlements: a problem and a solution', *Latin American Research Review* 2: 65–98.

Matrix (1984) *Making Space, Women and the Man-Made Environment*, London: Pluto.

Melrose, D. (1985) *The Threat of A Good Example?*, Oxford: Oxfam.

Merrick, W. and Schmink, M. (1983) 'Households headed by women and urban poverty in Brazil', in M. Buvinic, M. Lycette and W. McGreevey (eds) *Women and Poverty in the Third World*, New York: Johns Hopkins University Press.

Ministry of Health, Public Welfare and Housing (nd) *Notes on Housing*, Georgetown, Guyana: Government of Guyana.

—— (1981) *Guyana's Housing Drive*, Georgetown: Ministry of Health, Public Welfare and Housing.

(MINVAH) Ministerio de Vivienda y Asentamientos Humanos (1981) *Provecto Eduardo J. Mojica, Barrio San Judas*, Managua, Nicaragua: MINVAH/CONFER.

(MIPLAN) Ministerio de Planificacion (1980) *Programa de Reactivacion Economica en Benficio del Pueblo*, Managua, Nicaragua: Secretaria Nacional de Propaganda y Educacion

Politica del FSLN.

Miranda, G. (1977) 'Women's labour force participation in a developing society: the case of Brazil', in Wellesley Editorial Committee (eds) *Women and National Development: The Complexity of Change*, Chicago, Ill: University of Chicago Press.

Molyneux, M. (1985a) 'Mobilisation without emancipation? Women's interests, the state and revolution in Nicaragua', *Feminist Studies* 11, 2: 227–54.

—— (1985b) 'Women's role in the revolutionary process', in T. Walker (ed.) *Nicaragua: The First Five Years*, New York: Praeger.

Moore, R.J. (1978) 'Urban problems and policy responses for metropolitan Guayaquil', in W.A. Cornelius and R.V. Kemper (eds) *Latin American Urban Research, vol. 6, Metropolitan Latin America: The Challenge and the Response*, Beverly Hills, CA: Sage.

Moser, C.O.N. (1977) 'The dual economy and marginality debate and the contribution of micro analysis: market sellers in Bogota', *Development and Change* 8, 4: 465–89.

—— (1981) 'Surviving in the *suburbios*', *Bulletin of the Institute of Development Studies* 12, 3: 19–29.

—— (1982) 'A home of one's own: squatter housing strategies in Guayaquil, Ecuador', in A. Gilbert (ed.) *Urbanisation in Contemporary Latin America*, London: John Wiley.

—— (1983) 'The problem of evaluating community participation in urban development projects', in C. Moser (ed.) *Evaluating Community Participation in Urban Development Projects, DPU Working Paper* no. 14, University College, London.

—— (1985a) 'Housing policy and women: towards a gender aware approach', *DPU Gender and Planning Working Paper* no. 7, University College, London.

—— (1985b) 'Residential-level struggle and consciousness: the experiences of poor women in Guayaquil, Ecuador', *DPU Gender and Planning Working Paper* no. 1, University College, London.

—— (1985c) 'Women's work in urban protest and struggle', paper presented at DSA/BSA Study Group Meeting on Gender and Class in the Third World, London.

—— (1986) 'Approaches to community participation in urban development programmes in Third World cities', paper presented at Economic Development Institute Workshop on

Community Participation, Washington, DC.

Moser, C.O.N. and Chant, S. (1985) 'The role of women in the execution of low income housing projects draft training manual', *DPU Gender and Planning Working Paper* no. 6, University College, London.

Moser, C.O.N. and Levy, C. (1986) 'A theory and methodology of gender planning: meeting women's practical and strategic needs', *DPU Gender and Planning Working Paper* no. 11, University College, London.

NACLA (North American Congress on Latin America) (1976) *Nicaragua* X, no. 2, New York.

—— (1978) *Crisis in Nicaragua* XII, no. 2, New York.

Nelson, J. (1979) *Access to Power: Politics and the Urban Poor in Developing Nations*, Princeton, NJ: Princeton University Press.

Nimpuno-Parente, P. (1985) 'Gender issues in project planning and implementation: the case of Dandora site and service project, Kenya', *DPU Gender and Planning Working Paper* no. 13, University College, London.

—— (1986) 'Women in a site and services scheme, Dandora: a gender analysis of housing development', mimeo, Nairobi: Housing Research and Development Unit, University of Nairobi, Kenya.

Oakley, P. and Marsden, D. (1984) *Approaches to Participation in Rural Development*, Geneva: International Labour Organisation.

Overholt, C., Anderson, M., Cloud, K., and Austin, J. (1984) *Gender Roles in Development*, Connecticut: Kumarian Press.

Pahl, R. (1978) 'Castells and collective consumption', *Sociology* 12: 309–15.

PAHO (Panamerican Health Organisation) (1979) *Document No. 381: Conclusiones de Salud del Niño en Las Americas*, Washington, DC: Organización Panamericana de Salud.

Paul, S. (1986) 'Community participation in development projects. The World Bank experience', paper presented at Economic Development Institute Workshop on Community Participation, Washington, DC.

Peake, L. (1986a) 'Low-income women's participation in the housing process: a case study from Guyana', *DPU Gender and Planning Working Paper* no. 10, University College, London.

—— (1986b) 'A conceptual enquiry into urban politics and gender: formal and informal modes of participation', in E. Kofman and K. Hoggart (eds) *Politics, Geography and Social Stratification*, London: Croom Helm.

—— (1987) 'Guyana, a country in crisis', *Geography*, 72, 4.
Perlman, J. (1976) *The Myth of Marginality*, Berkeley, Calif: University of California Press.
Pickvance, C. (1977) 'On the study of urban social movements', in C. Pickvance (ed.) *Urban Sociology: Critical Essays*, London: Tavistock.
Population Council (1983) *The Performance of Men and Women on the Repayment of Mortgage Loans in Jamaica*, New York: Population Council.
Powell, D. (1984) 'The role of women in the Caribbean', *Social and Economic Studies* 33, 2: 97–122.
Pradilla, E. (1976) 'Notas acerca del problems de la vivienda', *Ideologia y Sociedad* 16, (January/March), Bogotá, Colombia.
Rakodi, C. (1983) 'The World Bank experience: mass community participation in the Lusaka Upgrading Project', in C. Moser (ed.) *Evaluating Community Participation in Urban Development Projects, DPU Working Paper* no. 14, University College, London.
Randall, M. (1982) *Sandino's Daughters: Testimonies of Nicaraguan Women in Struggle*, London: Zed Press.
Resources for Action (1982) *Women and Shelter in Honduras*, Washington, DC: USAID, Office of Housing.
Roberts, B. (1978) *Cities of Peasants*, London: Edward Arnold.
Robson, D. (1983) *Aided Self-help Housing in Sri Lanka*, London: ODA.
Roldan, M. (1985) 'Industrial outworking, struggles for reproduction of working-class families and gender subordination', in N. Redclift and E. Mingione (eds) *Beyond Employment: Household, Gender and Subsistence*, Oxford: Basil Blackwell.
Rose, H. (1978) 'In practice supported, the theory denied: an account of an invisible urban movement', *International Journal of Urban and Regional Research*, 2, 3: 521–37.
Saboia, J. (1985) *Salario Minimo, A Experiencia Brasileira*, Porto Alegre, Brazil: LPM.
Saffioti, H. (1978) *Women in Class Society*, New York: Monthly Review Press.
Sara-Lafosse, V. (1986) *Comedores Comunales: La Mujer Frente a la Crisis*, Lima, Peru: Grupo de Trabajo, Servicios Urbanos y Mujeres de Bajos Ingresosf.
Saunders, P. (1981) *Social Theory and the Urban Question*, London: Hutchinson.
Saunders, P. and Williams, P.R. (1986) 'The new conservatism: some thoughts on recent and future developments in urban studies', *Environment and Planning D: Society and Space*, 4, 4: 1–8.

Schlyter, A. (1984) 'Upgrading reconsidered: the George Studies in retrospect', *Bulletin of the National Swedish Institute of Building Research* M84: 4, Lund, Sweden.

Schmink, M. (1981) 'Women in Brazilian *Abertura* politics', *Signs* 7, 1: 115–34.

―――― (1982) 'Women in the urban economy in Latin America', *Women, Low-Income Households and Urban Services*, Gainesville, Fla: Center for Latin American Studies, University of Florida.

―――― (1984) 'The "Working Group" approach to women and urban services', mimeo, Gainesville, Fla: Centre for Latin American Studies, University of Florida.

Scott, J. and Tilly, L. (1982) 'Women's work and the family in 19th-century Europe', in E. Whitelegg, M. Arnot, E. Bartels, V. Beechey, L. Birke, S. Himmelweit, D. Leonard, S. Ruehl, and M.A. Speakman *et al.* (eds) *The Changing Experience of Women*, London: Martin Robertson/Open University.

Selby, H., Murphy, A., Cabrera, I., and Castaneda, A. (1981) 'Battling urban poverty from below: a profile of the poor in two Mexican cities', paper prepared for the Wenner-Gren Foundation Symposium on Households: Changing Form and Function, New York, October.

Senga, Ndeti, and Associates (1977) 'Monitoring and evaluation study of Dandora Community Development Project to the Government of Kenya', *Baseline Survey Report*, Nairobi, Kenya: S.N. and A.

―――― (1979a) 'Medis 5 – Tenure to land', *Baseline Survey Report*, Nairobi, Kenya: S.N. and A.

―――― (1979b) 'Medis 6 – building groups', *Baseline Survey Report*, Nairobi, Kenya: S.N. and A.

―――― (1979c) 'Medis 7 – employment and income, subletting, affordability, workshop clusters, house consolidation', *Baseline Survey Report*, Nairobi, Kenya: S.N. and A.

Sepulveda, J.R. (1977) *Algunos Elementos de Socializacion Politica en el Area Suburbana de Guayaquil*, Guayaquil, Ecuador: Departmento de Publicaciones de la Universidad de Guayaquil.

Singer, P. (1968) *Desenvolvimento Econômico e Evolucão Urbana*, São Paulo: Cia Ed. Nacional e Ed. d USP.

―――― (1982) 'Neighbourhood movements in São Paulo', in H. Safa (ed.) *Towards a Political Economy of Urbanisation in Third World Countries*, Delhi: Oxford University Press.

Singh, A. (1980) *Women in Cities: An Invisible Factor in Urban Planning in India*, Population Council: New York, mimeo.

Sorock, M., Dicker, H., Giraldo, A., and Waltz, S. (1984) *Women and Shelter*, Washington DC: Resources for Action, Office of Housing and Urban Programs, USAID.

Standing, G. (1979) 'Socialism and basic needs in Guyana', in G. Standing and R. Szal, *Poverty and Basic Needs*, Geneva: International Labour Organisation.

Statement of the International Seminar (1987) 'Gender-aware research or housing in Third World countries', *Trialog*, no. 11, 1: 4–7, Statement of the International Seminar in Lund, Sweden, 1985.

Strachan, A. (1981) 'Housing patterns and values in a medium-sized world city: Georgetown, Guyana', *Tidjschrift voor Economische und Sociale Geographie*, 72, 1: 40–6.

Sudra, T. (1976) *Low-Income Housing Systems in Mexico City*, PhD dissertation, Massachusetts Institute of Technology, repr. Ann Arbor, Michigan.

Thomas, C. (1983) 'State capitalism in Guyana: an assessment of Burnham's Co-operative Socialist Republic', in F. Ambursley and R. Cohen, (eds) *Crisis in the Caribbean*, London: Heinemann.

Tienda, M. and Ortega, S. (1982) 'Las Familias Encabexadas por Mujeres y la Formacion de Nucleos Extensos. Una Referencia a Peru', in Secretaria de Programacion y Presupuesto (ed.) *Estudios sobre la Mujer. 1. El Empleo y la Mujer. Bases Teoricas, Metodologicas y Evidencia Empirica*, Mexico: Secretaria de Programacion y Presupuesto.

Turner, J. (1968) 'Housing priorities, settlement patterns and urban development in modernizing countries', *Journal of the American Institute of Planners* 34: 355–60.

—— (1970) 'Barriers and channels for housing development in modernizing cities', in W. Mangin (ed.) *Peasants in Cities*, Boston, Mass: Houghton Miffin.

—— (1972) 'Housing as a verb', in J. Turner and R. Fichter (eds) *Freedom to Build, Dweller Control of the Housing Process*, New York: Macmillan.

—— (1976) *Housing by People*, London: Marion Boyars.

Turner, J. and Fichter, R. (1972) *Freedom to Build: Dweller Control of the Housing Process*, New York: Macmillan.

UNCHS (1983) *Formal and Informal Financing in Site and Service Projects in Kenya: A Case Study*, Nairobi, Kenya: HABITAT/UNCHS.

—— (1984a) *Community Participation in the Execution of Low Income Housing Projects*, Nairobi, Kenya: UNCHS.

—— (1984b) *Sites and Services Schemes: The Scope for Community*

Participation, Nairobi, Kenya: UNCHS.

────── (1985) *Community Participation, Cost Recovery and Afford-ability*, Nairobi, Kenya: UNCHS-HABITAT.

────── (1986) *The Role of Women in the Execution of Low-Income Housing Projects*, Nairobi, Kenya: UNCHS–HABITAT.

UNDP (1982) 'Analysis of housing in Guyana', *Discussion Paper*, Georgetown, Guyana: UNDP.

UNRISD (1979) *Inquiry into Participation – A Research Approach*, Geneva: UNRISD.

USAID (United States Agency for International Development) (1976) *Health Sector Assessment for Nicaragua*, USAID Mission to Nicaragua, Managua.

(US) Save the Children Federation (1982) *Adaptation of Save the Children's Community Based Integrated Rural Development Approach to the Urban Community Context in Sri Lanka: A Self Evaluative Statement*, Westport, Conn: SAVE.

Vance, I. (1985) 'Women's participation in self-help housing: the San Judas *barrio* project, Managua, Nicaragua', *DPU Gender and Planning Working Paper* no. 4, University College, London.

van Wijk, J. (1986) 'Women and planning and housing in the Netherlands', in *Women and the Man-Made Environment Reader*, Conference on Feminist Geography and Urban Planning, University of Amsterdam and Physical Planning Department.

Ward, P. (1976) 'In search of a home: social and economic characteristics of squatter settlements and the role of self-help housing in Mexico City', unpublished PhD dissertation, Department of Geography, University of Liverpool.

────── (ed.) (1982) *Self-Help Housing: A Critique*, London: Mansell.

Wekerle, G.R., Peterson, R., and Morley, D. (1980) *New Space for Women*, Boulder, Colo: Westview Press.

Wheelock, J.R. (1979) *Imperialismo y Dictadura: Crisis de Una Formacion Social*, Mexico City: Siglo Vientuno.

Whitehead, A. (1979) 'Some preliminary notes on the sub-ordination of women', *Bulletin of the Institute of Development Studies* 10, 3: 10–13.

Winch, R. (1978) 'Inferring minimum structure from functions: or did the bureaucracy create the mother-child family?' in A.F. Marks and R.A. Romer (eds), *Family and Kinship in Middle America and the Caribbean*, University of Netherlands Antilles and the Department of Caribbean Studies at the Royal Institute of Linguistics and Anthropology at Leiden, Netherlands.

Wise, A. (nd) *Women and the Struggle for Worker's Control*, London: Spokesman Pamphlet.

Women and Geography Study Group (1984) *Geography and Gender*, London: Hutchinson.

World Health Organisation (1976) *National Food and Nutrition Survey of Guyana*, Washington DC: Pan American Health Organisation.

Wright, G. (1980) *Moralism and the Model Home: Domestic Architecture and Cultural Conflict in Chicago, 1973–1983*, Chicago, Ill. and London: University of Chicago Press.

Name index

Abreu, P. 57
Adamson, P. 93
Afshar, H. 13
Agarwal, A. 19
Anand, A. 19
Anderson, P. 192
Angel, S. 34, 35
Ardener, S. 11
Arredondo, G. 26
Austerberry, H. 11

Bandaranaike, Madam 91
Barnes, C. 73
Barrett, M. 10
Barroso, C. 57, 58, 59, 65
Bend-Kirten-Holder, A. 136,
   137
Blumberg, R. 44
Bolaffi, G. 60
Bossert, T.J. 141
Bridges, J. 43
Bromley, R. 43
Brown, R. 192
Burgess, R. 5, 11, 35, 47, 48
Burnham, F. 118
Buvinic, M. 14, 136

Caplan, P. 19
Castells, M. 167, 191, 192
Chana, T.S. 71, 73
Chaney, E.M. 193
Chant, S. 7–8, 31, 34, 38, 39,

51, 53, 195, 199, 200
Chinchilla, N.S. 193
Clark, M.H. 70
Clarke, C. 34
Collier, D. 179
Connolly, P. 34
Cornelius, W.A. 179
Cueva, A. 170

Davidoff, L. 11
De Andrade, L. 61
De Azevedo, S. 61
Deighton, J. 165
Dick, C. 121
Doebele, W. 34
Dos Santos, C. 61
Downs, C. 167
Dwyer, D.J. 34

Eckstein, S. 179
Elm, B. von 14, 136

Fernando, M. 8, 111, 195, 199,
   201
Fichter, R. 5
Furtado, C. 56

Gamarnikow, E. 167
Gardiner, J. 10
Gilbert, A.G. 54, 128
Girling, R. 23, 27, 85
Griffith, M. 121

Subject index